T0158500

DANGER **CLOSE**

DANGER CLOSE

THE BATTLE OF LONG TAN, AS TOLD BY THE COMMANDERS TO BOB GRANDIN

Harry Smith, OC, Delta Company, 6RAR
Geoff Kendall, 10 Platoon Commander
Bob Buick, 11 Platoon Sergeant
Dave Sabben, 12 Platoon Commander
Morrie Stanley, Forward Obervation Officer, 161 Battery, RNZA
Adrian Roberts, 3 Troop Commander, No. 1 APC Squadron
Bob Grandin, Helicopter Pilot, 9 Squadron, RAAF

ALLEN&UNWIN
SYDNEY · MELBOURNE · AUCKLAND · LONDON

First published in 2004 as *The Battle of Long Tan*
This edition published 2019

Allen & Unwin
83 Alexander Street
Crows Nest NSW 2065
Australia
Phone: (61 2) 8425 0100
Email: info@allenandunwin.com
Web: www.allenandunwin.com

A catalogue record for this book is available from the National Library of Australia

ISBN 978 1 76087 726 2

Set in New Baskerville/American Typewriterby Midland Typesetters, Australia
Printed in Australia by SOS Print + Media Group

10 9 8 7 6 5

MIX
Paper from responsible sources
FSC® C001695

The paper in this book is FSC® certified. FSC® promotes environmentally responsible, socially beneficial and economically viable management of the world's forests.

CONTENTS

MAPS

FOREWORD

This is a very important book: an account of a battle that has become synonymous with the Australian Army and the Vietnam War—Long Tan. And it is particularly important because it has been written by the commanders who were closely involved in the fighting.

It was fought on 18 August 1966 by D Company of the 6th Battalion, Royal Australian Regiment, in torrential rain in a rubber plantation to the east of the Task Force Base at Nui Dat. D Company had the support of gunners of the 1st Field Regiment, who fired 3,198 rounds during the three-hour battle, and were dramatically resupplied mid-battle with ammunition by two RAAF helicopters. In a feat of arms that upheld the finest traditions of the Australian Army, D Company resisted overwhelming odds until a relief column arrived from Nui Dat.

The accounts by the commanders at Long Tan graphically show the face of battle, in all its uncertainty, bravery, fear, demands and danger. It is a valuable insight into what it is like to serve in an infantry company in combat. Also providing valuable insights are the chapters dealing with training for war and the first few months in Phuoc Tuy province.

Just what the Vietnamese intentions were is still unclear, but what is quite clear is that the Nui Dat base at the time was vulnerable to a major attack. Some sort of attempt at a decisive action was in prospect, but D Company's resounding victory put paid to that.

The final chapter deals with a number of issues, but none more contentious that the subject of *Honours and Awards* and the seeming lack of proper recognition afforded to those who so distinguished themselves.

It is hard to reach any conclusion other than that Harry Smith and a number of those who performed valiantly were treated ungenerously. Long Tan has become a battle that literally defines the Vietnam War for Australians, a battle so decisive in outcome that its anniversary has now become Vietnam Veterans' Day: and Harry was awarded a Military Cross for his efforts! The quotas implicit in the awards system then in place is said to have limited what could be done, but what about the flexibility and fair-play we as Australians are supposed to be renowned for? We have recently seen Second World War Resistance heroine Nancy Wake justifiably honoured by Australia, having earlier been well-recognised in British Commonwealth awards. It is not too late for retrospective recognition for those who served their country so well at Long Tan.

I am very honoured to write this foreword, for I have a particular connection with D Company. I was moved across from Charlie Company to join Delta as its artillery forward observer hours after its Company Sergeant Major, Jack Kirby DCM, was killed in a tragic artillery accident in February 1967. I subsequently came to know them as well as any outsider, particularly a Gunner, might. They were proud, somewhat guarded with newcomers, and resentful of their treatment in the aftermath of Long Tan, but self-confident and, above all, competent. You were in no doubt what you were doing with Harry Smith: he was a forceful and confident leader, who knew what he wanted.

This book tells the story of an action that could have been a disaster, but for the valiant efforts of those involved. How the victory was achieved is told in the words of the field commanders. It is a story that has been a long time coming, and I believe the book will take its rightful place as the definitive account of Long Tan.

Steve Gower AO
Director
Australian War Memorial
March 2004

PREFACE

THE STORY

This is a story of an incident in the lives of seven ordinary men who were brought together in extraordinary circumstances on 18 August 1966. They were born just before or during the Second World War and they reflect the thoughts and actions of the youth of the time. These are recounted in the autobiographies they have written about this period of their lives. While each had a very different upbringing, they all took part in active service in the mid-1960s. Their stories illustrate the sense of duty that was prevalent at the time and demonstrate the brashness of youth. The reader is also told about the training experiences that Delta Company, 6th Battalion Royal Australian Regiment (6RAR) went through before they left Australia, which were meant to prepare them to go into battle.

By June 1966 these seven men had arrived in Phuoc Tuy Province, Vietnam to be a part of the Australian Task Force that was given the responsibility of establishing peace in this district. Their number included members of the infantry, artillery, armour and air force. As they describe their initiation into the conditions of this foreign environment there is little awareness of what was about to happen.

The seven men who tell their story in this book could be called the 'commanders in the field' during the major battle that was to ensue. The infantry soldiers were members of 6RAR. They were Delta Company commander, Major Harry Smith; Delta Company platoon commanders, Lieutenants Geoff Kendall and David Sabben; and Platoon Sergeant Bob Buick. Bob took command of 11 Platoon when his platoon commander, Lieutenant Gordon Sharp, was killed early in the battle. The artillery soldier was the forward observer attached to Delta Company from 161 Battery, Royal New Zealand Artillery, Captain Morrie Stanley, who commanded the use of artillery during the battle. The armour soldier was the troop commander of 3 Troop, 1 Armoured Personnel Carrier Squadron, Lieutenant Adrian Roberts, who led the cavalry as they brought reinforcements to the battle. The airman was Flight Lieutenant Bob Grandin, a helicopter pilot with 9 Squadron, Royal Australian Air Force, who was co-pilot in the lead helicopter that provided an ammunition resupply at a critical time in the battle. Bob's contribution is included to represent the activity of the lead helicopter as Flight Lieutenant Frank Riley, commander of the lead helicopter, has since passed away.

The battle that is the focus of this story is the Battle of Long Tan. It occurred on 18 August 1966 and this date and the name of the battle are now used as the Day of Remembrance for the Australian involvement in the Vietnam War. The story is told in the first person to convey the way in which ordinary people respond under the intense and traumatic conditions of battle. It also allows the reader to recognise the way in which extreme pressure can convey a sense of chaos, yet an order prevails that allows independent entities to produce a coordinated and concerted effort that overcomes adversity.

On the morning of 18 August 1966 Delta Company was sent out towards Long Tan on Operation Vendetta. As the name indicates, the intention was one of retaliation for the enemy mortaring of the Task Force area some thirty hours earlier. The story of the events over the next few hours is an enthralling recount of how each individual battled for survival against overwhelming odds and established a place in Australian history. The story moves chronologically through the events, while moving from member to member to allow each individual to describe what was happening to him at the time. This provides an account of the Battle of Long Tan which has never before been told.

Many of the misinformed stories about the battle are exposed as the reader follows the experiences of those who were actually there. Many questions will rise in the minds of those who understand military tactics, while simple logic will cause others to wonder about the sequence of events. However, it is impossible not to marvel at the valour and resilience of the men in battle.

The writers have provided an epilogue on the battle and its aftermath which contains some fascinating reflections after the event. The veterans have raised issues that reflect the political and military climate of the period. There are references to injustices that should be rectified. All describe the way in which events can be transformed from objective reality into historical myth. This last section is a hard-hitting criticism of how historical events can be manipulated.

To allow the reader to follow the lives of these ordinary individuals, each has provided a story of the way in which his life has unfolded since that eventful day. It is fascinating to reflect on how individuals continue to evolve in similar yet different ways. That they could choose to re-form as a group after thirty-odd years and 'right the wrongs' about the Battle of Long Tan is fascinating in itself. I am sure that the reader will find this book an interesting commentary on both a piece of military history and the social fabric of those times.

OUR VIEW OF THE WORLD AT THE TIME

The Second World War ended in 1945 and signalled the beginning of the end of colonialism by the European nations. However, those countries that espoused the communist cause saw the turmoil of the time as an opportunity to encourage the growth of their ideology. They openly supported national revolution throughout the world, especially in Africa and South-East Asia. The British surrendered colonies in Africa, and India became independent in 1947. The French tried to retain or regain their colonies for a while and as a consequence became embroiled in a number of 'wars for independence' in Africa and French Indo-China. The colonies argued that they did this in the name of national independence.

Indo-China in 1946 was a collection of many ethnic groups, Vietnamese being the dominant one. Anti-French Vietnamese, under Ho Chi Minh, wanted independence and commenced a guerrilla war against their French colonial masters. It was these Vietnamese who began the First Indo-China War and defeated the French at Dien Bien Phu in 1954.

The subsequent peace treaty, called the Geneva Accords, determined that the French would withdraw from Indo-China and that the former French colony would be divided into four separate countries: Laos, North and South Vietnam and Cambodia. The victorious anti-French Vietnamese forces, the Viet Minh, under the leadership of Ho Chi Minh, formed a communist state in North Vietnam, while the South attempted to form a democracy. Under the Accords there were to be elections and the eventual unification of the North and South. However, neither of the parties complied with the agreement. North Vietnamese communist forces, who had been part of the Viet Minh, started military action against the Government of South Vietnam in the late 1950s.

The communist forces in the South were supported by the North and became known as the National Liberation Front (NLF) and were also called the Viet Cong (VC). The 'liberation fighters' became ever stronger and more successful in military actions against the Government of the South. Early in the 1960s it became clear that South Vietnam was becoming politically unstable. The USA supported the South Vietnamese Government in its endeavour to form a democratic system of government. In 1963 the South Vietnamese asked the United States of America for military assistance to combat the influence of the NLF and the North. Members of the US Army and a group of Australian military advisers went to South Vietnam to assist and train the Army of the Republic of Vietnam (ARVN). The Viet Cong adopted the tactical and revolutionary teachings of Mao Tse-tung and called their fight 'the People's War'. The tactics they used were also known as guerrilla warfare or insurgency.

The armed forces of Australia and New Zealand participated in the Korean War, under the United Nations flag. They had supported the British Government in Malaya, in the anti-guerrilla war against the communist terrorists, known as the Emergency. Also, the Confrontation between Malaysia and Indonesia saw the Australian armed forces in action against the Indonesian Army in Borneo.

When China vetoed the involvement of United Nations forces in

Vietnam, the United States of America called upon its allies to join forces in supporting the South Vietnamese Government. Australia and New Zealand responded to this call under the terms of the South-East Asia Treaty Organisation of which they were member states.

In a significant upgrading of its commitment, in 1965 the Australian Government committed the 1st Battalion Royal Australian Regiment (1RAR), supported by other arms and services including a New Zealand artillery battery. They operated under the direct control of US Headquarters out of Bien Hoa, near Saigon. When it became apparent that further commitment was appropriate, it was decided that the Australian troops should operate in their own area under their own command and control. The Province of Phuoc Tuy, south-east of Saigon, was chosen as the area of operations. It was decided that a task force of two battalions and supporting arms and services would be stationed in this area and would commence operations in June 1966.

The Australians built two base areas in Phuoc Tuy Province, an operational and a support base. Nui Dat, a small hill with a rubber plantation alongside, situated approximately in the centre of the province, became the main operational base. A logistical support group was established at Vung Tau, twenty kilometres to the south-west on the coast, where sea and air resupply facilities were available. The total manpower of these two establishments was about four thousand.

The positioning of the main operational base in the centre of the province, away from the provincial capital, Baria, which was the main population area, suited the Australian operational plans. The security of the base was easier to maintain without the local populace moving around the camp. Also, by limiting contact with the population, there were fewer opportunities for the VC intelligence service to gain information.

The Province of Phuoc Tuy was approximately 2,500 square kilometres in area. It consisted of coastal plains with sand dunes to the south, the Saigon River delta with mangroves and swamps in the

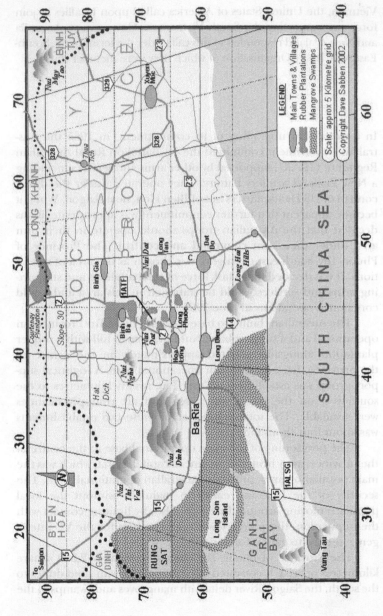

1 Phuoc Tuy Province, South Vietnam

west and three isolated jungle-covered mountain areas. These were the Nui Dinh and Nui Thi Vai mountains, ten to twenty kilometres west of the Task Force base and overlooking the Australian base, and the Long Hai hills, about 25 kilometres to the south on the coast, which were the highest features in the province. The balance of the province was a combination of a deciduous type of rainforest, light timber and small areas under rice, rubber or food cultivation. It was an ideal area of operations for the Viet Minh to wage war. They had been very successful against the French. Now the guerrilla fighter was to hear English spoken rather than French.

The French, on their return to the province after the Second World War, suffered one or two military defeats and could not neutralise the Viet Minh. They fell back to occupy and protect the large towns of Baria and Vung Tau. A series of forts spread along the main roads. The plan was to keep the roads open and control the lines of communication between the centres of population in which they had an interest. These forts, similar to those in the movie *Beau Geste*, served no useful tactical purpose because they isolated the French forces. The French dared not venture out in small groups, as they would be attacked.

The Viet Minh moved freely around the province and controlled the people in the countryside, although not in the centres of population. After the defeat of the French in 1954 the Viet Minh, who were from North Vietnam, remained in South Vietnam. In 1960 the Nation Liberation Front (the Viet Cong) commenced a revolutionary war against the South Vietnamese Government. The Viet Cong fighter in 1960 picked up the same rifle used against the French; nothing had changed in the six years after the French had left. So the Australians' enemy had had complete tactical and military control of the province since the early 1950s. The Army of the Republic of Vietnam (ARVN), like the French, occupied the towns and forts. The Viet Cong, like their fathers, the Viet Minh, were in control of the countryside. With this dominance they also had influence over most of the population outside the main centres.

In preparing its troops for Vietnam, the Australian Army had begun adapting the methods used in Malaya during the Emergency, developing what was to become known as counter revolutionary warfare. This was the Australian method of countering an enemy which employed the teachings of Mao Tse-tung on guerrilla warfare called 'A People's War', and was essentially developed from the British model.

The principle of the doctrine was to isolate the population from the guerrilla forces and place them under control of the government. Without the support of the local population, a people's war cannot progress through the three stages of Mao's teachings.

Stage One was the formation of revolutionary cells in all the hamlets. Through these they introduced anti-government doctrine, most crucial for success, and established the infrastructure with which to conduct political and military actions against the government.

Stage Two involved grouping the cells into platoons to conduct expanded military actions against the government. This included ambushing small convoys and attacking small army outposts. As the successes mounted, so did the political propaganda. Recruiting and support were able to expand. Platoons formed into companies and companies into battalions, which still operated in the local province and area. With Stage One and Stage Two supporting each other, the People's War expands until the government cannot contain the actions taken against it. The whole infrastructure within the country then collapses.

Stage Three then implements conventional-style warfare when victory over the government forces becomes certain.

Should the war not progress to the next stage then the doctrine was to remain at the then current stage. Should the tide turn against them, with the government forces gaining control, they were to revert to the previous stage. This type of warfare never ends, as the revolutionaries will wait for the opportunity to recommence military operations. In the meantime, they continue to promote the political doctrine and actively recruit for the revolutionary cause.

Phuoc Tuy Province in 1966 had been progressing towards Stage Three. D445 Provincial Mobile Battalion of Phuoc Tuy Province was a unit that had been successful against the ARVN on the battlefield and thereby encouraged the political cells, through anti-government propaganda, to recruit for units in a Main Force regiment and division. This led to every hamlet having a political and small military cell while the military units included a Main Force division with two regiments. Militarily, D445 Battalion was respected as a fine unit and one which had been successful in action.

This was the military and political situation of the province when the Australians arrived. The Australian counter revolutionary warfare plan was to neutralise and destroy Stages One and Two of Mao's teachings. It was similar to pouring oil on water. As the government control of the local population increased so the influence of the guerrillas waned. This control slowly expanded, like oil over water, as the military pushed out against the revolutionaries. By engaging the enemy in battle, and consequently reducing the lines of communication and supply, the Australians planned to increasingly restrict the enemy's effectiveness throughout Phuoc Tuy Province.

CHAPTER ONE
AUTOBIOGRAPHIES OF THE
COMMANDERS

Each of the following is designed to paint a picture of the participants as they grew into the men who fought in the Battle of Long Tan. Through their stories they illustrate the types of activities in which young men of this generation participated and the values by which they were taught to live. It is fascinating to reflect upon the resilience of their spirits and the sense of adventure that prevailed. These characteristics were to provide them with the grit and determination by which they were able to withstand overwhelming threats to their very survival.

THE COMPANY COMMANDER, DELTA COMPANY, 6RAR:

MAJOR HARRY SMITH

I was born in Hobart, Tasmania in July 1933, son of Ron and Ann Smith. Dad served in the Second World War as a sergeant in the General Grant tanks of the 2/9th Armoured Division. He worked at Cadbury's Chocolate factory in the Production Department for 48 years, starting as a messenger clerk and retiring as a director. Dad was awarded an OBE for services to the community in 1966.

I attended Hobart High School where I served five years in the school cadet corps, reaching the rank of cadet lieutenant in my last year, despite having been dishonourably 'stood down' from the school unit for a short period some years earlier. I had 'borrowed' some ammunition after a Vickers machine-gun range practice so I could shoot rabbits with my issue .303 rifle while at Brighton Military Camp. On this particular range day, the Regular Army officer decided to actually inspect webbing pouches in addition to the usual verbal warning and caught me red-handed with twenty or so .303 rounds, an offence that required punitive measures, albeit more embarrassing than serious. I think that my father's admonition was more frightening than being disciplined by the headmaster and the cadet corps officers.

In those days, Brighton Camp had a large undeveloped land area to the north that abounded with rabbits. During summer holidays, I used to get out of bed early and stalk rabbits up and down the sandy gullies and ravines, blowing many to pieces with the overly large calibre rabbit gun. These exploits probably contributed to me earning a marksman's badge in range shooting.

After leaving school at the end of 1950, I chose to enrol in a seven-year-long diploma course in metallurgy at night school rather than go to university, much to my father's disgust. At that time I worked as a laboratory assistant with Austral Bronze at Derwent Park, just north of Hobart. I was attending night school five nights a week, but I still managed to skate and sail when time permitted.

Unlike youths of today I led a very sheltered and disciplined life, having to explain to my father if I was an hour late home after work. Once, I recall falling asleep on the train and having to return from New Norfolk by a later train at 2.00 a.m. I then had to try and explain to Dad where I had been since 10.00 p.m. My zest for work, study and sporting activities left me no time for interests in such things as girls, hotels, drinking or smoking. Guided by Dad, who was a good carpenter, I built a new Rainbow dinghy and took out the Tasmanian Rainbow Championship and was runner-up in the Australian Championship in the summer of 1950–51.

Towards the end of 1951 my number came up in the original 90-day National Service ballot for eighteen-year-olds, and I was inducted in January 1952, serving again at Brighton Camp. With my earlier cadet training and military aptitudes I soon rose to the exalted rank of lance corporal and then to full corporal; I was enjoying army life despite the cold Tasmanian weather. After the 90 days' National Service, I returned to work at Austral Bronze to find my job was no longer available. I gave the seven-year diploma a big miss and joined the Regular Army in May 1952.

After a non-commissioned officer's (NCO) course I was given the temporary rank of corporal and the job of section instructor, training National Servicemen, back at Brighton. It was a job that required me to be up and dressed by reveille and to stay up to lights out daily—fourteen hours a day, often seven days a week for the fourteen-week intakes. It was at Brighton, in the NCO's mess at age nineteen that I first tasted alcohol and took up smoking—both socially required habits for a new corporal. Girls were still not on the agenda, given the long work hours and the camp being so far from town.

At about this time Dad suggested to me that if I seriously insisted on staying in the army, I should use my educational qualifications and apply for the new Officer Cadet School (OCS) at Portsea, Victoria. I was duly selected, and travelled across Bass Strait by ship, my first 'overseas' trip, to commence the Second Course OCS intake in July 1952. This was six months of rigid discipline plus physical, military field and academic training at the highest level outside of the Royal Military College (RMC) at Duntroon. Some of the activities that occurred might be described these days as bastardisation, but we took it all in good spirits. Unlike many of the students, who had come straight out of civvy street, I already had some insight into military life.

I enjoyed and excelled at practical work in the field and did fairly well in academic studies, coming out first in the Field Prize and second in the Staff Prize at the end of the course. I graduated near the top of the class as the lowest form of officer in the army: a 'one-pip' second lieutenant on less pay than a corporal. I felt that most regular soldiers and officers, especially RMC graduates, despised us. This attitude appeared to continue for many years, in fact right up to the late 1970s when a few OCS officers finally rose to the rank of colonel and brigadier.

In the latter weeks of OCS, cadets were asked where they would like to be posted and in which corps they wanted to serve. Following in my dad's footsteps, I requested the Armoured Corps School at Puckapunyal in Victoria for corps training. I was hoping for a posting to sunny Queensland, well away from the cold Tasmanian and Victorian climates. As it happened, I was posted to Infantry and the Corps School at Seymour—I suppose not far from my first choice of Puckapunyal, which was only 25 kilometres away!

During the three months' Infantry School corps training, my previous experience managed to get me top marks in all phases of weapons and fieldwork. I was then posted as a platoon commander—not to Queensland—but back to the winter frosts of 18 National Service Training Battalion at Brighton, Tasmania. Perhaps I was sent there to help keep the rabbit plague in line! These were days when showers were out because all the water pipes were frozen and we pulled on uniforms over warm pyjamas. It was here we had to stand under tin shelters hour upon hour, day after day, intake after intake, controlling rifle and machine-gun practices—without ear protection—and the medical experts later wondered why most army people had 'industrial or high frequency deafness'.

I went through nearly three years of fourteen-hour days and nights training intakes of National Servicemen, along with further education in officer training—at the hands of RMC officers fresh from active service in Korea. My experience with them and Regular Army NCOs taught me a lot about things military. And in the brief breaks between National Service intakes I was able to find time for the odd visit to the ice-skating rink and to learn something about normal life.

I learnt too much too quickly, and despite family wishes, and the advice of my seniors, married Kathleen at an early age—much too early! I was only able to travel the thirty kilometres home to my wife's flat once or twice a week, if reluctantly granted overnight leave by the CO, who of course lived in married quarters right on the Brighton base. My parents helped me finance a small soft-top convertible Morris Minor tourer that I unfortunately ran under the tray of a turning truck. Veering to the right, I assumed it was turning right at a country road intersection, but it then went left as I steered around that side to pass. I converted the Morris to a topless model, fortunately ducking instinctively just in time to avoid being decapitated. Consequently, I was without wheels for some weeks and not a favourite son at home.

An RMC officer who visited Brighton regularly from a CMF adjutant's posting at Launceston to see a pleasant WRAAC officer, who later became his wife, was Captain Colin 'Mousy' Townsend. Thirteen years later, he was to be my battalion CO in Vietnam in 1966.

In retrospect, one bright light in the Brighton period was being sent off to the RAAF base Williamtown, NSW, to get my parachute wings, considered as requisite training for all young officers. I remember looking at the 30-metre-high 'Polish Tower' jump trainer with pangs of nervous fear at the thought of leaping off attached to a flimsy line slowed by a fan, let alone the thought of jumping out of an aeroplane eight times to get the prized wings badge. Yet, after the three weeks of intensive and repetitive ground training the drills became instinctive and when the time to jump finally came, that was also instinctive, despite a very rapid pulse pumping adrenalin and the butterflies in the pit of my stomach. Of course, as is human nature, instructors who were already well qualified had to add nervous colour by humorously highlighting what could go wrong!

This was my first step into what was to become a career allied to parachuting and other Special Forces activities. It was also the first of five hundred enjoyable jumps in later years. Unfortunately in 1975, parachute jumping put an end to my career after I suffered serious disc injury in a military free-fall parachute accident.

After three years training National Servicemen at Brighton, relief came in mid-1955 when I was posted as a platoon commander to service in Korea. But before I left, the war finished and I was re-posted, in December 1955, to the 2nd Battalion, Royal Australian Regiment (2RAR) in Malaya as a platoon commander reinforcement officer for active service in the Malayan Emergency. Here I was assigned to be 9 Platoon Commander, Charlie Company, at Sungei Siput operational base, about a hundred kilometres south from the main barracks base on Penang Island, a tourist resort area to which leave was granted about three days a month.

I had to leave my young pregnant wife in Hobart until British Army-sponsored married quarters accommodation became available many months later. We had decided on having a baby on the strength of my posting to Korea and my possible loss in action. At the time, we felt it was bound to be a son, to continue the family bloodline.

The Emergency was a daily routine of ambush, village food checks, security patrols and jungle patrols. I was sent down to Singapore and across to Kota Tingi by train to attend a four-week UK jungle patrol course. It was on the return train trip that I first saw blood and gore in a big way. The train, the Singapore Express, travelling at high speed, hit a British Army Saracen armoured car which had stalled at a road crossing, opening it up like a can of sardines and spreading the mangled corpses of the eight British soldier occupants along the railway line for hundreds of metres. I was involved with others in picking up fingers, arms and other pieces of bodies, an experience that matured me significantly and a sight which has always plagued my memories thereafter, surpassed only by what I saw on the battlefield at Long Tan.

Around May 1956 I was able to get married quarters on Penang in the Military Complex for my now very pregnant wife. On the base officers' wives addressed their counterparts by their husband's rank—and of course my wife was married to a lowly second lieutenant and therefore had few friends. She was not impressed by this situation, nor with all the time I was away at Sungei Siput. Fortunately a faithful and friendly *amah* (Malayan housekeeper) was provided under the British Army system to help with our baby girl, Deborah Anne, born in June 1956. The *amah* was also company when I was away, which was most of the time.

While based at Sungei Siput, I came to fire my first angry shot. I was ordered to take out a small patrol with a tracker dog to try and locate a wounded communist terrorist. When I went on forward of the dog handler, who had led us to him, to investigate the find I saw a terrorist about ten metres away, appearing to be removing a grenade from his belt. I shot him with my .30 calibre M1 carbine. I recall firing far too many rounds into him—it was an overreaction, but I just wanted him well dead and unable to throw the grenade at the patrol or me. We did not find a grenade. This operation was written up as 'based on good information, was well planned and efficiently executed by the Platoon Commander'. 'Executed' was perhaps an appropriate term as the killing might not have been necessary, but at that stage I was not taking chances and we faced similar situations later in Vietnam.

It was over the Christmas period of 1956–57 that I earned the lasting nickname of 'Harry the Ratcatcher'. I was required to carry out the duties of orderly officer at the battalion base at Kuala Kangsar for about three weeks. I was extensively briefed by our strict disciplinarian ex-Scots Guards adjutant, Captain Don Ramsay, to curb the noise emanating from some of the huts after lights out. After many successive but unsuccessful investigative incursions into the barracks area, I walked into the offending hut some nights later to discover a group of well-oiled soldiers noisily playing poker and two-up. I announced something like 'At last—got you—you rats.' From then on, my nickname followed me everywhere, although after Long Tan some changed the name to 'Cong-Catcher', but I am quite happy to live with 'Harry the Ratcatcher'.

The battalion was ordered to lay ambushes on the Thailand border near a town of Kroh. I was selected to lead the Charlie Company patrol and moved off to Kroh for two months. We laid ambushes on likely tracks atop high mountains but my group saw no action. But we gained considerable and valuable experience in jungle ambushes, resupply by aircraft and helicopters, along with the use of artillery and air support supplied by British forces.

I returned to Sydney where I continued serving with 2RAR. The lonely existence in Malaya plus the lack of a stable family home and close friends had not endeared service life to Kathleen. We had two other children, Sharon and Brett, born in 1958 and 1961. Sharon was another lovely girl, although my wife and I were still hoping for a son and so we continued on to a third child, to whom I gave three Christian names in case he wanted to become an RMC officer. Years later Brett wanted to join the navy, but was refused because of a medical history of sporting injuries.

After a period of Special Forces training with 2 Commando Company in Melbourne, in 1965 I was posted to 6RAR at Enoggera, outside Brisbane, and promoted to acting major and company commander of Delta Company. I discovered the battalion commander was Lieutenant Colonel 'Mousy' Townsend, who did not take kindly to my commando green beret and promptly ordered me off to the quartermaster's store to get the regulation British-style cumbersome peaked cap. I suppose I should have gone to the store before reporting to the CO. He also did not take kindly to my 'modus operandi' of training my company along commando lines with eight-kilometre runs each morning. I was accused of elevating my company above the standards required for an infantry battalion, apart from also leading young officers astray by teaching them to do parachute rolls out of the top-floor officers' mess windows, with at least one broken ankle resulting from these hijinks.

Colonel Townsend and I rarely saw eye to eye on any subject. In my first annual confidential report he intimated I was disloyal, but then agreed we were training for what was a company patrol action war and that each company commander had the right to use his own personal techniques. The colonel had seen a year in Korean service in cold, open country, whereas I had seen two years of tropical patrol warfare in Malaya, in terrain similar to Vietnam. I wanted to implement what I knew of tropical warfare and Special Forces techniques. Maybe a 'Mouse' and a 'Ratcatcher' were incompatible!

During the pre-Vietnam training exercises I continued to push my company harder and further than others. While I attracted the wrath of the CO, it put a feather in the company's hat. My company, as a group, knew they could always do what was required of them under pressure and this put them in good shape for what was to happen in Vietnam. From then on, it always seemed that whenever there was a long patrol or quick reaction required the job always fell to Delta Company. While Colin Townsend was a very popular commander, he and I often seemed to be in conflict, which was probably a combination of two factors. I was far more outspoken than most of the other company commanders and refused to be what was known as a 'yes man'. Also, I could make quick commonsense decisions and get on with the job, rather than sit around and procrastinate, which may have given him the impression that I was at risk of making hasty decisions.

Nevertheless, in early June 1966 I found myself saying goodbye to friends at Enoggera and embarking onto a chartered Boeing 707 which flew us north via a brief stopover in Manila to join our Advance Party at Vung Tau in South Vietnam.

I was born in 1941, a war baby into a struggling working-class family. My dad was a sergeant in the Transport Corps, serving in both the Middle East and New Guinea during the war. My first memories are of Samford outside Brisbane, where we lived until I was about seven. We then moved to Manly and subsequently Lota, where we lived until I left home.

The first significant event in my life occurred in 1954, when I was selected in the Queensland under six-stone rugby league team. This set me on the football path, which dominated my early life. I left school at fifteen with a reasonable junior pass and started my working life as an apprentice electrician. To become a tradesman, in my family's opinion, was the top of the ladder. I'm sure they were disappointed when, after a couple of years, I decided that crawling around ceilings for the rest of my life wasn't for me.

I left the apprenticeship and started work as a trainee executive for the old electrical retail firm Chandlers. Trainee executives in their early stage of development look remarkably like junior storemen and office cleaners and I spent a year or so at the company's big warehouse at West End. The next senior storeman above me at the time was Les 'Shorty' Turner, who turned up as a sergeant in 6 Battalion some years later.

In 1960, just prior to my nineteenth birthday, I was picked in first grade for Wynnum Manly in the Brisbane rugby league competition. By 1962, I was the regular first grade half-back for Wynnum. My elder brother, Brian, who had an electrical business in Tara, a town in south-western Queensland, suggested that I come to work for him selling TV sets. He reckoned that I would get the job of player/coach of the local side in the next season if I applied for it. This eventuated and I spent the end of 1962 and most of 1963 in Tara. At 21 years of age, I probably wasn't the best qualified coach they could have had but we had a reasonably successful and, from my point of view, incredibly enjoyable season.

Then I saw an ad which asked 'Would you like to be an officer in the Australian Army?' As I read the details, it seemed that all one had to do was spend a year at a sort of holiday resort called Portsea, with sport, a hectic social life and eventual graduation as a dashing young lieutenant. Several weeks and many aptitude tests later I was called before the selection board. I drove down from Tara the night before. I remember thinking I'd better listen to the news so as to be up on current affairs. A general called 'Big Minh' had just taken over a place called Vietnam, and there was quite a long report on the goings-on in that country. Next afternoon, when asked by the board about Vietnam I was able to give an up-to-the-minute résumé of the situation there. Luckily, they didn't ask me to show them on a map where Vietnam was. I wouldn't have had a clue!

When I got the letter saying I had been accepted for Portsea, I rang my folks to let them know. My dad said, 'Nothing wrong with the army—it's the bastards who are in it that'll give you a problem!' Talk about prophetic!

After graduation, I had six months in the almost peace-time army that existed in early 1965. Suddenly, however, the game got serious. It was announced that Australia was sending a battalion to Vietnam (that place again) and 2RAR split to form 6RAR. June 1965 was very significant for me: I was posted to Charlie Company, 6RAR, photographed in the *Courier Mail* leading my platoon in the 6 Battalion birthday parade and I met the lady who is still my wife today.

My first OC in Charlie Company was Peter Philips, later decorated in the Tet offensive, who finished up as a major general and later the National President of the RSL. He is as fine an officer and a man as you would wish to meet and taught me quite a bit about leadership in the short time he was my boss.

My first clear memory of Delta Company, 6RAR is seeing them run past as a company, all wearing camouflaged bush hats and led by Harry Smith. My recollection is thinking, 'Christ, what a shower!' At that stage somewhere late in 1965, the company was primarily National Servicemen, many of the experienced NCOs had not yet arrived, and from the vantage point of a Regular Army officer, comfortably ensconced in the primarily Regular Charlie Company, I was perhaps a little supercilious.

Little was known, at least among the 'baggies' (subalterns) about the company commander of Delta Company. We knew his nickname was 'Ratcatcher' but we were unclear about its origin. We knew from our casual contact with him that he was a cranky little bastard, who was quite prepared to tear a strip off a subaltern if you got across his anchor rope.

Similarly, my initial opinion of the National Servicemen can best be described by the following encounter. One morning I was moving between the mess and Charlie Company HQ. A National Serviceman (actually it was Phil Duncan) in uniform passed me in the classic 'thumb in bum, mind in neutral' mode. I let him get about five metres past and then roared, 'Don't you salute officers?' He turned, and with a quite genuinely contrite look said, 'Oh, Jesus—sorry, mate!'

I therefore had some mixed feelings when I learned I was to be transferred to Delta Company to take over Graham Cusack's 10 Platoon.

Very shortly after I arrived in Delta Company, Jack Kirby joined the company on return from Malaya/Borneo. For a very short while Jack was platoon sergeant of 10 Platoon before being promoted and made CSM.

Jack was a perfect foil for Harry. As well as being physically at opposite ends of the scale—Harry short, fit and feisty; Jack big, slow and methodical—they, perhaps unwittingly, provided a great combination of drive, example and humour which resulted in the crack rifle company that fought at

Long Tan. That, however, was somewhat further down the track.

What follows are my memories of some of the things that happened between late 1965 and August 1966, and the way I saw them.

We went to the Jungle Training Centre at Canungra for infantry minor tactics training—why the hell, I'll never know. Most of the training was done at section level so the platoon commanders were forced to watch the sections being exercised by a group of allegedly experienced senior NCOs. My most vivid memory is watching in fury while an aged Scottish WO2 from Signals Corps berated one of my corporals after a section attack. 'Why didnae ye use ye're EY rifle, mon?' says Jock, blissfully unaware that the EY rifle (extra yoke—a standard .303 rifle bound with wire to prevent breaking when firing a M36 grenade) had been out of service for at least ten years! Each evening we would have an Orders Group where the OC would tell us which parts of that day's training we were to discard as either useless or downright dangerous. Sadly, on my return to JTC as an instructor two years later, soldiers en route to Vietnam were still being taught stuff which could have got them killed when they went into action there. That's another story, however.

Back at Enoggera we were getting new equipment and weapons and could actually start to feel we were going to war. And then came our big pre-embarkation exercise. We went off to Shoalwater Bay where from the very first day Harry Smith made it clear that Delta Company was going to be better, faster and more aggressive than anyone else. Strangely, after several days and nights of forced marches, night raids and totally frustrating the exercise's umpires and enemy, the company was right on side. We started to feel that we *were* better than the other companies in the battalion and so started to look for ways to prove it.

At one stage in the first phase of the exercise we were so far ahead of the rest of the battalion that we were taken out of the exercise for a day to allow the rest to catch up!

Between phases of the exercise, we had a tactical route march of about thirty kilometres to another part of the exercise area. We set off in alphabetical order of companies. A couple of hours into the move, 10 Platoon on point, my forward scout reported friendlies coming toward us. Shortly thereafter, I met one of my mates, Bill Kingston, leading the point platoon of Bravo Company. We were passing in a diametrically opposite direction. As we passed I gave Bill a look which I hoped he would interpret as 'Where the hell are you going?' Bill's look in reply I will never forget. With a raise of the eyebrow and a shrug of the shoulder he answered, 'Don't ask me—I'm just doing what the dickhead behind me says.' Shortly thereafter I passed the OC of Bravo Company who asked me, 'Where are you going, Geoffrey?' I replied that I was heading for our rendezvous (RV) that was roughly north-east. He said something like, 'Oh no, my dear chap, you must read the ground.' I left him shaking his head at the folly of actually walking towards the place one was trying to get to. What was said when the two company commanders passed each other I don't know, but would love to have heard. Incidentally, Delta Company arrived at the RV first, before nightfall. The other companies straggled in over the next day or so, Bravo Company arriving about thirty hours after us.

After the completion of the exercise it was back to Brisbane for the wind-up before embarkation. Suddenly, it was not so much fun. I packed off my beautiful brand-new wife to live with my folks in South Australia and as she climbed the steps of the plane I felt very much alone.

Embarkation took place from Amberley via 707 jets. We passed through Manila, where we were not allowed off the airport and there were armed Philippine military police to keep us there. Nonetheless, ten days after arrival the first of our troops reported sick with gonorrhoea, which could only have been contracted in Manila. How the hell did they do it? I still don't know, but may I suggest to today's young officers that they never underestimate the ability of the Australian soldier to find booze, women or gambling.

I was born in South Africa to an Irish father and an English mother on 31 August 1940. The Buick family of five arrived in Australia in 1954 to settle first at Maylands then Bentley in Perth, Western Australia. I attended Forrest High Technical School at Mount Lawley, a school that taught the trades as well as all the other subjects. I enjoyed the subjects but my marks didn't impress my parents.

I left school at fourteen and my first job was as a deckhand on ferries operating across the Swan River from the Barrack Street jetty to South Perth and weekend cruises down the river on the SS *Perth*. Unfortunately I was sacked for failing to refuel a ferry, causing it to become stranded on the mud mid-river. Other job experience included time with Wormald Brothers as a factory hand and time as a storeman with Harris Scarfe and Sandovers, a retail store in Hay Street, Perth. I was sacked from those jobs too. My short working career had been a disaster, sacked from the lot. I took the bold step of enlisting in the army and on 4 February 1959 I signed on for six years.

Joining up in the 1950s was a ticket to leave Western Australia and see the world. Army life during the late 1950s and early 1960s was like being in limbo between the Second World War and who knew where. A private, like a mushroom, is 'kept in the dark and fed on bullshit'. From day to day he had no idea of the big picture or even the little picture; he just had to do his duty as required and enjoyed his down time. The affairs of the state or any other subject that required thought, opinion or comment were not discussed. Any interest in non-military-matters was usually discouraged with, 'Don't worry, son, the army will look after you!'

I went to Malaya with 2RAR and it was there that I learned the final graces of being a 'digger'. Military training, drinking and social skills were all passed on from the older members of the battalion. A few had served in Korea and most had completed the previous tour to Malaya with the battalion. Not only did you become skilled as a soldier in the art of warfare, but you also learnt how to relax. Success at work and play, with the maximum use of valuable rest time, was the secret of success.

The experience I gained in Malaya was to be critical when only a few years later I went to war in Vietnam with 6RAR. My mates and I had no idea what the future had in store for us. The important story of life is to learn to do things properly while you can, as it is too late when the bullets are flying.

Returning to Australia in 1963 I fell in love and married Beverley. I first saw Beverley at the Majestic Hotel in Brisbane, now sadly demolished like most of our drinking holes of the time. Unfortunately, soon after I was off with the battalion (2RAR) and away for nearly three months. We were the enemy forces to 1RAR and a British unit on Operation Sky High. I was determined to make 'an impression' on returning to Brisbane and so bought a MkII Ford Zodiac to impress her. Luckily, I had discovered her name while on exercises, from a mate, Jim 'Smiley' Myles, who was also taken by this good-looking girl and had written her name on his arm. We married in June 1964 and I took discharge in February 1965 as I saw no future in the peacetime army. We celebrated the birth of our daughter Tracey during March and I joined the RAAF in April. Three months later, in July, I rejoined the army. The war in Vietnam offered a challenge and excitement. I wanted a piece of the action.

I enlisted in the army for six years and although I had been out of the green uniform for only five months, this made no difference and in August I was off to Kapooka, home of the Army Recruit Training Battalion. Little had changed since my first visit in February 1959. Recruits still lived in the Nissen hut buildings of the 1940s that looked like large galvanised water tanks cut in half lengthways and laid on the ground.

These huts were airless and hot in the summer and bloody cold and bleak in winter. The instructional staff was in a new building and luckily I was to spend only a few days in one of those huts before moving in with the staff. What a difference in standards: hotel-type rooms with four to a heated room, while back in the old huts there were twelve blokes in a water tank. There I met an old digger mate, 'Blue' Harris from 2RAR days, and we were to go on to Delta Company, 6RAR together. He was with Company Headquarters at Long Tan. I have no recollection of him leaving the company and I cannot remember the last time we met, but I think he is living in Sydney.

Because we were not really recruits, the staff were at a bit of a loss as to what they should do with us. To keep us busy we had to attend a lesson on the self-loading rifle (SLR) given by a lance corporal. The lesson was about safety, stripping and cleaning, the very first lesson every soldier has with the SLR. The standard of instruction was so poor that at the break after the first part, we told him that he was to report to someone. Off he went thinking he would be back soon. We had completed the lesson before he returned, as he of course had not found the person he had to report to. I have seen that lance corporal quite recently. He is now a major, and in 1995 he still was unaware of the switch we pulled on him.

Those with previous service completed tests to determine the level of skill they had in relation to the final standards required for passing out. The results of the tests determined at what stage you entered the training system. I was above the required level to complete recruit training and therefore I did not require any refresher training. It was just a matter of waiting to leave the place—the sooner the better. The day to march-out could not come quickly enough. I had a couple of weeks to fill in, so off to the diggers' mess to clean tables, make the tea and coffee, clean the floor and cut the bread. My orders finally arrived. I was to return to the Corps of Infantry and at the end of August left for 'The School'. The School of Infantry is located at Ingleburn near Liverpool, NSW where all infantrymen completed their training in the skills required to be an infantry soldier. Again 'Blue' Harris and I did our training and tests, this time as section commanders (corporals) in the bush while the staff noted our relevant skills and knowledge. This of course allowed the staff to take it easy as we did the instructional periods and completed the tactical drills. I would have done the same if I was in their position: why bark yourself when you have another dog to bark for you? We completed the relevant tests within a few days of arriving and again we were waiting for the paperwork to catch up and to move on. Late in September we were both posted to the newly formed 6RAR based at Enoggera.

At the time I was not happy having to go 'through the mill', but it was time well spent and focused my mind on what I had to do. The skills and procedures that I had not practised for a few years brought the mind and body back to life. I was ready to be a digger. For the three months that I was playing soldier boy, Beverley and our daughter, Tracey, were in Brisbane. We had not seen each other since April and it was wonderful to be united as a family again. We were not to know then that for the next two years or so we would be together for about fifty days, as training and duty in Vietnam took over.

THE COMMANDER OF 12 PLATOON, DELTA COMPANY:

SECOND LIEUTENANT DAVE SABBEN

I was born in January 1945, in Suva, Fiji. My father's father had also been born in Fiji, and his father had come from England to Fiji in the early days of the then colony. All three had been in the government services. My father was in what was then the British Colonial Customs Service, and my mother was a double-certificate nurse before taking up the even more challenging role of rearing kids.

When I was nine, Dad got a promotion and transfer to the colony of British Honduras (now Belize), becoming the Collector and Comptroller of Customs and Harbour Master. Among his other duties and titles were 'Receiver of Wrecks' and 'Inspector of Lighthouses'—all very exciting to a nine-year-old boy. The latter title made him responsible for the lighthouses, navigation beacons and channel markers on dozens of coastal reefs and islands, which he then had to inspect twice a year. Being an avid fisherman, and the waters of Belize a fisherman's paradise, it took no great push to have Dad out on the government launch on inspection trips.

In the three years we were there, the family had many trips up and down the coast, stopping at the various inspection sites and exploring the often uninhabited islands. Being in an area frequented by some of the more notorious pirates and privateers of the Caribbean, and being nine, ten and eleven years old, I was always having adventures about discovering real pirates' treasures.

After three years in British Honduras, Dad was once again promoted and transferred—this time to the then-British island of Mauritius. We arrived there in 1957, with me about to turn thirteen and to enter high school. Since French was the language used most commonly in schools, my parents sent me to boarding school in Sydney for the next five years. I took with me a love of the outdoors and a preference for a field rather than an office life. I also had the sense of adventure that can only come from having walked in the imaginary footprints of the great Captain Sir Henry Morgan, not to mention other adventurers and bands of pirate cutthroats!

I disliked school. It was indoors, regimented and—to my young mind—'pointless'. I resisted the wonders of English grammar, the intricacies of Latin and the obscurity of algebra and calculus. I liked ancient history—they more or less lived outdoors in Egypt, Greece and Rome—but I found the endless succession of kings and cardinals in the modern history of

Europe dead boring. Geography and geology were fine, but where was the career path for either of these? Physics and chemistry were presented in such a grossly theoretical way that I couldn't grasp their relevance to the rest of my life. There were no art courses for me to hone a natural instinct and ability, but there *was* music for this individual who couldn't carry a musical note in a paper bag.

I was not good at team sports, but while at school, I did join the cadets and spent two years earning two stripes, mastering a sub-calibre .303 (a Lee Enfield housing a .22 bore) and rather enjoying the exercises at Singleton Army Camp. This, however, did not give me enough of a taste to consider a career in the Armed Forces.

Approaching my final year at school, I realised that in order to pursue my favoured career path of marine biologist or ornithologist I would have to go to university. Even if the heavens opened and my report card fell out with straight A's, neither my family nor I had the money to support me through a uni course, so it was into the work force for me.

With both parents regular church-goers and having for five years attended a Church of England boarding school (with two church activities each day and three on Sundays!), I had by eighteen developed more of a respect for the Bible than for church services and sermons. In time I came to accept the Bible as an authoritative rule book, applicable to my times and me.

Further 'study' (by which I mean a rather casual and unstructured reading, leading to a serious pursuit of knowledge on selected subjects) revealed to me that somewhere in my future I should undergo military training. My logic, which I haven't had cause to alter in the following thirty-odd years, is that if God loves me as much as He loved Israel, then I should do as He told Israel to do. Among the many instructions given to 'His People' but never subsequently altered or rescinded is the command for all males twenty years and older to be trained for war (for example, Numbers 1:2 & 3).

My older brother Frank had joined the Citizen Military Forces (CMF—now the Reserve) after leaving school, before he became a patrol officer in New Guinea, so I thought that perhaps I should join the CMF, too. However, I decided to delay joining until I got a career under way. Besides, I had until I turned twenty to apply.

On leaving school in December 1962, I took a job with a store in Sydney, joining their advertising department. I started as everybody's slave and coffee maker, of course, and honed my layout, design and artwork skills between brews. I enjoyed the relative freedom of the work force after the regimented boarding-school life and compensated for the office job by spending as much time as I could on weekends driving an FJ Holden up and down the back roads and fire trails inland from Gosford, NSW.

At about this time, the Indonesians announced that they were adopting a policy of 'confrontation' towards the proposed Federation of Malaysia. Because Australia had troops in Malaya and Borneo, there was every chance that Australia might become involved.

As a result, a new National Service scheme was established which would call up a selected number of twenty-year-old Australian males for two years' full-time service in the army. The first step in the National Service process was for all Australian males to register during the half-year in which they turned twenty. The selection process was then by a ballot of birthdays followed by strict medical and other examinations of those called up to weed out the unfit and the undesirable. I was determined to be a part of this National Service contingent. I was not called so I packed my bags and presented myself at Victoria Barracks. I argued with them until they put me on a train to Kapooka. Their initial reluctance was because my status was unclear as I did not have my own passport, having entered the country on my mother's at thirteen. My determination to join created notoriety for me as I became the subject of newspaper articles and a cartoon.

Once there I volunteered for officer selection. The typical selection experience started with groups of eight recruits being isolated in a sandpit, surrounded by officers with clipboards and being bellowed at by a sergeant who was explaining the 'rules'. The rules were along the lines of 'The sandpit is a river.

Here are some ropes and poles. Get that barrel across the river without touching the sand. You're being timed. Go.'

The idea (though we didn't know it at the time) was for the natural leader to emerge from among his peers by motivating the others to conform to *his* plan. There were six of these tasks, from which one or two recruits were selected from the group. In some groups, none were selected, even after all six tasks. The selected recruits were then formed into new groups of eight, which were then set harder tasks, requiring more thought, direction and the exercise of more intense influence over their peers.

After the first two days, I believe there were still three hundred or so candidates at Kapooka. The following two days were more academic: the candidates were required to speak both on their own chosen subject and on nominated subjects. Current affairs were discussed to sort out the thinkers from the sheep. We were given reports and press clippings and expected to present our assessment of them with just a few minutes' notice.

We were assessed in all things—even how long it took us to change from PT to parade ground gear. Our showers were timed, and our barracks room was inspected after each change to ensure we were stowing our gear properly and not taking shortcuts.

Each candidate had to address the officers individually and collectively. This weeded out the shy types, but by then my shyness had become more a deep sense of reserve, so I was able to rise to the occasion. There was a written exam that included prose responses. At each stage, candidates were removed without explanation, and we never knew whether those removed were being selected or rejected.

Finally, there was a 'social drinkies' event in one of the classrooms, to determine who could hold a wineglass and not disgrace the Officer Corps with such brutish behaviour as stubbing a cigarette out on the carpet or spilling wine on the commanding officer. At the end of this evening—after some candidates were removed even at this stage of the selection process—it was announced that the survivors would be transferred to the Officer Training Unit next day. There were 25 of us in that particular group.

The only piece of advice I remember receiving during all this selection process was from a Regular Army corporal. Once, when I was first to arrive on the parade ground puffing but smiling, he fixed me with the sort of a glare that only an NCO can master and growled, 'Don't think this assessment's jus f'yer selection, wetback. If yer in, yer next six munths gunna make yer think this wuz a picnic.'

He wuz right!

A few days later, 160 or so recruits of the first intake of National Service arrived through the gates of the Officer Training Unit (OTU), Scheyville, NSW. There, on the parade ground to meet and greet us, was the Regimental Sergeant Major (RSM) Larry Moon, and his very efficient-looking array of warrant officers and sergeants. The buses drove onto the parade ground and we all got out. Moon made us feel that it was our fault the buses had driven onto his parade ground, and for the next six months, he never looked like forgetting it.

My memories of OTU are mostly about struggling just to keep up. In later years, I found that most of the others felt that way too. If there were good times at OTU, I missed them. Yet I relished the course. I had never been so challenged before, and I had a vision of the end result. I recognised that this experience was building a better 'me', and I actually found the development deeply satisfying.

Some found the uniforms, the regimentation, the high pressure of constant activity and the pedantic nature of the training to be onerous. I had no problem with any of that. I didn't find the uniform or regimentation a problem—boarding school had prepared me for both of these. I didn't find the studies a problem—at last I found logic in everything I was taught. I didn't find the incessant activity a problem—most of it was outdoors and all of it was challenging.

And the pressure (some might call it mild bastardisation) wasn't a problem—I had learned to simply retreat into my shell when things got too rough, yet to still pull my weight regardless. 'Suppress the ego; maintain the output.' I could put up with whatever was thrown at me because I knew we were training for situations where worse would be thrown and I'd be expected to still pull my weight.

In the first three months, we went from generally fit to superbly fit, from vaguely able to purposefully able, from 160 ragged and raw recruits to a strongly bonded unit of about 120 officer cadets. And we were only halfway through.

In October 1965, we watched the second intake of National Service officer cadet hopefuls spill out of the buses onto the RSM's parade ground. This time we understood why Larry Moon 'hated' us. The army was expecting him and his team to take this civilian mess, dressed in greens and pretending to be soldiers, and to convert them into the leaders of Australia's finest—and then in only 22 weeks!

I think it was then that I realised how far we'd come. The change had been gradual and there'd been no time for reflection. But now, each of the first intake was made responsible for a second intake recruit, with not a drop but an increase in our own training activities. The sixteen-hour days became eighteen-hour days, with more PT, exercises and classroom tasks. While 'enjoy' is still not a word I would associate with the Scheyville experience, perhaps 'satisfying' would be. I began to feel that I was, in fact, doing well. I topped some of the subjects—notably map reading in which I excelled (and actually got 100 per cent on one occasion, I believe), and did well in most others.

Towards the end of the course, the subject of corps allocations arose. Although the basic OTU course was aimed at producing infantry platoon commanders, there was a need for junior officers for the other arms and services, so a limited number of OTU graduates were posted to non-infantry units. Most, however, were posted to an infantry battalion or went to other infantry postings.

Five OTU graduates—myself among them—were posted to 6RAR, recently formed in Enoggera, Queensland, by the splitting of 2RAR into two infantry battalions. All of us were to be posted as platoon commanders in the rifle companies—exactly what all our training had been directing us to!

The end of the six-month OTU course saw 86 officers (about half the original intake) graduate in December 1965 and return to their families for Christmas. I daresay most of their families had some trouble recognising their boys from the Christmas before. In a society where Beatle haircuts and sloppy clothes were the norm for twenty-year-olds, our short hair and uniforms were pretty conspicuous.

In mid-January 1966 I reported to the 6RAR adjutant, on the day after my twenty-first birthday. Crisp, ironed polyester uniform, single pip shining and looking oh so very impressive on each shoulder. Heart pounding and breathless, anticipation throbbing under my officer's peak cap. The only thing non-regulation about me was my pair of non-issue shoes, but they were black, well polished and almost army-issue shaped. I'd seen that the captains at OTU had had a winking relationship to dress regulation shoes, and so had chosen comfort over uniform. However, only a stickler for details would notice them and even then, he'd have to be insanely committed to standards to even pass comment—much less discipline me!

Standing in front of my new company commander later that same day, I got both barrels.

Major Harry A. Smith, OC Delta Company, 6RAR, was a stickler for detail and insanely committed to standards. He made it well known to everyone within a hundred metres of his office that hand-made Italian shoes were not represented in the army supply system. Further, that when the army saw the obvious error of its ways and began to provide them, then—and only then—would I be entitled to wear them. But not before!

Of course, they weren't anything like his description, but it didn't matter. Neither Harry nor I ever saw those comfortable shoes again.

Harry had acquired the nickname 'Harry the Ratcatcher' in Malaya some ten years earlier. The army was small enough for just about every officer to know just about every other officer of equal or senior rank, so it wasn't too hard for me to get an insight into Harry. I put the word out with my girlfriend's father, who was an ex-army senior NCO and had many serving mates and back came the reports. The common thread was 'keen type'. He'll set his rules and standards. If you don't shape up, you'll be shipped out. And so it proved to be.

The Artillery Controller for Delta Company:

Captain Maurice Stanley: 161 Battery New Zealand Artillery Forward Observer

I was born in March 1931 in Christchurch, New Zealand, but I grew up in Napier on the east coast of the North Island. In the same year, much of Napier was devastated by a major earthquake and was rebuilt in its present Art Deco style.

It was a good area to grow up in, and I was able to spend many hours swimming, sailing, fishing and cycling. During my last couple of years at high school, winter meant rugby union with practice midweek and competition on Saturdays. During the war years, a few warships called into the port and many cargo ships came in to load meat, wool and fruit for Britain. My friends and I used to swim out past the wharves and sometimes it seemed we were very close to their huge propellers. For a period, my father was a weapon-training instructor at the local drill hall, and I enjoyed helping him with his 'homework', stripping and assembling small arms.

My years at high school—until the end of 1948—were quite pleasant. I favoured science, technical subjects and mathematics and do not recall getting the cane very often. Out of the classroom I was in the second rugby team, captain of the shooting team, prefect and RSM of the school cadet unit. At that time, I did have thoughts of being a technical-school teacher. However, I suspect that some of my schoolmasters and others, such as my favourite uncle who had returned from active service a few years previously, had an influence on me and I decided to apply for the army.

In January 1949 I enlisted in the only option available at my age, the Regular Force Cadet Unit. This was a special unit established at Trentham Camp, Wellington, to educate and train young men between the ages of $16^1/_2$ and 18 years to provide tradesmen and instructors for the Regular Army. Most of the cadets were in effect completing their final year or two of high school, and the program was generally school in the mornings and military training in the afternoons. As I had matriculated, I was given the opportunity to attend Victoria University, Wellington, to study pure and applied mathematics, part-time. Unfortunately, for each of the four lectures and one tutorial per week, I had to travel 90 minutes each way. Usually I returned to camp just in time for a quick lunch, and then had to prepare myself for the afternoons of 'square-bashing', weapon-training, PT and so on. While I did not do very well at my university studies, I was in the first rugby team and a qualified marksman with the rifle and the Bren gun.

Later in 1949 I attended a selection course for entry to the Royal Military College, Duntroon. I heard nothing of the matter until just before Christmas, after I had already graduated as a sapper in the Royal New Zealand Engineers. In typical style I received an order to go to the Orderly Room, where the OC had something to tell me—what had I done now? Consequently, I felt quite relieved when told that on returning from my Christmas holiday break I should be ready to go to Australia for the four-year course at RMC with nine other New Zealanders.

We were all about nineteen years old when we sailed on the MV *Wanganella* to Sydney. As we were the juniors we supported each other during this adventure and were guided by the senior classes, who were returning to complete a further year of their courses. On board, I met Don Kenning, who was to become my first battery commander at Bien Hoa, Vietnam. Don was returning to graduate at the end of 1950.

Some readers may know something of the initiation ceremony that was conducted at RMC in those days. It is sufficient here to say that the trial was strenuous and stressful. When I was instructed to sing 'Waltzing Matilda' during the ordeal, I took exception and persisted in singing 'Maori Battalion', a well-known New Zealand marching song. After all, how could I be expected to know the words of an Australian song? No doubt I received some attention for my impudence.

Four years of a 6.00 a.m. to 9.00 p.m. routine of academic and military studies followed.

'Fango' Watson, the famous Duntroon RSM, selected me to stand in front of the whole unit on many occasions as a drill demonstrator to assist in our preparation for the many ceremonial parades which were conducted. Also for a couple of years, I was the RMC member of the Armed Forces Catafalque Party when one was mounted at the Australian War Memorial. As a result of these activities I received more than my fair share of 'Fango' yelling orders and sweet words in my ears.

While at RMC I still wanted to be an engineer, and in my third year the academic work was focused in that direction. In my final year, however, I transferred to specialise in artillery and graduated into the Royal New Zealand Artillery. Incidentally, one of the infantry instructors at RMC in my time was George Chinn. Would you believe it! When I was attached to 6RAR in 1966 he was the RSM, and he was in one of the helicopters that resupplied D Company with ammunition during the Battle of Long Tan.

Apart from the military work and academic studies, a most significant event for me was meeting a lovely Canberra girl at church! During the first few weeks at RMC, local leave was not granted, except that after a period, we could go to church. It was simply a matter of getting onto a bus heading for the denomination of your choice; amazingly, many of us identified as Presbyterians, and went to St Andrew's. Later, we could go out to lunch in Canberra, provided that we had a written invitation. After four years of relevant manoeuvres,

Alva and I became engaged on the day I graduated as a lieutenant in December 1953, and we were married six months later. We are still together today with three sons in their forties and we have seven grandchildren.

My first real job came in 1954 at Waiouru Military Camp, which is located in the mountainous centre of the North Island, where there can be harsh winters with heavy frosts and frequent snowfalls. It is a great place for military training and I suppose I was fortunate in that regard, although I do not think my Canberra girl was very impressed with the isolation. While I was there I was first attached to the School of Artillery for three months' training, after which I was appointed to the Compulsory Military Training (National Service) Depot as an instructor and later became Staff Officer—Training. I was to learn a great deal during those three years through teaching and from the experienced officers and NCOs in the unit.

Even at Waiouru, the army trained for jungle warfare, and I was one of four officers sent to the Jungle Training Centre, Canungra, for an officers' jungle tactics course. What a change in climate! The outdoor part of the course was tough work, but I enjoyed it. The war veteran instructors were not there to play and said that some sections of the course would be made as close to battle conditions as permitted during peacetime. On one occasion, a few of us chickened out and asked that some explosive charges, which had been placed only a few feet above our heads, be moved. On the other hand, the confidence course, firing the Bren gun from the hip, the rum and prawns in the mess, were all great fun.

In 1957 I was posted to the HQ of an infantry brigade in Christchurch. The brigade comprised three large Territorial (CMF) battalions. My job was staff captain and I took a liking to the operational administration, particularly when all the units were in the field.

Still as an artillery officer, I landed the job of mortar officer in a Regular Force infantry battalion in 1959. That unit was destined to proceed to Malaya and trained for a year at Waiouru. During that period I developed a great respect for the infantry as I shared many of their experiences.

Following this time in which I was virtually in the infantry, I at last scored an artillery appointment to Auckland as adjutant of a Territorial light anti-aircraft (Bofors) regiment. As two of the batteries were based a couple of hours' drive away, I was able to become familiar with another part of the North Island.

In 1962 I was battery commander of a Regular Army field battery at Papakura, just south of Auckland, and although the battery was under-strength it was almost ready for overseas duty.

Soon after I took up my next appointment as battery captain of a medium (5.5 inch) battery in Hamilton and shifted my family there in 1964. I was then selected for a contingent to go to the UK. A total of 150 troops from the Artillery and Armoured Corps were to travel to England courtesy of the RAF to perform public duties by providing guards for Buckingham Palace, the Tower of London and the Bank of England. In addition, we were able to exercise with British Army units on Salisbury Plain. Our ceremonial training was conducted in New Zealand under the guidance of a drill sergeant from the Welsh Guards, and we received further training at Woolwich. I did four duties as Officer of the Tower of London Guard, which involved 24 hours on duty followed by 48 hours off duty, which gave me some opportunities for sight-seeing around London.

Fifteen months later, I was in a completely different military environment.

In January 1966 I received a telephone call in my Hamilton office from Army HQ inviting me to get ready to go to Vietnam at short notice because another officer from the first contingent had to return to New Zealand. Initially, that meant a rushed job to get myself inoculated as protection from all manner of dread diseases.

Although I had been in Papakura with 16 Field Regiment two years earlier, I was not in the original 161 Battery when they began training for Vietnam. They deployed to Bien Hoa near Saigon in mid-1965. Because I knew most of the men in the battery very well, having worked with them for some time, I felt as if I was just rejoining the old team when I arrived at Bien Hoa as the replacement battery captain.

At that stage, the battery was in direct support of 1RAR, and we were attached to 173 Airborne Brigade. When I arrived I could see how much work the men in the battery had already done during the six months they had been in the theatre. The area was quite well established with guns, the command post dug in, a few buildings for stores, and tents for messes and accommodation. Provided that the generator and the projector were working, we even had movies to enjoy on some evenings and the sight of tracer and flares in the night sky did much to enhance the realism of the Audie Murphy films that were shown.

During my early weeks at Bien Hoa the place was at times strangely quiet, except when the guns were firing, because the battery commander and FO (forward observation) parties were out on operations with 1RAR. When they returned I would see how tired they were and that their tents were festooned with laundry while they rested in the sun or in their tents out of the rain. I learned a lot from them and later I was to get first-hand experience.

In late February my battery commander offered me the opportunity to join Operation Rolling Stone as an FOO with 1RAR for a couple of days. 161 Battery had already been deployed near 1RAR as part of a protection force for a US engineer battalion base and its road construction task near Ben Cat, about thirty kilometres from Saigon. During one of the nights with the rifle company I heard conversation between the Company HQ and a listening post and was informed that VC were passing in front of the company. Some were allowed to pass and then the small arms fire started, causing me to consider what might develop. In the end there was no call for fire support, but I got a hell of a fright and next morning I saw bodies being buried with the aid of a bulldozer.

1RAR was engaged in Operation Denver in April, near Song Be, about a hundred kilometres north of Saigon and 161 Battery had moved in by air from Bien Hoa in support of the operation. During this period the battery commander returned to New Zealand for a short period and I took over his role for a few days. After walking with Battalion HQ and wondering what was going to happen next and what I should do about it, I was relieved to find that I was not personally involved in any contacts. When I returned to the nearby battery area I found it necessary to cool down a situation which arose when a padre who was learning how to play his guitar commenced playing at last light 'Stand To'. An irate (large) gunner had told the guitarist what he could do with his instrument and was about to assist him. At about the same time, unfortunately, a soldier suffered a nervous breakdown and had to be extracted for medical attention and eventual return home.

Near the end of April the battery commenced dismantling the base camp at Bien Hoa in readiness for the move to Phuoc Tuy Province to form part of 1ATF. A friend of mine, 'Red' Potts, had arrived from New Zealand to take over the position of battery captain and a month later, the battery commander, Don Kenning, commanded the Task Force set up for the movement of units by road from Bien Hoa to Vung Tau and Nui Dat. The force included 161 Battery RNZA, 105 Battery RAA and several ordnance, transport and police units. I found that rather than moving by road, I was to move by air to Vung Tau and join D Company, 6RAR as their artillery FOO, at the ripe old age of 35 years.

THE COMMANDER OF THE ARMOURED PERSONNEL CARRIERS: LIEUTENANT FRANCIS ADRIAN ROBERTS, OC 3 TROOP, 1 APC SQUADRON

I was born in Western Australia, the eldest child in a large family. My father had seen service in the Second World War as an RAAF navigator and bomb aimer in Europe and he inculcated in me strong values about service. This sense of service in a period that was the height of the Cold War led me to a military career. I was brought up to honour God, serve the Sovereign and love my country; simple, clear, strong values that have guided my life. My father believed, as do I, that a 'good name', honour and being 'one's own man' are central to good character. At the same time being temperate, modest and self-effacing were also stressed. These latter qualities were not necessarily helpful among ambitious peers.

On graduation from Teachers' College I taught until 1962 when I was selected to attend Officer Cadet School (OCS) Portsea. In parallel with my teaching studies and employment, I had enlisted in 1959 into the Citizen Military Forces in 10 Light Horse.

I was enthusiastic about the Regular Army after a visit to Puckapunyal in 1962 and although I had just married, the adjutant of 10 Light Horse, Captain Templeton, and the RSM, WO1 Arthur King, both encouraged me to seek selection for OCS.

I had married in my wife's home town, Melbourne, in January 1962. Gillian and I had met at a church social club, the 'marriage market' of our day. After only six months of marriage she was to know the curious life of a soldier's wife as I trained for twelve months with only Saturdays and Sundays at home, if I was lucky, and OCS allowed the time. Tough times on an officer cadet's pay, but forty years later we are still married.

OCS Portsea was the hardest year of my life. The OCS regime was intensely physical and mentally demanding. The staff was determined to weed out the weak and to ensure that only the very best survived to graduate.

I remember the commandant, Colonel S.T.G. Coleman, standing, arms akimbo, and addressing my class at the beginning of our course. He said that he had seen officers in New Guinea give up because they thought that they had reached their limits; he was therefore going to teach us our limits so that in war we would not give up. Never has a course aim been so clearly and honestly stated—and applied.

OCS was a tough, manly school in which the very best of officer and soldier values were inculcated into students by a highly select staff. Fair, firm and friendly sums up officers, warrant officers and NCO instructors alike. The warrant officers were a library of practical experience that stretched from New Guinea to Malaya. Every detail, every skill that they had learned in operational circumstances was driven home to cadets. WO2 Rosenburgh's bayonet fighting classes were terrifying experiences. RSM Brennan's drill and ceremonial lessons were wonderful in welding a group of individuals into one body. WO2 'Wee' Jock Richards, himself an example of forceful personality, was always willing the unwilling to greater efforts. I remember them all as fine men and outstanding soldiers. Our officers taught us the higher level skills and knowledge required of an officer, as well as social skills. Among the latter were dancing lessons conducted under the watchful eye of the quartermaster's wife who supervised the bevy of local maidens who provided not only dancing partners, but also partners for the splendid balls held twice each course. Many of these girls later married their cadets.

About half of my course were 'other ranks'—soldiers from the Regular Army. A large percentage of us were from ordinary homes. Under the careful tutelage of OCS we were given social and human skills that enabled us to mix with anyone—from morning tea with the Queen to meals with Montagnards in South Vietnam.

There was no bastardisation. If anyone defaulted, the punishments were not humiliating. This contrasted to the behaviour we saw at RMC during a visit in 1963, where we were amazed to see 'custard races', where the first cadet who finished dessert put his bowl on his head and all the others, no matter the contents of their bowl, had to do likewise. What a contrast to the correct, formal atmosphere of the OCS cadet mess which was a perfect replica of an officers' mess.

OCS Portsea claims only the happiest of my memories both as a cadet and subsequently as an instructor.

I graduated from OCS in 1963 and was posted as a troop leader in B Squadron, 1st Armoured Regiment. It was an army that set great store on formality in the life of an officer and provided endless field training opportunities and major exercises, which made great demands on family life, especially as a second lieutenant.

During this time I went to Queensland as a troop leader in B Squadron and spent months exercising near Tin Can Bay as well as a short time in the Paluma area, west of Ingham. The latter provided valuable experience in the difficulties of operating armoured vehicles (Centurion tanks) in jungle, while Tin Can Bay's dreadful sand crust floating on seemingly bottomless mud was to relate directly to many subsequent Vietnam circumstances.

I did, however, enjoy my one and only Barrier Reef cruise, in a tank landing craft shipping Centurion tanks back from Ingham to Tin Can Bay!

I had been sent to Queensland immediately after our son was born, leaving my wife, with two small children, to cope alone on a second lieutenant's pay, most of which went on a rented cottage in Seymour. In my absence my wife, the baby, and our small daughter (born during my OCS time), were shifted, using an army truck and five willing troopers, to married quarters at Puckapunyal.

In the first ten years of our marriage I was to spend a total of five years away on various exercises and Vietnam postings. Somehow my wife held things together with the children and created a home. In those years there was no family support system except for one's regiment, as the army was indifferent to family problems and needs. Happily that has gradually changed over the years. Nevertheless, I salute the heroic efforts of service wives of that era and of my wife in particular.

In 1965 I was warned for service in Malaysia with the Life Guards but subsequently I asked to serve in the newly raised 1 APC Squadron. It was a decision I've often wondered about. 1965 flew by with the brand-new squadron raised with officers, then NCOs and gradually troopers, then being equipped with the new M113A1 armoured personnel carriers (APC). The squadron ran endless courses, trained on the vehicles and had the prospects of replacing 1 Troop then at Bien Hoa, Vietnam, with 1RAR.

While our training was intensive and produced a 'well-oiled' team it was notable for the absence of training with infantry. It meant that the use of APCs had not been inculcated into battalion thinking beyond simple transport and load-carrying tasks. While the squadron used the British Army training manuals, these did not appear to be available to infantry and so they were unaware of the drills associated with the integrated use of armour. These drills were in fact learned during operations in Vietnam—hardly a desirable process.

It is important to recognise some of the capabilities and limitations of the APC to understand their use at Long Tan. The M113A1 APC is really just an aluminium armoured box, proof against small arms fire and shell splinters, but not against armoured weapons or anti-tank mines. It could travel at 30kph, but was very rough for both passengers and crew when travelling across country. While it is possible to travel inside the carrier with hatches closed, it provides limited vision and the .50 calibre machine-gun cannot be used. Crew commanders tend to remain in their position, exposed from the waist up behind a gun shield, and communicate by radio with the driver and infantry commander. The noise of the engine still makes it very difficult to communicate within the vehicle. The infantry are seated either side of the vehicle, totally enclosed unless the cargo hatch is open. They exit the vehicle through a rear door ramp that lowers to the horizontal. However, it must be stressed that at the time of Long Tan the soldiers of Alpha Company had limited training with APCs.

On 1 May 1966 I arrived at Bien Hoa with a group of NCOs and troopers intended to take over 1 Troop vehicles. We went off on an operation with 173 Airborne Brigade in War Zone D and subsequently with the brigade on Operation Hardihood to secure the Phuoc Tuy area for 1 ATF. When the brigade withdrew, the troop was in position at the arrival of 5RAR. We were the first troops from 1 ATF in the area.

I must have been destined to be a pilot as I have a photograph of my first birthday cake with an aeroplane on top. I can only ever recall wanting to be a pilot, nothing else. While others recognised the difficulty of achieving this aim, I never doubted I would fly aeroplanes one day.

My father joined the army as a stable boy in the horse-drawn artillery in 1937 and was to serve in Artillery throughout the Second World War. I was born in the bush nursing hospital across the road from the fort in Queenscliff. My memories of Queenscliff are living by the beach surrounded by women, including my grand-mother, mother and aunty. I do not recall any male influences. I was an independent, some would say naughty boy, who once wandered off to the beach by himself at age four for a whole day, initiating a police search. I am not sure if it was as a punishment, but I was sent to school at this early age, as I was obviously independent enough.

When my father returned from the war he was offered a commission in ordnance. This meant a move to Bandiana, which was established as a dump for Second World War military equipment as it awaited disposal at auction. This created a wonderland for boys of servicemen to play war. All we had to do to play soldier was get through the barbed wire, not be seen, and 'we were there'. It was also the time of the rabbit plague and so we often wandered the hills hitting rabbit 'squats' with sticks or digging out burrows; collecting skins and making some pocket money. I often did this alone, packing a lunch, and signalled home by semaphore or mirror on schedules set by Dad, to indicate all was well. Our scout leader was an army officer who had served in India and he brought a reality to the stories of Baden Powell and the *Jungle Book*. He also trained us in the fashion of military scouts, or what I would now reflect on as being the modern-day SAS reconnaissance patrol. During the seven years we spent in this area I developed independence and resilience.

When we moved on posting to Adelaide the difference in education systems created the situation in which I moved ahead another grade. My family decided to send me to a private boys' school, Pulteney Grammar. I was now two years younger than the average age of the class and four years younger than the oldest boy in my class. I am sure this influenced my social maturity adversely. I was often the target of jokes, but had a determination to get others back, no matter the consequences. I managed to cope with all the challenges, both physically and academically. I particularly remember a trip to the Flinders Ranges with the scout troop. We prepared for months, walking in our heavy, hobnailed boots, carrying heavy packs, making our own pup-tents and planning our supplies. I still remember the colours of the outback, the wildlife, and the challenge of walking for so long with all our supplies. I also enjoyed the opportunity to play lots of sport at school. When I turned fifteen I joined the Air Training Corps and worked my way up to cadet under officer. After completing my matriculation year I was still too young to be accepted into university so I did a Leaving Certificate Honours year. I finished this year and was selected to enter the RAAF Academy in January 1957. I was the youngest member on course at sixteen.

The RAAF Academy was a continuous challenge for me as I decided to try and prove that, no matter how young or small I was, nobody could break me. I coped academically, but my continuous 'insubordination' to senior cadets saw me attend many punishment parades. As in Duntroon and OCS, this usually involved getting up early and running with your .303 rifle at arms-length for a period of time; however, many other tasks were incorporated to break your spirit and obtain obedience—what became better known as 'bastardisation'. I still regard this period as a great part of my life. We were challenged both academically and physically. We were given many opportunities to test our ingenuity, be it in making our own skis and learning to snow ski, or building our own canoes out of bamboo and canvas and travelling the rivers. We were taken to interesting places like the Snowy Mountains Scheme, Woomera, Darwin and the outback, plus the Newcastle and Wollongong steelworks. Sport was a major part of our lives and I learned to play rugby, something of a sin for an Australian Rules footballer, but there was no choice. As I approached my final year, my immaturity led to the authorities recommending that I be 'back-coursed' one year, as it was felt that I was not mature enough to be commissioned.

The years in the Academy were a period of growing up. It was a time of getting to know the opposite sex, about social drinking and about motor cars. My first car was a 1927 Armstrong-Siddeley soft-top that cost £25. From this I graduated to a Singer Sports, MG Magna, and MG TC, before settling down with a Holden. Despite all the trials and tribulations, I grew fifteen centimetres and survived to graduate. In my final year I met and courted a young WRAAF lady, something we cadet officers were forbidden to do, who would become my wife Jan.

After graduation I flew Dakotas at the School of Navigation out of Sale, Victoria. These aircraft were flying classrooms for the practical training of navigators. It was pretty boring work, although it took me to New Zealand on one trip. I kept my sanity through playing and coaching the local RAAF Australian Rules football team, along with participating in inter-service sports. Subsequently, volunteers were called for to train on Neptunes in 11 Maritime Squadron at Richmond, NSW. I volunteered and when Jan and I returned from our honeymoon to Sale we were informed that I was posted to Richmond the following week. We didn't get to unpack our presents or boxes.

For the next three and a half years I spent my time chasing submarines across the oceans of the Asia-Pacific region. With thirteen members aboard, it was a great experience to become a captain of a crew. It was the early 1960s and the slogan on the side of our aircraft was 'A Hard Day's Night', from the Beatles. International cooperative exercises took us to the Philippines and Hawaii, as well as all around the coast of Australia. In mid-1965 our crew was a part of the support mission for HMAS *Sydney* as it transported 1RAR to Vietnam. We flew to Lae in Papua New Guinea and operated from here, fully armed with live torpedoes, as we escorted the convoy through the straits south of the Philippines. During this experience, our electronic counter measures operator intercepted a signal that could have been the attack radar frequency of an enemy submarine. Everyone went to battle stations, the ships started weaving through the water, troops were stood on alert, and we searched down the line of the signal. Everyone was chattering away about what could happen next. Were we about to start the Third World War? Intelligence had indicated that the Russian Fleet had submarines that may have been in the area. After several hours of tension had elapsed everything settled back down. It turned out that one of the squadron aircraft that was positioning to the Philippines to take over from us had tested its attack radar with a couple of sweeps.

At that time, there was a call for pilots to train on helicopters. It was obvious that this call was associated with the Australian Government planning an increased involvement in South-East Asia. I was always looking for a new adventure and an opportunity to be posted overseas, so I volunteered for training. This involved a move to Canberra, and I commenced my conversion in January 1966, along with a dozen other pilots from various RAAF squadrons plus several RAF ex-chopper pilots who had been recruited in the UK.

It was a frantic time, as we all underwent our conversion to the Iroquois (Huey) or Bell UH1B helicopter. Initially it was a matter of getting control of this craft that flew according to different rules of flight. It was very sensitive, with its hydraulically assisted controls, and of course you had to fly close to the ground, allowing a very small margin for error. I remember that as I came to the hover one day, intensely concentrating, my instructor casually remarked that my wife was watching, at which point we hit the ground and bounced around, most ungraciously.

Once we were in control, we were taken out into the hills and practised operations in close proximity to obstacles. At this stage a real sense of three-dimensional control started to emerge and I recognised how finely I was able to operate the aircraft. A real test was to hover over a mushroom patch with the crewman hanging out picking mushrooms for all to share, while you remained in the hover!

Our only operational training was the major exercise at Shoalwater Bay just before we departed for Vietnam. It was the only time we carried troops and got experience in operating our aircraft with a load on board.

I remember listening to the announcement by the Prime Minister on 8 March, as I was sitting on the front steps of our house having a beer with Geoff Banfield, that the squadron had been nominated as part of an increased involvement in Vietnam. The next day I was included on the roll of six crews who were to move to Vietnam on 14 June 1966.

CHAPTER TWO
DELTA COMPANY PREPARES
FOR VIETNAM

The following is the story of the 6th Battalion Royal Australian Regiment's training program leading up to embarkation for Vietnam. The character of Delta Company was formed during this time. Its determination to be the fittest and the best was driven by the commanding officer, Harry Smith, who only knew one way: 'his way'.

JUNE TO DECEMBER 1965

The 6th Battalion Royal Australian Regiment (6RAR) was formed on 6 June 1965 at Enoggera, a suburb of Brisbane and an army camp since the First World War.

In the next month the first intake of National Servicemen entered the Australian Army. This first intake completed their recruit training at the army's Recruit Training Battalion located outside Wagga Wagga, NSW or Puckapunyal, Victoria. Later intakes completed this training at Singleton, NSW. For those allotted to 6RAR, infantry training was then completed at Enoggera, Brisbane. As there was also a need to select and train officers from each intake, those who met the criteria moved to Scheyville, a reconstituted army establishment that was prepared as 1 Officer Training Unit (1OTU).

Delta Company was one of two companies in 6RAR that was designated to accept and train National Servicemen in the many skills needed to be a competent infantry soldier. In early September some three hundred arrived at 6RAR from Kapooka to commence three months of intense training that was to be completed before Christmas 1965. These skills included bayonet fighting, patrolling and tracking, navigation and map reading, and mine drills. The weapons they needed to master included small arms, machine-gun, light anti-tank gun, hand grenade, grenade launcher, mines and booby traps. These skills were honed through repetitive practice until they became instinctive.

The corporals and lance corporals conducted this section training under the watchful eye of the sergeants. They developed a team approach, as the smooth functioning of the group would become the security of the section and platoon when under the stress of enemy action. Luckily, the sergeants of 6RAR were experienced soldiers who had served in Korea, Malaya and Borneo and were able to provide very practical supervision in the important skills.

Although the non-commissioned officers, the sergeants and corporals, of the company had trained the National Servicemen in the required skills as infantry soldiers, there was still much to learn and practise in order to create a confident and highly skilled combat unit. This was the training that commenced in January 1966 and continued relentlessly until the unit embarked for Vietnam during May and June of that year.

The combat unit, a rifle platoon, had 34 men. They comprised an officer commanding (lieutenant or second lieutenant), a platoon sergeant, three sections of ten with a corporal as commander, a lance corporal and eight privates. There were also two private soldiers on the Platoon Headquarters, a radio operator and an orderly/runner. There were three rifle platoons in a company, which also included additional specialists to administer and support the company. These were cooks, a medical orderly, stretcher-bearers from the battalion's band and a small party from artillery for combat operations. The company with all attachments was about one hundred strong but in Vietnam the operational strength varied from the mid-90s to about 110.

Delta Company was still short of two platoon commanders in December 1965 and these were to march in in early January of 1966. The day after David Sabben and Gordon Sharp joined the unit from 1OTU, the CO placed 6RAR onto a 'semi-war footing'. This was in response to the possibility that 5RAR and 6RAR might embark for Vietnam in the middle of the year. The battalion's training schedule entailed ten-hour days and six-day weeks. Training started at 0730hrs each day except Sundays and would end at 1730hrs on each day except for at least two nights per week, when it would continue until 2130hrs.

These training times did not include time for normal administrative activities and increased to seven-day weeks when the battalion was out of the barracks area for exercises.

The CO was under instruction to bring the battalion to a level whereby it could enter an operational area by mid-May. Thus the target was established: be ready by mid-May. That left us just sixteen weeks.

Two days later the training schedule for the sixteen weeks was promulgated:

17 Jan–24 Jan	Junior officers to Lever's Plateau
24 Jan–10 Feb	Battalion section-level training to be completed
10 Feb–15 Feb	Mount Byron and Kenilworth State Forest area for platoon/company exercises
15 Feb–21 Feb	Platoon training at Enoggera
21 Feb–26 Feb	Tin Can Bay for a live firing exercise and platoon-level exercises
28 Feb–01 Mar	Greenbank for a range shoot
07 Mar–12 Mar	Spring Mountain and Kenilworth State Forest for a battalion exercise
12 Mar–24 Apr	Rotate through Jungle Training Centre, Canungra by companies Delta Company slots: 13–20 Mar, 13–14 Apr and 22–24 Apr
15 Apr–21 Apr	Shoalwater Bay for a battalion exercise
25 Apr–03 May	Mount Spec for a battalion exercise
04 May–	Battalion administration, pre-embarkation leave, etc.

Reviewing the times out of camp and the heavy training schedule while in camp, most people who harboured ideas of seeking the pleasures of the night-life of Brisbane or the Gold Coast thought again.

After only two days in the unit and still without having met their platoons, all the captains and below (subalterns) were whisked off to Lever's Plateau to refresh them on section-level formations and contact drills in close country. Whoever designed Lever's Plateau obviously had section-level training for junior officers in mind and our instructors made the most of it. In places it was near vertical. In places it was rock and in other places swamp. It had leeches and the dank smell of rotting vegetation. Stagnant slime from fetid pools clung to boots and clothes for days. There were vines and moss and thorns to contend with. All had to be ignored. Dave Sabben thought the Scheyville instructors had taken all the best training places, but obviously there were some left over.

The instructors were some of the 2RAR senior NCOs, and some of the ex-2RAR junior officers experienced a few 'paybacks' during the course of the week. For some who had filled the roles of assistant adjutant or specialist platoon commanders, it was a reintroduction to activities they'd given up some time ago. A spirit of competition developed between these young platoon commanders.

While the officers of the battalion were being trained in the vagaries of procedures and practised solving battle and tactical problems, the platoons continued to train and develop combat skills. There was a need for section commanders to command their men and ensure all members of their section were motivated, adaptable and highly skilled in all the requirements to survive battles. By the end of January, Delta's sections were practising movement formations, field signals, camouflage and concealment, obstacle-crossing drills, harbour drills, contact drills and the hundred other skills an Aussie soldier had to develop to live and fight in the bush. These skills were the key to efficient movement and survival when under the incredible stress of battle. The Battle of Long Tan was to be the ultimate test for these soldiers and their precise use of these training skills was a critical factor in their surviving that engagement.

On their return from Lever's Plateau, the young officers finally met their platoons. There's a day in the life of any commander at any level that he will never forget. It's the day he meets his command for the first time. Geoff Kendall's dry sense of humour set the scene for Gordon Sharp and Dave Sabben as they waited, sweating into their uniforms under the Brisbane January sun. 'Moment of truth, fellas . . . They'll fall about, laughing . . . Bet you fluff your first salute . . . What'll you do if one faints on you? . . . What'll you do if they *all* faint on you?' Kendall was a tower of strength! No wonder they sweated.

The next two weeks were a whirl of finalising section-level training and introducing platoon-level training. The task at that time was to get the platoons ready for the exercises that would weld the sections into smooth-operating platoons. Then would come the company exercises, where the platoons would be welded into company sub-units. The battalion exercises would come later, where the companies would hopefully combine into a cohesive battalion on operations.

The platoon commanders found that the corporals had done an excellent job and the platoon sergeants had excellent control of the platoons both tactically and in administrative matters. The sergeants provided the young officers with the wisdom of their experience, most of whom were smart enough to listen. A few days into platoon training and the fear of being commanded by a civilian in greens abated somewhat.

It was during the platoon-level training that Harry Smith gently (at first) applied his standards. He would come around the platoon training areas with his CSM, WO2 Jack Kirby. They'd chat, make notes and leave. At the evening de-brief, he'd have hints, criticisms and guidelines for each of the platoons.

Jack Kirby was by no means the silent partner in the OC/CSM pair. He had a solid build, but nevertheless was fit. Jack also wore Malaya ribbons and had a great deal of input towards the running of the company. He was firm with the NCOs and gently but respectfully dismissive of the junior officers. He'd show it in his exaggerated terms of respect for the rank: 'Mr Sabben, Sir, with respect, Sir, get a haircut . . . Sir.' All the while he was bright-eyed and suppressing an infectious chuckle. They couldn't take offence and they always knew he was on their side after all. Between them, Harry Smith and Jack Kirby first moulded and then polished the company.

It started with the individual soldier. Delta demanded its troops patrol with shirt sleeves rolled fully down, fronts buttoned up and dogtags (personal identification discs worn around the neck) taped together with black electrical tape to prevent noise and any possibility of reflecting light. Face, neck and backs of hands were to be smudged with ash or dirt. Kit was where the book said it should be, so everyone knew where to find whatever they were looking for on someone else in the dark.

Delta insisted on well-developed field signals and before the first company exercise, the platoons were able to train all day and, while 'tactical' (on the job), never to use a spoken word. As the training developed into overnight practices of harbour drills, Delta gave up shaving. The reasons were simple, but multiple: the natural camouflage after the first few days, the time and smell of the act of shaving, the scarcity of water during summer exercises, the possibility of slight nicks becoming infected, and the possibility of bad water. It all made sense and the company responded to the professionalism of every suggestion or 'command'.

It had its lighter side. During one memorable Orders Group (O Group) following a night harboured out in the bush, Harry Smith decreed that in future soldiers would neither cough nor fart in the mornings. This was somewhat of a surprise to those like Dave Sabben, who had assumed that somewhere in the Bible God must have made allowances for such natural events. Imagine that in such an unnatural circumstance as a grown man waking to find he's spent the night fully dressed, cuddling a loaded rifle and sleeping on stones among the grass, he's not allowed even a quiet fart in protest!

However, the decree stood and over the next few weeks, several chronic coughers and farters either suppressed their natural urges or found new fields to cough and fart in. Delta was a silent company in the mornings thereafter. Harry did not allow for failure; if you could not make the grade he arranged for you to move to someone else's company.

Harry Smith's worth was not only in what he did, but also in how he did it. His company didn't invent new formations to move in or a new harbour drill to observe. Rather, he did what he did meticulously, attending to every detail as if someone's life depended on it, which most of the company understood but hadn't taken to its logical conclusion.

MT BYRON AND KENILWORTH STATE FOREST AREA FOR PLATOON AND COMPANY-LEVEL EXERCISES

This was the first time the platoons operated as platoons in the bush. In a way, it was the new platoon commanders' initiation to the platoons as well. This was the first time that they would see whether they 'had what it took'. So far, the platoons had only seen their commanders as an observer of their actions and a debriefer of their section commanders. Now it was them out there with the platoons, nominating formations according to the ground they were crossing, setting the pace, navigating, using voice procedure on the radio, directing contact drills, selecting harbour sites and placing weapon pits.

This was the time when they could be in the bush with the corporals and talk to them outside the formal barracks atmosphere. The state of the uniform often corresponded to the state of the relationship: the more starched the greens, the more stiff the formality. By day two in the bush, the O Group—meetings where daily actions were reviewed and new plans developed—became more relaxed; a few jokes and some light banter became apparent.

PLATOON-LEVEL TRAINING IN ENOGGERA AND LIVE FIELD FIRING AT TIN CAN BAY TRAINING AREA

Back in base, they concentrated on the weak points observed during the preceding exercise. The foothills of Enoggera echoed to the firing of blanks and the yells of 'Contact front', 'Ambush left', etc.

During each day, Harry Smith would call in at some time or the other and observe for a while before moving on. Sometimes he'd have Kirby with him, sometimes other people. He'd make notes and talk with whoever was with him, but never interrupt. At the O Group he would outline his observations and give 'direction'.

The battalion got experience at getting into and out of APCs during this time. While they practised their own movement drills as they deployed from the carrier, there wasn't any practice in the tactical use of APCs. Similarly, very limited experience was gained in getting into and out of helicopters. While these utilities would become integral parts of activity, the battalion did not develop operational efficiency until inefficiencies were revealed in actual operations in Vietnam.

At Tin Can Bay the soldiers honed their skills as marksmen through a range shoot. They also watched firepower demonstrations, where they got to see some of the possible supporting fire that could be brought to bear on a location. Other activities involved the officers being given a platoon or section 'stand' to run. Each group arrived and carried out the drill, for example, an ambush drill, under the watchful eye of the officer.

After a month of fairly continuous activity the sections and platoons were becoming well drilled. While time in the bush was hot, dusty and tiring, there was also a melding of teams as they worked through the hardship together. Being able to support each other when things were not so 'sweet' became an essential requirement. Spending days on end in trying physical conditions was the norm in jungle warfare.

GREENBANK FOR A RANGE SHOOT

This shoot was used to adjust the sights on all individual weapons. The armourer and his assistants checked each individual's target results and make the appropriate adjustments, then sent the individual back for a re-shoot. Each soldier has his own natural tendency when firing his weapon and must gain the confidence that it will hit what he is aiming at. This weapon would always be within reach in Vietnam and was cared for like 'one's life' depended upon it—because it did.

BATTALION EXERCISE AT SPRING MOUNTAIN AND KENILWORTH STATE FOREST

BATTALION EXERCISE AT SPRING MOUNTAIN AND KENILWORTH STATE FOREST

The next week the whole battalion moved into the hinterland behind the Sunshine Coast for a battalion exercise, to test the battalion's procedures and train everyone in deployment and other battle procedures. It was about this time that the unit was officially notified of service in Vietnam and training became 'deadly earnest'. As the other companies clicked up the training ratchet, Harry Smith simply raised the level for Delta yet again.

The exercise this time took everyone through the four phases of war: defence, withdrawal, advance and attack. Digging in for a defensive position on Spring Mountain was no easy chore with all its shale and rock. As part of the advance phase, they did an air-porta-bility exercise, which entailed loading the fully equipped company into a Caribou and flying to Coolangatta Airport and back.

When the battalion physical training tables were issued, showing the levels of fitness to be attained by the battalion, Harry Smith went to his Special Forces library and Delta went into over-drive. If ever there was the time for a rift between Harry Smith and Jack Kirby, this was the time, because Kirby struggled with the demands, but no rift occurred. Where the battalion specified ten kilometres, Harry ordered twelve. Where it specified fifteen-kilo packs, Harry ordered twenty-kilo packs. Where an activity specified sandshoes, Harry ordered boots and gaiters; this was to strengthen the legs and general fitness needed in battle.

Apparently, the battalion CO was furious, but Harry Smith persisted. At the time, the NCOs knew what was going on and maybe so too did the regular soldiers, but the National Servicemen just accepted it all as part of the army. Because they knew no better, they just buckled down and did it. If they had the time to compare lots with the other companies, they didn't think to do so.

Over the next few months, Delta came to be the fittest, fastest, most tactically proficient, most secure company in the battalion.

And the CO responded when he got his chance. As soon as the battalion exercises got under way, it became obvious it was 'payback time' for Delta. On every exercise, it seemed that Delta got the outside leg of the sweep, forcing them to move further and faster than anyone else.

The thing that must have irritated the CO was that Delta simply relished the task. By now, all the faint hearts and weak minds had joined the coughers and farters in some other location and Delta was a company confident in any task.

JUNGLE TRAINING CENTRE AT CANUNGRA

The Jungle Training Centre (JTC) at Canungra provided a battle efficiency course. Realism was developed through isolating the group and only allowing an issue of shelter or supplies that could be expected in Vietnam. The weather, being tropical, also represented the conditions they would encounter. It was a real taste of the perspiration and fatigue associated with high temperature, rain and humidity.

There were also mock Asian villages. They included all the 'trimmings' that could be expected: animals, tunnels, caches, 'enemy' and booby traps. Canungra was the place where individuals and sections honed their skills in close-quarter fire and movement through live-firing targets. Targets would pop up as they were advancing down a track. Soldiers were required to fire two shots from a rifle and three to five rounds from an automatic weapon. This was often a Second World War vintage Owen machine carbine—the famous OMC—that proved to be unsuitable in Vietnam and was eventually replaced by the Colt AR15, later to be developed as the M16, the Armalite. Of these three to five rounds at least one round had to hit the target. The soldier thus developed the skill of 'shooting to kill'.

The PT instructors at Canungra took particular delight in pushing everyone to their limit. They had a sadistic approach to an obstacle course they had designed, where they continually attempted to prevent soldiers successfully completing it so that they would have to repeat the exercise. The obstacle courses became a section activity with the stopwatch being dug out for company and battalion competition, with Delta Company determined to always be a winner.

When not involved with individual or section training, Delta continued with its own 'get fit' program. Each morning there would be a compulsory run in long pants and boots—starting at three kilometres on the first day and building to sixteen kilometres on the last day. Other times of the day were devoted to static exercises under a PT instructor. Harry Smith selected the top tables of the Special Forces fitness regime and applied it to all without exception. He revelled in it himself and demanded no less than 100 per cent compliance from everyone in the company.

SHOALWATER BAY FOR A BATTALION EXERCISE

The battalion travelled to this exercise in relative style: by train to Rockhampton, eight to a compartment, 64 to a carriage. The first leg took them from Brisbane to Gympie, where the train stopped about midday. Lunch was set up on the opposite side of the platform; it was a hot meal of ham and vegetables, to be served into metal dixies and eaten on the platform. All the diggers lined up for lunch. Some had been served and were eating, some were being served and the rest were waiting to be served. Into the opposite platform pulled another train, loaded with pigs. It stopped and it stayed. For some strange reason, a lot of diggers departed Gympie hungry that afternoon!

They arrived at Rockhampton where the battalion was formed up and marched down the main road to the Showgrounds. A corral was allocated to each platoon, and everyone was told to settle in but to be on one-hour's notice to move. Hexamine stoves were lit and a brew prepared. Late in the afternoon, when boredom had set in, they were told to prepare to stay overnight. As if by magic, the Showgrounds quickly became deserted. It was a busy night for the military police as they returned over-enthusiastic soldiers to the camp.

In the morning, the place looked like a battlefield. Diggers had arrived during the night—mostly drunk—and not being able to find their own corral, had slept (or passed out) wherever they could find a horizontal surface. The army chose 0700hrs, with the diggers at their worst, to become efficient and arrange transport to the exercise area. In the mad scramble to be ready, breakfasts and shaves were missed. The clothes of the night before—many showing distinct signs of second-hand beer—remained unwashed and unchanged. By mid-morning they were in the exercise area and the routine started again. Settle in, be on one-hour's notice to move, don't wander from the camp. The old saying 'hurry up and wait' was certainly the norm.

The exercise itself began with the Delta OC being declared an exercise casualty and 'evacuated' to Rockhampton. Everyone felt that this was no 'accident'!

Delta was flown by helicopter to a hillside some 22 kilometres away and started digging in for the night. Next morning it was a five-kilometre advance to contact, followed by a company assault on an 'enemy' landing zone (LZ). At this point, Harry Smith joined the company again as it camped overnight on a hillside and pondered its next task.

The battalion was spread over a whole map and was to concentrate its force over the next few days in order to put in a battalion attack on an 'enemy' camp. When Delta commanders plotted their orders, they found that they had been given the outside sweep of the battalion advance: a trek of some 35 kilometres to be done in two days. At the O Group, Harry Smith specified the 35 kilometre hike, but after the accompanying directing staff (DS) had moved off, began planning a subterfuge that would allow the company to reduce the length of the march. The 35 kilometres would take the company up the west side of a series of hills to the first pass between the hills perched on top of a steep and forbidding ridge line and then down the eastern side, in the form of a giant inverted U. Harry decided that the company would patrol up the west leg to a particular saddle about halfway up the line of hills, then try to blaze a trail across the saddle to the eastern side. If this worked, the company would cut across. If not, it would repeat the exercise on each subsequent saddle until it could cross. While this could be interpreted as cheating, Harry Smith believed that it was 'creative routing' and that he was using his ingenuity.

Next morning Harry set a cracking pace. At the lunch break, the company commanders convinced the DS that they were just to the west of a hill, further up the line than where they actually were, and reported the false location as if it were true. During the afternoon, Harry forced the pace again. At an early dinner stop the company again established a false location, now two hills ahead of where it really was. After dinner, Delta Company saddled up again and covered the last hill to its anticipated crossing point, continuing to convince the DS that it had reached the supposed 'real' crossing place.

What the DS thought were the three normal early morning clearing patrols were actually six half-section patrols sent out to find a way down the other side. A route was selected and Delta started down the eastern side of the ridge. On the flat ground again, it turned south and headed to the battalion rendezvous. During the day, when the company stopped for a brew, Harry Smith provided adjusting location references. At the lunch stop, the CO changed his orders and Delta was required to step up the pace in order to be at a different location at a different time. By the CO's map, the company would not be able to make it. By Harry Smith's map, it would be a stretch, but he felt the troops were fit enough to do it.

At the CO's O Group next morning, Harry Smith didn't own up to the deception. Delta had still covered more than any other company, and it was still on its objective before any other company was on theirs. Why not let the deception stand?

Someone in the company had brought a transistor radio and the local Rockhampton radio station was playing the latest Nancy Sinatra song, 'These Boots Are Made For Walking'. It was an instant hit with Delta Company and became its theme song. In his O Group that day, Harry Smith commissioned Dave Sabben to design a company logo incorporating the boots, the letter D and the company colour, red. (Dave finally produced an acceptable logo using a red Greek capital delta, which is a triangle, with a pair of golden boots. Later, in Vietnam, when they were issued with the new shin-high general purpose boots, the logo was revised to show the new boots, and this has been the Delta 6RAR logo ever since.)

Exercise orders for the next day set Delta another 5-kilometre patrol to locate and take an 'enemy' camp. Harry chose to achieve this by dividing the company into three independent platoon patrols and converging on the area from three different directions. Doing this, he cut off the escape routes and 'captured' the three 'enemy' in the camp. Radioed orders then told the company to camp there overnight. Suspecting that they would be set up for a busy night, the officers again colluded in a deception. After giving their location and having dinner, they settled into the night routine. While the clearing patrols were out, Harry Smith had one of the signallers render the directing staff's radio unserviceable. This was achieved by placing a piece of cardboard inside the handset connection so the contact points were kept apart. As soon as the clearing patrols were in, Harry got the company up and it moved about five hundred metres down a dry creek bed to a new harbour position. The DS was unable to report the new location.

All through the night, the company could hear the 'enemy' trying to draw a reaction from the empty patch of scrub it had previously occupied. In the morning, the signaller 'repaired' the directing staff's radio, putting the blame for the malfunction down to moisture, despite the fact that the only water evident in the area was in their water bottles or running down their backs.

Delta's next task was to cover fifteen kilometres and put in three separate platoon attacks on three separate targets. All platoons were in position about eight hours before they were expected, while the 'enemy' were still digging in and camouflaging themselves. All platoon attacks took advantage of the surprise element and put in their assaults by the book. The DS waiting at the 'enemy' camp nearly wet themselves when the attacks began, as all the 'enemy' soldiers were out in the open, cutting camouflage and brewing up.

Delta then linked up with Bravo Company for the final advance and assault of Phase One of the exercise. Over these days, Delta had tactically covered 50 kilometres fully kitted out and at all times moving in correct formations. It was at this point of the exercise that some felt the bond within Delta Company had been formed and they moved from being a collection of good platoons to a company. With a new spirit and pride in their collective achievement, the soldiers set out on Phase Two of the exercise: to clear the peninsula to the east. Delta once again took the outside loop in its stride—one might even say, with pride—and for the next week, advanced up the peninsula in a series of leg-numbing marches.

Finally, the 'enemy' camp located, it was Delta Company who infiltrated the camp, providing the details of the layout and vital distances to the battalion CO, who was then able to put in a textbook assault to end the exercise successfully.

BATTALION ADMINISTRATION AND PRE-EMBARKATION LEAVE

The battalion went into administration mode. All the Q-Store equipment had to be cleaned after the exercises and packed for departure. There were rounds of vaccinations and introductory briefings on the war and the area of operations. Somewhere in all this, there was a march through the streets of Brisbane, drinks for the officers at the Brisbane Victoria Barracks and the whole battalion was sent on pre-embarkation leave.

And then it left for Vietnam.

CHAPTER THREE
THE FIRST TWO MONTHS IN
PHUOC TUY PROVINCE

In this chapter we use the voice of Harry Smith to illustrate how Delta Company and others settled into Vietnam. It was a time of new experiences, some hardship and frustration. But overall it was a period of initiation to the rigours of a war zone. The 'hurry up and wait' syndrome was still prevalent as the company carried out its routine duties and waited to engage the enemy.

For most of the diggers in the company, arriving in Vietnam was like arriving in another world. Not just because it was a war; but because the countryside, the people and their way of living was so different. It's often difficult to remember that in the 1960s, most twenty-year-old Australians hadn't been overseas. Travel was very expensive and even when it was possible the destinations were more often America and Europe than South-East Asia. Unlike today, there was little television in the early 1960s; it was in black and white and most of the programs were almost exclusively British or American. Consequently, very few of the soldiers had the global awareness that is associated with the young today. There was still the tradition, if not the policy, of a 'White Australia'. No one had heard of Vietnam. Up until the early 1960s it wasn't even called Vietnam—it was called Indo-China.

Although not all the battalion had arrived in Vung Tau by 6 June 1966, a small parade was conducted to celebrate 6RAR's first birthday.

Delta Company arrived in Vietnam by air on 9 June 1966 and the battalion was given 'acclimatisation' training among the sand hills of the Australian Logistic Support Base (ALSG) at Vung Tau. Vung Tau was an area noted as a rest and recreation centre (R&R), for both Allied and VC troops, as well as a holiday destination for the civilian population of Vietnam. This was an interesting coexistence. Consequently, bars and other forms of night-life proliferated. The number of cases of VD evidenced the nature of the night activity after infrequent leave breaks.

For Delta Company the first week at Vung Tau was supposed to be for acclimatisation, to get everybody used to the monsoon humidity and equatorial temperatures. It was only 10 degrees of latitude above the equator—nearer to the equator than Darwin or even the very tip of Cape York. But that didn't stop the intense activity. Day One was devoted to equipment and stores issues, lectures and briefings. On Day Two there were lectures and demonstrations for the officers at the nearby American air base. Day Three was an all-day range shoot, with virtually unlimited ammo to expend! Day Four was taken up with helicopter ('chopper') familiarisations and introductions to new weapons. And Day Five was devoted to a full battalion exercise in the nearby mangrove swamps and mudflats.

Among the briefing papers were the histories of the conflicts in the country since the Second World War, accounts of recent American operations in the province and background to the politics of the conflict. Delta was also provided with organisation charts and intelligence summaries for the enemy formations they might expect to find operating within the province from time to time. The officers had to read and digest all this information among all the other activities. The diggers had time to swim and play beach cricket between the training activities.

Morrie Stanley had been in Vietnam for six months and his two operators, Willy Walker and Chris Cooper, had been there a lot longer. As a result his forward observation party had a bit of a bludge until 6RAR got themselves settled and organised. Eating tropical fruit, swimming and hanging around was good therapy for them. Even when they did join up with Delta Company and Morrie attended O Groups in the first few days, they felt that the company really needed time to sort itself out without there being too many hangers-on. They helped with acclimatisation and orientation, but the most important thing was that they came to know everyone and to feel part of the company.

9 Squadron arrived in Vung Tau on 12 June by Qantas Boeing 707 to Saigon and then 35 Squadron Caribou for the last leg of the journey. Bob Grandin remembers moving into Villa Anna, an old French villa on the foreshore that was currently the home of the 35 Squadron pilots. 'The villa was in need of repair, became very overcrowded with seven or eight to a room, but was far preferable to living in a tent,' he recalls.

The squadron flew its first operational mission the next day, taking small arms ammunition for 5RAR to Nui Dat.

Meanwhile, Adrian Roberts remembers that at the end of his acclimatisation at Bien Hoa he participated in an operation with 173 Airborne Brigade in War Zone D, as well as an operation lifting South Vietnamese troops. They also did normal 1RAR patrols in APCs in 1RAR's tactical area of responsibility (TAOR). The troop moved as part of Operation Hardihood to Phuoc Tuy and participated in the clearing of the 1ATF base area, including the 173 Airborne Brigade clearance battle for Long Phuoc. During this action he was on a carrier in a blocking position near the crossing point on the Suoi Da Bang that would later be used en route to the Battle of Long Tan.

Adrian Roberts recalls that with the arrival of the 1 APC Squadron the members of 1 Troop's replacements were dispersed to 2 and 3 Troops while the original vehicles became 3 Troop's. What this meant was that there was a fair leavening of 'experienced' officers and NCOs, but it also meant that 3 Troop had some rather mechanically 'tired' vehicles, albeit with radios and crew intercommunication facilities (the latter the only ones in the squadron).

When the 173 Airborne elements left Phuoc Tuy the APC, with Adrian in temporary command, moved into a position on the western side of Route 2 just opposite that to be occupied by 5RAR. They were there when that battalion arrived and later were joined by the whole squadron in a position further south and immediately south-west of Nui Dat that was to be their home for the next year. Often overlooked, the troop was the first element of 1 ATF actually on the ground.

It was while 6th Battalion was 'acclimatising' at Vung Tau that the 1st Australian Task Force (1ATF) base was being established around a small hill twenty kilometres to the north. This small hill didn't even have a name. On the maps, it was marked as 'Nui Dat', which is Vietnamese for 'small hill'. On other maps there were three hills so marked, and more on adjoining maps. However, the Australians adopted the name 'Nui Dat' for their small hill and the 1ATF base became known as Nui Dat from then on.

5RAR currently occupied the area around Nui Dat along with other elements of what would become the Task Force. 5RAR was intensively patrolling the general area and trying at the same time to dig in and get defensive wire up around its part of the base. However, from the very early days, VC reconnaissance units were constantly probing the base and bumping into the 5RAR patrols.

It wasn't long before the VC worked out that they could take on the lone battalion at Nui Dat. Information filtered through to the ARVN and to the United States intelligence networks that the VC were planning a regimental attack on Nui Dat within a few days. What was to have been two weeks of acclimatisation for 6RAR was cut short with this news and the next day they flew in to Nui Dat.

This move from Vung Tau took place on 14 June. The battalion was airlifted by Chinook helicopter into the Nui Dat base area, which was to become Delta's home for the next twelve months—a muddy existence in an old rubber plantation. 6RAR was allocated the east and part of the south perimeter of the Task Force base, with 5RAR allocated the north, the APCs the west and the artillery and engineers the south. By

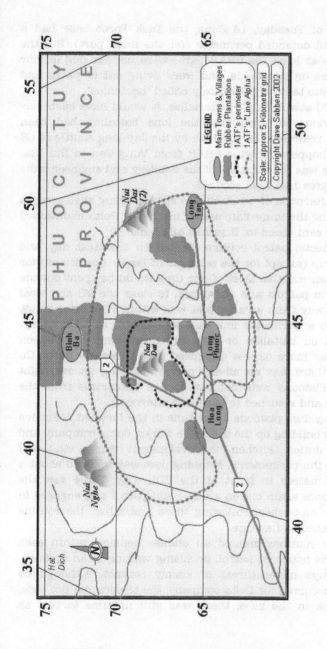

PHUOC TUY PROVINCE

LEGEND

Main Towns & Villages

Rubber Plantations

1ATF's perimeter

1ATF's "Line Alpha"

Scale: approx 5 Kilometre grid

Copyright Dave Sabben 2002

Nui Dat (2)

Long Tan

Binh Ba

Nui Dat

Long Phuoc

Hoa Long

Nui Nghe

Hat Dich

N

2   Task Force area showing 'Line Alpha'

the night of Tuesday, 14 June, the Task Force base had a defined and defended perimeter (for the most part). But the defenders—at least the 6RAR part—were neither dug in, nor behind wire or minefields, and were living out of packs and under plastic tents affectionately called 'hootchies'.

The VC attack didn't materialise. It would have been perfectly obvious to them that the lone battalion had been massively reinforced on the 14th by the day-long shuttle of US Chinook choppers ferrying 6RAR from Vung Tau to Nui Dat. Then there was the shuttling of the artillery and engineer units after the area had been secured.

The afternoon of 14 June was spent digging shell-scrapes and clearing the immediate area. That night, Delta maintained a 100 per cent stand-to. It rained all night.

The hectic patrol routine started on the next day and didn't let up (except for the calendar of larger operations) for the next ten months. Most of our time would be spent outside the base on patrols and ambushes, to clear the VC and local civilians away from an area that was within VC mortar range and out to a perimeter line that was known as Line Alpha. When not on battalion or company operations, the platoon routine was more or less organised on a three-day basis. On Day One there was an all-day patrol following an overnight ambush. Platoons went out two to five kilometres from the perimeter and returned to base late afternoon.

On Day Two platoons spent time in the forward defensive line (FDL) building up the defensive works, doing company and battalion duties (kitchen or development works etc.) and defending the perimeter. A listening post was manned about a thousand metres in front of the FDL. Day Three saw the platoons once again out on a day/night patrol and engaged in setting up ambushes. Following these ambushes, the routine then returned to Day One.

These routines created an endless tension within each soldier. The hours on patrol, or sitting waiting in an ambush, were always under threat of enemy contact. Although no contacts occurred for Delta company, the tension did not ease. When back in the base, there was still no time to rest as defences needed building and routine watches had to be carried out. The stress of the heat and dust, or mud, combined with the never-ending threat of an unseen enemy, bore heavily on everyone's shoulders.

For Dave Sabben the cycle seemed endless.

For the first few weeks, patrol followed patrol, FDL duties followed ambushes, the day not spent outside the 'wire' was the day we worked for Company or Battalion HQs. The one night in three we had 'off' was usually in someone else's FDL. The only relief to this routine was when it was Delta's turn for a three-day operation, when our own FDL became another company's rest night. But then, for the three days in the field, the company was fully on duty each day and on 50 per cent stand-to around the harbours each night—not much of a break from the base routine!

Dave Sabben's 12 Platoon had only varied from the patrol routine to the extent that they had been attached to (and formed the FDL for) the APC squadron. Duties with the APCs included riding shotgun on the now-daily supply convoy between the ALSG and the Task Force base. The APCs would trundle down the road to Vung Tau in the morning with us aboard and meet the truck convoy forming up at the ALSG. The platoon would be distributed onto the trucks and the convoy, interspersed with the APCs and would trundle back up to Task Force. In the afternoon, the same would happen in reverse and they'd spend the night in the APC FDL.

It irked Dave to see the 'I'm all right, Jack' attitude of the ALSG troops and their officers.

Every time I went to the ALSG I saw instances of the base troops and their officers looking after them-selves rather than supporting the field troops. In the early days, for example, we were still in boots and gaiters long after each ALSG warrior had been issued out the new shin-high general purpose boots.

The Armalites we carried were damn near worn out, having been third-hand from 1RAR, who got them second-hand from the US 173 Airborne Brigade. The fibreglass stocks and butts were faded and splitting, yet I often saw the ALSG warriors sporting brand new Armalites that they would never fire in anger. This was, in my humble view, bordering on the criminal and would have resulted in a Board of Inquiry had our senior officers taken their jobs seriously.

Dave was also concerned by what appeared to be other misplaced priorities.

On a less individual scale, for months after we arrived at Nui Dat we were in desperate need of trench diggers for FDL trenches, drainage ditches and latrines. At the ALSG, we observed tractors with backhoes being used as mobile ladders to put up telephone wires and electric power lines from the generators. The ALSG warriors were using *for luxuries* exactly the equipment that was so sorely needed at Nui Dat for life-saving weapon pits. The soldiers who had to dig the latrines and drainage pits by hand could only watch in quiet rage as the ALSG looked after number one at Vung Tau.

He felt that this was another case for a Board of Inquiry.

Bob Grandin, along with all the other squadron pilots, was flying regular missions in support of the Task Force. This involved troop lifts and logistic support by carrying loads inside or slung under the helicopter, plus medical evacuations. All these flights were to be in and out of secured landing zones. At the same time they were training on the use of M60 machine-guns mounted on the side of the aircraft, with which they had had no experience in Australia. Many of the flights involved flying supplies from 1ALSG to Nui Dat and sometimes to troops in patrol locations. Bob recalls: 'I remember one trip being a planeload of fresh bread, straight out of the oven in Vung Tau and still warm. Another involved taking hot meals of steak and vegetables out to patrols in the field'.

Bob also remembers that the most exciting flying involved developing tactics with the Special Air Service (SAS) for immersion and extraction of patrols into and from known enemy territory. This involved flying at treetop height and landing in very small clearings in the jungle.

> I felt one with the helicopter and believed that it was an extension of my person as we operated under testing conditions. However, the relative isolation we achieved from the 'war' by returning to Vung Tau each evening, meant for me that I did not feel the sense of imminent terror that may be associated with being under threat of the enemy at all times.

The 6th Battalion's first operation was called Operation Enoggera and ran from 21 June to 5 July. The village of Long Phuoc had been the site of a bloody battle for the American 173 Airborne Brigade when it conducted some preliminary operations prior to our arrival. The VC used villagers to stop the passage of the Americans through the village and then opened fire on them from the flanks, killing 34 and wounding many more. The Americans counted 43 bodies of VC and there could have been many times that number wounded. It was clear then that the VC would make every effort to retain control of Phuoc Tuy Province. As a consequence of this operation, the civilian inhabitants of Long Phuoc and Long Tan were moved to a controlled Malayan Emergency-style village complex at Hoa Long by US Army and ARVN forces. After all the villagers had been relocated, their houses were destroyed by aerial bombardment. Our job on Operation Enoggera was to complete the destruction of the village. We were to destroy or remove any caches of food and other supplies, and then destroy the tunnels and hides that honeycombed the area.

It was on this operation that the battalion suffered its first casualty when Alpha Company corporal, Mike Martin, was shot in the forearm by a sniper. However, only minor contact was made with VC and only a few odd shots were fired. We found some tunnels, but only a few of the larger underground complexes that were supposed to exist. Rather than smash and destroy everything, we purloined some souvenirs from the vacated village, such as mother of pearl plaques and religious brass ornaments. One of our soldiers found a brass figurine within a wall niche in a temple whose skirt lifted up to reveal a huge brass penis. I don't know what religion that was!

It was during this operation that one of the incidents that did not engender good relationships between Brigadier Jackson and 9 Squadron involved Bob Grandin.

I was on a mission to take the brigadier out to Hoa Long on an inspection of the area. We were most concerned about whether the landing zone was secure. He responded that 'Anywhere the Brigadier goes is secure'. After we landed we stayed in the aircraft with it cocked ready for a rapid departure if necessary. After a short time gunfire erupted on the edge of the LZ. We immediately started the aircraft, looked around for the brigadier. He wasn't to be seen so we departed. The radio suddenly screeched with comments of 'Get the hell back here, the brigadier is hopping mad'. We asked that the LZ be secured before we would return. After a while we returned and brought him home. He let us know in no uncertain terms that we had disobeyed orders, that we were chicken and asked why we had come to war if we were not prepared to fight. This difference in opinion on how to effectively operate helicopters, in which the army continually argued that they should be in command of the helicopter rather than the air force or the individual aircraft captain was to continue to be a point of contention. This was despite the fact that assigned tasks were always carried out by the squadron. Just not the way the army would have done it.

For Adrian Roberts, June to August is recalled as an endless work cycle of establishing their base while supporting both battalions in operations. 'We also provided support to the ARVN battalion in Baria,' he remembers.

And in between times we carried out cavalry-style reconnaissance tasks, endless convoy escort duties, and protection of road clearance teams. While our experience built up, the vehicles wore down and by August 3 Troop had critical serviceability problems in track replacement. Our operations with infantry were really confined to personnel lifts. The detail of operating with APCs remained unknown to most infantry users. So the month of August and Long Tan saw us hardly ready for what was to follow.

Operation Brisbane was mounted in great haste in response to a report from the Allied Headquarters in Saigon (11FFV) that a VC regiment (1,500–2,000 soldiers) had concentrated in the mountains just to the west of Nui Dat with the intention of attacking the Australian base. 6RAR and 1APC Squadron searched the area for three days without finding anything of significance. Although headquarters in Saigon quickly downgraded its estimate to an enemy company (80–100 soldiers), this incident was a factor in our subsequent attitude to intelligence reports of enemy strengths and intentions.

The Task Force HQ liaison officer at Hoa Long Village attended daily HQ 1ATF 'morning prayers' briefings and added weight to the knowledge of a VC build-up to the east. This information supported Captain Mike Wells, the senior Australian Army Training Team Vietnam (AATTV) Phuoc Tuy Province adviser at Baria. But the general attitude had developed that this information came from unreliable sources.

The next operation on 24 July was Hobart. Delta Company was sent way out to the east, the farthest march, some 5,000 metres east of the Long Tan area, but we saw little action, unlike the other companies. 'However, this was to be a good operation for all of us,' Bob Buick remembers: 'It was the first time everyone used the procedures and drills we had trained for and practised in Australia.'

'Operation Hobart was our initiation into the VC battlefield,' recalls Dave Sabben.

> And what an initiation it was. On Day Two of this, our very first field operation, the battalion had more casualties than it was to suffer in any single day for the rest of the tour other than for the battle at Long Tan and Operation Bribie. The loss of two killed and seventeen wounded in action was made more bitter by the fact that, although several were reported, no VC KIA (killed in action) were confirmed on that day.

Bravo and Charlie Companies were the ones to experience plenty of action. On 25 July Charlie Company, using small arms and artillery fire, engaged an enemy force of company strength. The enemy retaliated with small arms and mortar fire before withdrawing south. In the meantime, the commander of 6RAR had deployed Bravo Company into a blocking position across the enemy's likely avenue of escape. The enemy used this route as expected and a bloody battle ensued with Bravo Company using artillery and small arms fire to repel enemy attacks using small arms and mortars.

At one stage on the night of 25 July, artillery was called on a suspected VC patrol movement. Unfortunately, the result was that one round went well astray, off line and short, and landed in Alpha Company. It wounded the company commander, Major Peter Smeaton, and three signallers, all of whom had to be evacuated to hospital. Charles Mollison was recalled from Task Force HQ on 26 July to become acting OC Alpha Company.

The casualties suffered by the enemy and the subsequent destruction by us of many camps and storage areas were a great loss to the VC in an area he had previously regarded as his own territory. This action alerted us to the fact that the enemy could concentrate his forces and the battalion commander decided that, henceforth, patrols in depth would only be conducted in company strength.

Not only did the battalion learn the misfortunes of war in two swift and terrible lessons—it also learned that the VC were well armed, aggressive, well trained and prepared to 'have a go'. This was not the local 'shoot and scoot' VC we'd been told about. These were seasoned VC troops, and we were operating in their area. They were a force to be reckoned with, and we realised that we'd better recognise the fact.

Delta had the outside sweep on Hobart, and was for almost all the time the company furthest from the Task Force base. Hobart was Delta's first real opportunity to exercise its company-level training, and we did. The platoons operated independently during the days and regathered for the nights. Much of the time the Delta platoons of 25 to 28 diggers were patrolling 1,000 to 2,000 metres apart from each other, 5,000 metres from the nearest artillery, and 10,000 metres from the base. After the Alpha and Bravo incidents, it was uncomfortable to realise that VC forces of up to company strength were actually between Delta and the base. This, along with the 6RAR casualties, sobered up the Delta diggers considerably.

Towards the end of Operation Hobart the battalion CO made a change of plans which required Delta to switch from being the easternmost company of the sweep east of the village of Long Tan, to become the westernmost company of the cordon around the village itself. It was the sort of routing that we'd become used to in training, so we simply saddled up and slipped into overdrive again.

In the process of changing positions, Delta on 28 July traversed east to west through the rubber plantation that they would again visit on 15 August and would become the battleground of the Battle of Long Tan on 18 August.

In reviewing Operation Hobart, I was told that the VC had been a company of the local Provincial Battalion D445 which had fought hard to escape the blocking force established by Bravo Company after they had rebounded off Charlie Company. The scope of this contact should have woken us up to the fact that we were involved in something a little more significant than a Malayan guerrilla-style conflict. But we continued to overlook the written intelligence brief and to regard the enemy as disorganised local guerrillas, which would take flight rather than attack us.

While HQ 1ATF was apparently made aware, I recall that down at company level I was never given specific information that we were likely to encounter organised Main Force and certainly not North Vietnamese battalions. Information was available that two VC regiments could assemble anywhere in the province in 24 to 48 hours, but the gravity of the threat was not stressed. We had it embedded in our minds that at worst we might run into the odd platoon of the local D445 Battalion, and there was absolutely no suggestion that we might be attacked in the Nui Dat base.

I was aware that reports of large VC groups had been regularly received by intelligence staffs, but they always proved unfounded and often the reports coincided with our own patrol movements, leading the Task Force HQ to believe the informants had only seen our patrols. Consequently, an attack on the base was not considered a probability and therefore it was very poorly defended. There was little barbed wire of note out the front of the FDLs, and no anti-personnel minefields. It was preposterous to suggest the base might be in danger. We believed that the local VC were not about to take on a two-battalion Task Force with its supporting artillery regiment, mortars and armour, and with US Air Force fighters and bombers not far away on CAP (combat airborne patrol).

Advised not to worry about VC attack and told not to work on traditional defence needs of protective anti-personnel minefields and larger wire obstacles, I had the company work like Trojans to improve living standards. This was carried out in our spare time between patrols, security of other areas, standing patrols and ambushes. We scrounged odd bits and pieces of huts from the Americans. Items such as ammunition boxes became prized possessions as seats or tables to keep things off the red mud. We even had TV from the outset, with a set donated by the American Special Services Unit. TV news programs were broadcast from a plane circling around high above the Saigon area, about 50 kilometres to the north-west.

We dug drains to divert the run-off from daily monsoonal downpours, and with the aggregate gravel excavated by shovels from under the muddy red soil, we made proper raised paths and roads. We raided old plantations to the south and planted banana tree avenues along the paths and, although questioned by the CO, erected a barbed-wire concertina fence between Delta and Charlie Companies and behind Delta Company along the boundary with battalion HQ and Support Company. I was concerned in case there was an enemy patrol intrusion through another company area, given at times large areas were undermanned when companies were out on patrol and with a large gap between us and the engineer area to our west. My policy was to protect my company from all directions, within reason, with obviously the best wire facing the open area to the south-east.

In our base camp every piece of clothing and equipment we used soon became stained a uniform red mud colour and anything we were not using every day soon became covered in green mould. Every afternoon the rain just bucketed down and quickly filled our carefully dug weapon pits with water. From sundown until sunrise we had to keep shirts on with sleeves rolled down to reduce the chances of catching malaria from the bites of mosquitoes. All exposed parts of our bodies we kept covered in repellent. Even if the sun shone during the day there was little point in taking off our shirts because the sun rarely penetrated through the canopy of rubber tree leaves. All in all, it could hardly be described as a good time. However, we were so busy there was little time to think about the appalling conditions and no time to complain about them. We just got on with it although the lack of mail from home because of slow delivery sorely tested our patience.

I worked my company hard and gave them little time to relax, much to the disapproval of a few reinforcements who had served some months with 1RAR at the comfortable Bien Hoa airfield base complex, where they had ample time to spend in the canteens. Private Terry Burstall, who later became a controversial author of some note about the Vietnam War, was one of the reinforcements and was not overjoyed at all by the hard work after his short stay up at Bien Hoa with 1RAR. But it was my policy that 'any fool can be uncomfortable but with a little effort life can be made more comfortable', so we all worked very hard and long when other units might well have been in their canteens before the evening stand-to.

I wanted a comfortable Malayan Emergency-type base complex where my soldiers could relax after strenuous patrols. Others in the area were happy to sit around and wallow in the mud and my platoons detested having to tenant other areas when the landlords were out on patrol. Major Brian McFarlane, who had served in Malaya and who commanded the neighbouring Charlie Company, sympathised with the need for comfort, yet those who had served in Korea or who had not been outside Australia seemed unwilling to improve their lot in base life. Colonel Townsend and I often argued about the development of my area: he suggested I was still pursuing the attitude of elevating Delta Company above a normal standard.

Anyone who should have been charged for minor offences was given the choice of going up to the CO or of taking 'my punishment'. This involved digging pits, making paths and improving the area, under the supervision of the Company Sergeant Major Jack Kirby—a huge ox of a man, a very loyal and reliable warrant officer, respected by all. The only misdemeanours I had to send to the CO were those of absence without leave (AWOL) reported by military police, and UDs (unlawful discharges). Both were mandatory charges to go to battalion HQ. However, many of the offences were kept within company circles, even one occasion when my own 9 mm Browning pistol nearly put a hole in my foot when it fired as I was pulling it out of the holster for an armourer's check. I used to wear a pistol around the base, but carried an Armalite M16 rifle on patrol

Suffice to say we had ample 'volunteer' labourers and Delta Company area was eventually transformed from a muddy cesspool into a 'relatively pleasant' place, given the monsoonal rains, mosquitoes and insects, plus a few cobras and scorpions the size of a small spade blade. I achieved the aim of a comfortable yet defendable area. We built a nice diggers' canteen first, then a combined officers/sergeants' mess so we could all relax and share a joke over a beer. Our cook, Sergeant Bill O'Donnell, and the quartermaster sergeant, Ron Gildersleeve, made sure we had the best supplies and food when we were in base camp.

Apart from my own company personnel I had others on attachment. There were two signallers from the battalion Signals Platoon—Corporal Graham Smith and Private 'Yank' Akell—as well as the mortar fire controller, Sergeant Don 'Jack' Thomson, and the New Zealand Artillery Battery mobile FO party, comprised of Captain Morrie Stanley and two signallers.

'The FO party,' recalls Morrie Stanley, 'also made itself pretty comfortable.'

It comprised signallers Willie Walker, Chris Cooper and myself. Willie and Chris had transferred from the Armoured Corps in New Zealand to become radio operators with the original battery deployment to Vietnam in 1965. I was therefore very fortunate to be with men who had had twelve months' operational experience. They somehow had been able to purloin a Landrover to carry our kit and some home comforts. The boys produced a well-worn tent from the back of the Landrover so we slept in that initially and later furnished it with ammunition boxes etc. Our weapon pit was more a sludge hole, like others in the company area, but we had made a table and stools from ammunition boxes and our patch became quite a focal point. The table was used for eating, playing cards and cleaning weapons and we had hands of bananas tied up in the rubber trees overhead. At night we often had the company of blokes from the locating troop listening post and sometimes during the day we were able to listen to the Armed Forces Radio or 'Hanoi Hannah'.

Units deployed around the Task Force area provided artillery support. These included 103 and 105 Field Batteries RAA and 161 Field Battery RNZA plus an American self-propelled, 155 mm battery, Battery A, 2/35 US Artillery. The battery affiliations were: 105 Field Battery in direct support of 5RAR; 161 Field Battery, RNZA in direct support of 6RAR; 103 Battery and Battery A, 2/35 in general support of the Task Force. The Artillery Tactical Headquarters was co-located with the Task Force Headquarters Tactical Operations Centre.

Major Ian Darlington, HQ battery commander, sought from the infantry battalions on the Task Force perimeter the distance from the wire that they estimated they could prevent deployment of mortars. It was about 1,500 to 2,000 metres. A circle of this distance and a circle of the maximum range of the enemy 82 mm mortars were described around the Task Force perimeter. This gave an area in the shape of a 'tyre' or 'doughnut' within which the enemy could deploy mortars and possibly not be detected. This area was studied in detail and possible enemy mortar positions earmarked. These numbered about 120 and were each given target numbers and grouped into threes. Each group was given a nickname.

Each field battery was allocated a target within each group and this became the Task Force counter battery fire plan, nicknamed 'Tin Trunk'. Each field battery had about 40 counter battery targets for which they were required to keep data up to date. When calibrating the batteries the right-angle road bend at Xa Long Tan was used as a datum and a fall of shot was observed from a 161 Reconnaissance Flight helicopter.

By this stage, it seemed to Morrie Stanley that the diggers were having a tough time of it.

> While I may have had some understanding of infantry units and the way they worked, that cannot compare with being actually in a section or platoon in an operational base or in combat. I feel bound to refer to their most uncomfortable existence because I could see it and almost feel their (usually) silent acceptance. Few writers describe with skill the effects of routinely repetitive activities such as digging, clearing patrols, night pickets, ambush, filling sandbags, erecting wire, eating and attending to personal hygiene. Add to these, heat, rain, mud and the apprehension of danger. The product is dirty, tired men who still need to be tough and prepared for battle. That is why I believe that those of us who are not diggers should do everything possible to help them.

Living conditions began to improve in the base by August when tents arrived from Bien Hoa. The logistic plan devised in Australia envisaged 6RAR using much of the equipment that had been used by 1RAR for the previous twelve months. Unfortunately, after twelve months in the tropics, tentage was one of the items that had already passed its use-by date. Also, some luxuries such as tables and chairs for mealtimes, public (very) showers and some beer became available. Morrie Stanley moved in to share a tent with Captain Iain McLean-Williams, the company 2IC. He recalls: 'We had different work patterns and were rarely in the tent at the same time, because when I was out he was by himself and when I was in he was usually working while I had some horizontal recreation and monitored the artillery radio net.'

'Growing outside our tent were bloody hot chilli peppers,' Morrie remembers.

> I know that the company cook, Bill O'Donnell, used to nick some of them to make some of his concoctions

more interesting. I had also acquired a pet turtle that I called 'Wally'. He already had a small hole drilled near the back of his shell, to which I attached some nylon cord and much of the time he was tethered to a corner peg of the tent. Wally liked sauerkraut and when he went missing and the cook 'found him', I strongly suspect that Bill had walked Wally over to the kitchen early that morning for a sauerkraut breakfast.

During a short operation at about this time, Chris Cooper, one of Morrie's radio operators, was bitten by insects and developed a serious infection. They had all spread banana leaves around their bedding areas for comfort, and Chris had set himself up on an ant nest. It seems that he may also have angered some centipedes and he had to return to the gun area for treatment and confinement to bed. Murray Broomhall, a competent battery surveyor/technical assistant, replaced Chris. In view of later events, these two men must have considered the possible effects of these job changes on their lives.

'During Operation Hobart there had been a lot of enemy activity,' Bob Buick recalls.

All companies located and searched recently vacated camps, some built to accommodate 100 soldiers; there were signs that the VC were close by and in strength. These signs kept some of us on our toes, while others still proceeded casually down the track. We should have expected enemy activity and signs in the jungle because we had not seen anything of him around the Task Force base. Forced from their homes in the hamlets of Long Phuoc and Long Tan when the Task Force moved in, the VC had been pushed into the bush and further to the east. This was the counter revolutionary warfare plan, making the enemy live in the jungle with longer lines of supply and communication. It was isolating the VC from his support and made him endure the lack of homely comforts he had enjoyed for so long. Something would eventually break, the VC would have to move further away or have a crack at us and try to force us to leave.

The northern part of Phuoc Tuy Province, according to all reports, was the location of 5th VC Division, consisting of 274 and 275 Regiments. Roaming the southern sector of the province was D445 Battalion, a local VC battalion-size group supported by a number of small political and administrative groups. These enemy units were our main threat. Each had been very successful in previous battles against ARVN. Also 274 Regiment was known to be near the province border to the north-west.

Reports continually came into the Task Force HQ that the VC were in the province in force and the 1ATF commander anticipated an attack against the base. Patrols from both the 5th and 6th Battalions had seen signs of the VC, but there was nothing to confirm or verify the reports. 274 Regiment of 2,000 men was reported to the north-west of our base and 275 Regiment with a similar strength to the north-east. Both units were near the province border and there did not seem to be solid information on their intentions or location that could be substantiated.

The Task Force sent patrols out all over our area of responsibility. These included SAS patrols of four or five men and company patrols of about a hundred men from 5RAR and 6RAR. We found no signs confirming the enemy division's presence. There was an incident in which the VC fired on a US Army Chinook helicopter just west of the base.

D445 Battalion had been identified as our most likely enemy in the province. They were local forces or provincial forces. However, 274 and 275 Regiments were Main Force units, and thus were better equipped, more highly skilled in the art of warfare and of a greater danger to us. They were all regular soldiers with similar skills and discipline to ourselves, and not village part-timers.

'One of the problems with intelligence was that when an item got reported too often and did not prove correct, people downgraded it automatically when they heard it again,' Geoff Kendall remembers.

This was certainly the case with the intelligence reports about VC regiments in the Long Tan area. They were reported there so often and never seen that no one in mid-August 1966 would have believed that some two thousand enemy could be sitting just three or four kilometres away from our base camp.

I remember an incident, somewhere around early August. I had a brush with a mortar bomb which dropped short one night, perhaps due to a faulty or incorrect cordite charge. One bomb landed and exploded just three metres from my tent. Luckily, most of the shrapnel hit the low sandbagged sidewall, but odd pieces went over the top and through the tent, just above where I slept in my bed. One piece the size of a five cent coin went through my plastic wardrobe, neatly making a hole through both sides of the folded trousers and shirts on hangers, including the formal summer mess kit that someone aloft had ordered us to bring to Vietnam!

As we had been given a small allowance of about $48 to purchase clothes for R&R, I reckoned it was fair enough to make a claim for reimbursement—in the order of $48. Well, it took me two years of infrequent correspondence and finally a letter to the minister to get that $48 paid, which was much less than the cost of the time of all the public servants involved—typical! But that was the bureaucracy then, and I gather it still is the same today, more than 40 years down the track.

In early August, the patrol routine was twice interrupted for Delta Company. The first time on the 8th and 9th was to be part of a 5RAR operation to cordon the village of Binh Ba, to the north of the Task Force base. The second was to have two days' R&C (rest and convalescence) in Vung Tau, after two months of non-stop operational duty in-country, 24 hours a day, seven days a week.

The R&C was spent at the newly opened villa around the coast from the township of Vung Tau itself. A small core of platoon diggers actually stayed there, but many of the others disappeared into the back streets upon arrival and only re-emerged in time to catch the convoy back to Task Force. For many of us, it was our first opportunity to mix with the Yanks in the bars and clubs and we found them to be generally friendly and generous.

About mid-August, patrolling to the north-east of the base was increased, although we at company level were not really made aware of the exact reasons. It seems that warning had been given to HQ 1ATF of suspected Main Force VC moving to attack the base. Delta Company returned to base on 15 August after a patrol to the north-east and back via the Long Tan rubber plantation and the rubber-tappers' hut with nil contact. Although, I vaguely recall I thought we heard a bugle call once, somewhere north of Nui Dat 2, a large hill north of the rubber and sometimes called Nui Dat East. Alpha Company was sent out to replace Delta Company on the 16th and was based just north of the Long Tan rubber plantation, patrolling south and over the Nui Dat 2 hill.

There'd been a warning order drawn up for the next battalion operation—Vaucluse—that was to go into the Nui Dinh hills to the south-west of the base from 8 to 24 September. The Nui Dinhs were suspected of being the base area for the provincial communist political cadre—the Chau Duc Commission. That'll be a tough nut to crack, everyone thought.

CHAPTER FOUR
THE DAYS PRECEDING THE
BATTLE OF LONG TAN

Events on 16 and 17 August provide an interesting prelude to the battle in the Long Tan rubber plantation on the 18th. Company patrols by Alpha Company and then Bravo Company detected activity and signs that indicated the presence of a substantial enemy force. The vulnerability of the Task Force area became apparent as the enemy launched a mortar and rocket attack.

Charles Mollison had returned as acting OC Alpha Company, 6RAR. He was leading the routine three-day patrol, commencing on 16 August, into the TAOR. The plan was to patrol to the east, over Nui Dat 2 and back through the Long Tan rubber plantation. Intelligence reports had indicated that there may have been significant enemy activity in this area. They discovered signs of the enemy by the middle of the first day. Later in the afternoon they had several contacts with enemy soldiers dressed in green uniforms. During one of these an enemy officer was killed who appeared to be carrying details associated with the firing of mortars. All these details were reported back to the Task Force.

The company harboured for the night of the 16th/17th near Nui Dat 2. In the early hours of the morning they were startled by the sounds of mortar fire. A quick check indicated that the mortars were targeting the Task Force area, and Alpha Company soon passed on a bearing of the direction from which the sound was emanating. This assisted the placement of the counter bombardment.

Lieutenant Peter Dinham recalls how on the first night out the peaceful slumber of 2 Platoon, Alpha Company was rudely disturbed by the sound of mortars firing. 'I instinctively knew that the mortars were enemy and dreaded the prospect that they were being fired at us. However, it soon became evident that the Task Force base was the target. In accordance with normal procedures each section commander took a compass bearing to the enemy base plate site (based upon the sound of the firing) and estimated their range from our location. I took my own bearings and these were consolidated and conveyed to Company HQ to assist with friendly artillery counter bombardment. The Task Force artillery then commenced counter bombardment missions on suspected enemy mortar sites. During this counter bombardment Alpha Company was ringed by friendly fire and bracketed by one salvo with shrapnel scything through the air and clods of earth raining down. This concluded in the early morning—not a restful night.'

Peter recalls that they had not dug-in and were lying in shallow 'shell scrapes'. This did not give them much sense of security against the shrapnel of the returning fire from the Task Force. Everyone was relieved when the firing stopped and no one had been hurt. The threat of a round falling within our area was very real as we were ringed by the returning fire. Everyone had snuggled as deeply as possible into whatever protection they could find. There was also a lot of tension from the fact that the mortaring of the Task Force indicated that there was VC in the area. After a long and tense wait it was approaching dawn and company personnel prepared for morning routines.

In fact members of 3 Platoon heard movement during the night. They had not engaged the movement with fire as they were not able to determine if it was the enemy, one of our own moving around, or a stray animal. This is always a difficult decision. Any effort to engage this type of movement has the secondary effect of giving away your position—a very dangerous situation if enemy are in the vicinity.

Prior to dawn the company stood to and waited for first light to send out clearing patrols. Corporal Smith of 8 Section 3 Platoon moved forward of his position hoping to determine what had made the noise earlier that morning. He reported that the rain, which had stopped overnight, had made the ground soggy and he was able to see footprints in the shape of Ho Chi Minh sandals. Approximately five to ten enemy had passed their position that night. He believed that it could have been the enemy mortar or rocket attack squad returning to their base after the attack on the Australian Task Force base.

Orders from Battalion HQ directed Alpha Company to retrace its steps and set up a defensive position to the north-west of Nui Dat 2. The Company was disappointed that they could not pursue the enemy. They continued to see signs of enemy movement and discovered a telephone cable, which they cut.

MEANWHILE BACK IN THE TASK FORCE AREA

Of course, members of Delta Company had also been involved in the mortaring on the morning of the 17th. Harry Smith remembers that he had had a late night on the 16th entertaining pilots from Bien Hoa in the combined company officers/sergeants' canteen. The pilots had come to see those that they supported on a regular basis. The relative peace of the night was interrupted by the distant *pop, pop, pop, pop* of mortars firing at about 0245.

> Lying in bed in my tent, I recall awakening and listening to the noises and thinking, that's odd, wonder what's up out there to the east? Thirty seconds or so later, the mortar bombs, along with RCL rockets and (as later discovered) some 75 mm field artillery shells, hit the base area. They landed well away, over in the engineers' and artillery area. All hell broke loose as officers, NCOs and soldiers shouted orders to take cover and prepare for an attack. I rushed out of my tent, boots on the wrong feet. Cursing, I ran fifty metres across to the Company Headquarters command post, standing the company to in their weapon pits and awaiting further action and orders.

Was this a preliminary to an attack on the base? That was the big question. Surely not! Things started to fall into place. Someone recalled a small VC patrol had been seen out the front of the base area earlier— obviously counting the paces for the ranging of their mortars. But no attack came. All went quiet after our own artillery guns had fired back by way of counter bombardment on suspected positions calculated from listening post angles of the enemy mortar sounds. We spent a sleepless morning—wondering, watching, listening and waiting for the dawn. In an early morning Sitrep to Battalion, I suggested we had heard guns as well as mortars. The 6RAR Operations Log Serial 3 records my report at 0450hrs 'that I believed we heard a gun firing three rounds towards the end of the mortaring from a bearing of 1500 mils'.

Morrie Stanley recalls exclaiming, 'What the hell was that?' as he suddenly awoke to the sound of mortar fire.

I do not recall looking out of the tent to see what was happening, I just put some clothing on, slipped into my boots, grabbed my webbing, my M16 rifle and radio, and headed for the Delta Company command post (CP). It was frightening, even though I thought the explosions were not close to me, and I was first to arrive at the CP. Perhaps because I knew there were sandbags around the CP at that stage, I was able to summon some extra speed. Anyway, we sat out the morning listening to reports of the effects of the mortaring and to the artillery net carrying counter bombardment fire orders. The enemy mortar fire soon ceased.

On the night of the 16th Bob Buick with 11 Platoon was security platoon in 6RAR Alpha Company's position. They were providing perimeter security because Alpha was out on patrol.

When the enemy fire hit Task Force, Second Lieutenant Gordon Sharp, Private Ron Eglinton and a couple of other diggers were playing cards in the command post tent; it was the only tent that had power connected and hence lights. No one took any notice or cared, all too engrossed to consider incoming enemy fire. There was money on the table being lost and won.

I told Gordon Sharp that it was incoming and went outside to see and hear from what direction the enemy fire was coming. Moving out from a tent, which was lit, into the dark, the eyes need time to readjust to the variation of light intensity. I had no time to consider this and walked a few metres falling into a bloody deep hole. It was the preparation for the construction of the Alpha Company CP. I suppose it was about a metre to two metres deep. This only heightened my anger over the lack of interest and urgency shown by Sharp and others. Falling into the hole only topped up my anger.

I got a compass bearing to the VC firing positions and moved back to the tent and sent the relevant bearing to Battalion HQ. With a group of bearings plotted on a map the position of the enemy can be determined by using a grid system. For the whole of the time, some five to ten minutes, Sharp and the others continued to play cards. I again said that the enemy was firing mortars into the base. He said, 'This was nothing to do with us—it's over the other side of the Task Force.' I went off like a free keg of beer at a wharfies' party, abusing my platoon commander and ordering everyone to stand to. Everyone including Sharp bolted out of the tent, stumbling in the dark to take up his respective position ready for action.

The rest of the morning passed quietly for Delta Company. All the activity was on the southern side of the base, near the artillery positions and in the Task Force HQ location. The guns opened up with counter bombardment fire and the VC stopped firing their mortars.

11 Platoon remained in the Alpha Company area for the next 24 hours. Alpha Company was due back on the 18th. Bob Buick remembers:

> On the afternoon of the 17th I went to Delta Company to pick up two reinforcements for the platoon. They were Privates Colin Whiston and Frank Topp. Sadly, I didn't know that 24 hours later they would both be killed in action. Infantry can really only live from day to day as they never know what will happen next.

'On the night of 16/17 August my 10 Platoon was providing perimeter security and "shotgun" for the APC troops,' Geoff Kendall recalls.

> We were, like everyone else in the Task Force, awoken by a different set of sounds that we finally identified as incoming fire. None of it landed in the APC Squadron area so apart from standing to all morning we took no real part in that action and only heard what was going on over the net.
>
> It was suggested that the bombardment might be preparation for an attack on the Task Force. At the time I thought this was ridiculous. To my fairly inexperienced eye the Task Force was virtually impregnable. We had our barbed wire, weapon pits, artillery etc. Surely no enemy would dare to attack us. It is only after reading accounts of attacks on American bases that I understood how vulnerable we would have been to an enemy prepared to blast its way in at one point in the circle, get into the soft centre with satchel charges and wreak havoc. The VC and NVA (North Vietnamese Army) did this to US bases at regular intervals during the Vietnam War with great success. If the first contact on 18 August had been at 2200hrs, in the form of an assault on,

say, the engineers' squadron area with bangalore torpedoes and the works, I wonder how different history would be today.

Dave Sabben recalls that 12 Platoon was in Delta's FDL on the night of Tuesday 16 August.

At about 0300hrs Wednesday morning, I was woken by soft explosions to the east, followed by the whistling of projectiles overhead and the louder explosions of mortars and recoilless rifles closer to me on my west. This placed them in among Task Force HQ the newly arrived SAS unit, the artillery lines and the engineers. I relayed the compass bearings of the primaries to Company HQ who relayed them to Battalion HQ and a little later there was counter bombardment fire from the artillery into the general area of the primaries. We remained at 100 per cent alert for the rest of the morning, expecting an assault or at least a strong probe on the perimeter, but nothing eventuated.

In the APC area, Adrian Roberts woke when the mortars or shells began landing to the south-east of 1ATF HQ in the engineers' area or thereabouts.

Awoken by the *crump* of landing rounds 3 Troop gathered near the headquarters' tent, puzzled by the nearness of the flashes and bursts, thinking at first it was close defensive fire then realising that it was incoming enemy fire. Moments later we went to stand to on Squadron Headquarters' orders, which meant all APCs were fully manned in their night positions on our perimeter. Sometime later after the incoming fire had ceased we went to 50 per cent manning, that is, one crew member on watch at each APC gun. Eventually, with the dawn, we stood down and aside from rumours about what type and how many rounds had fallen on the other side of the ATF Headquarters, it seemed like 17 August 1966 was to be just another day.

The mortaring on the morning of the 17th affected the artillery batteries in two ways: rounds were falling in their area and they were providing the returning fire. Captain Ian Darlington was due on duty at 0300hrs on 17 August and was moving to the TAC HQ at about 0240hrs when the mortar attack commenced. He was relieving Chuck Hendrichs (US Army 155 mm Battery) and was greeted by him with 'They're not outgoing, Sir' as bombs exploded in the rubber trees nearby.

He was joined in the FSCC (fire support control centre) by Jim Townley and Barry Campton. The radio net was chaotic: reports of secondaries (bombs exploding) were coming from primarily 103 Battery and 161 Battery. Requests for Mortreps, particularly bearings to primaries (mortars firing) brought reports from every direction around the perimeter. It was obvious that the radars couldn't cope. The problem was that the radars needed to track a bomb for twelve seconds to locate the source. Unfortunately they were 'flicking' to other bombs (stronger signals) before the twelve seconds' track had been achieved and thus the results were nonsense. It was clear that the targets of enemy fire were the engineers' perimeter, 103 Battery, 161 Battery and Task Force HQ.

There was an enormous sense of frustration at the inability to get people with compasses to give bearings to primaries. Ian Darlington can recall at one time a figure standing at the entrance to the FSCC tent keeping people out so they could get on with their work. It was the Task Force commander, Brigadier O.D. Jackson, and for that he remains most grateful.

It gradually became apparent that the fire was from the east in the general direction of Long Tan and the guns were ordered to 'lay' in that direction.

After a reliable bearing came in from 6RAR, which passed through one of the (Counter Battery) CB list targets, Ian Darlington ordered ten rounds fire for effect (FFE) from the three field batteries, followed by about two repeats, possibly with some adjustments.

　　　　　　　　　　　　　　　　　　　DANGER CLOSE

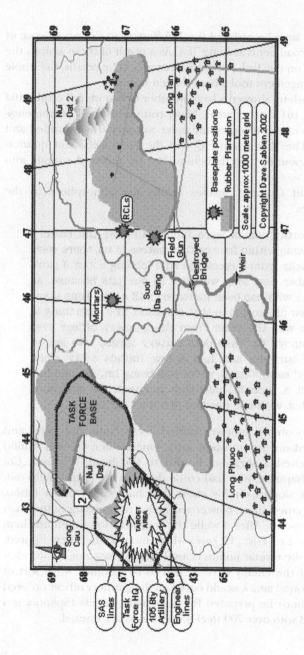

3 Task Force base attacked

Labels on map:
- Nui Dat 2
- Long Tan
- RCLs
- Field Gun
- Destroyed Bridge
- Suoi Da Bang
- Weir
- (Mortars)
- TASK FORCE BASE
- Nui Dat
- TARGET AREA
- Long Phuoc
- Song Cau
- Baseplate positions
- Rubber Plantation
- Scale: approx 1000 metre grid
- Copyright Dave Sabban 2002
- SAS lines
- Task Force HQ
- 105 Bty Artillery
- Engineer lines

At the same time he ordered the 155 Battery to fire on a copse of trees at the road bend at Long Tan. As a result of these actions the indirect fire on the Task Force base ceased. As he recalls, the whole artillery engagement took about sixteen minutes.

The wash-up showed a large number of rounds fell on the 103 Battery and 161 Battery areas. Many rounds also fell on the engineers' perimeter, a troop commander was seriously wounded and lost a leg. The Task Force HQ and the Field Regiment quartermaster compound, directly behind it, also received rounds into their areas.

Sergeant Graeme Smailes recalls the atmosphere in the artillery lines.

> The mortar bombs were falling all over the battery area, some within four or five metres of us, there were also shells from a recoilless rifle lobbing about. I can't remember how long we were in our pits because, as any one who has been mortared will agree, time takes on a new dimension in that situation. The next thing to happen was the order from the gunnery officer over the tannoys to 'Take post battery target'. We leaped out of our pits and had a few rounds away when 'Cheesy' said, 'Christ, we're still being hit.' No one had given it a thought until that moment. We continued firing but with our heads down a lot further.

The incoming mortars shifted away from the guns and concentrated on the transport area. One soldier, Gunner Phillip Norris, received a shrapnel wound to the head. A driver, Col 'Chappy' Chapman, who had come down to the gun to help out, had a flesh wound on his chest that had wiped out a tattoo. 'Chappy' seemed more concerned about the missing tattoo than the actual wound. After a while the mortars moved behind them and onto the Task Force HQ area where more soldiers were injured.

When the mortar bombs ceased falling it was not known what the plans of the enemy were. It had to be assumed some sort of follow-up frontal attack would occur, so the gunnery officer ordered Splintex rounds be prepared for open sight targets (Splintex is a shell packed with over 700 steel darts). No attack ensued.

The artillery kept firing high explosive (HE) on and off for the rest of the morning and at first light Lieutenant Doug Heazlewood, the section commander, came to see how everyone was and gave them all a swig of rum, which was appreciated. In the light of day those in the artillery lines could see just how close most of them had come to being either seriously injured or killed. They set to cleaning up the site and restocking their bunkers.

The gunnery officer informed them during the day that it appeared 103 Battery had received a large percentage of the mortar hits of the previous night compared to the rest of the Task Force. It must be said that the VC (or North Vietnamese) knew how to effectively deploy and use their mortars.

BRAVO COMPANY ORDERED OUT ON PATROL

At first light on the morning of 17 August Bravo Company was ordered out to locate and investigate the positions from which the mortars had been fired. Second Lieutenant John O'Halloran, 5 Platoon, Bravo Company remembers that they were still recovering from the action during Operation Hobart.

> During that operation the enemy had used mortars and the company had heard bugles for the first time. 6 Platoon and Company Headquarters took heavy casualties: two killed and fifteen wounded. I remember that on 16 August Corporal Robin Jones and I were allowed leave to visit the company's wounded who were in the hospital on the beach at Vung Tau. This was the first time since early June that I had been to 'Vungers' and also the first time we had worn 'greens' that had been starched by the laundry in Baria. We had a very heavy day in Vung Tau, not arriving back into the Task Force area until last light. After visiting friends over at the engineers' area where the chopper dropped us, we eventually arrived back in 5 Platoon lines late and worse for wear.

Consequently, he was hard to wake when the mortaring commenced. Shortly after he was woken for the second time, he went to the Platoon HQ pit as the rest of the company was standing-to.

From the weapon pit they were able to see the flashes of mortars that were being fired from a position directly in front of Bravo Company either between the two Suoi Da Bang rivers, or over the second one. The mortars were not falling in their area, but down to the right at the rear of Delta Company area. While they could hear the RCLs being fired, they could not see their location. Major Noel Ford called an O Group at Company Headquarters. During this briefing they were given orders for a company fighting patrol to go out on the bearings taken off the mortar flashes and locate the mortar base plate positions.

As it was thought the mission would be accomplished in a short time, orders were not to take rations or bedding. As they moved out at first light, Second Lieutenant O'Halloran was still wearing his starched greens and underwear. He was glad they were only going for three hours as after the first hour he was badly chafed. The next five days did not improve this situation.

At first light on the 17th Bravo Company moved through the opening in front of 5 Platoon and headed straight out through the young rubber, bananas and thick jungle on the Nui Dat side of the first Suoi Da Bang. The mortar base plate position was located between the two creeks in thick jungle and bamboo. There were five or six base plate positions and evidence that between 20 and 30 men had been in this location. The base plates had been dug in using rocks to support them. The enemy had vacated the position in a hurry, as some small personal items were located, such as a tobacco pouch and rice.

After reporting this discovery new orders were received for Bravo Company to split up into three platoon patrols. Second Lieutenant O'Halloran and 5 Platoon went east over the second Suoi Da Bang and then north and around in a circle, eventually meeting up with the company on the flat ground to the south of the ridge between the rivers. While numerous tracks were located they all eventually petered out, not giving any real idea of the enemy withdrawal route. However, Corporal Jones reported locating the recoilless rifle position a short distance to the south of the company harbour area. Bravo Company settled into a harbour over the night of the 17th/18th. 8 Platoon, Charlie Company arrived with a resupply patrol, as by that time both lunch and dinner had been missed. It was to be an uncomfortable night, as they had no sleeping gear or mosquito nets.

Major Ford, Second Lieutenant O'Halloran, Corporal Jones plus others returned to the RCL position. Three or four large rubber trees had been cut down, which indicated the RCLs had been set up in daylight with the trees for protection from sight and during the night the trees had been cut down to allow for clear firing. It appeared that our artillery counter bombardment fire had been accurate, as there were signs that a round had hit an oxcart. There were empty shell cases, human parts and clothing that indicated some casualties had occurred. In this area there were pits for a platoon. A track led from the RCL position east back into the rubber. This track was fresh and well used.

They returned to the company harbour and the findings were reported to Battalion HQ. At this time they were told that Delta Company would be bringing out rations and that they would relieve them early afternoon.

Forty-eight men who had been rostered to go to Vung Tau on R&C returned to Nui Dat on the morning of the 18th. Such was the concern at this stage for the declining health of these troops that despite the combat circumstances it was considered absolutely vital that they go. This reduced Bravo Company to 32 men for the next day or two. Those remaining were ordered to continue to search for the enemy rocket launcher sites and any other signs of elements of the VC.

Charlie Company, under Major Brian McFarlane, was also carrying out patrols from the Task Force area. 7 Platoon searched its sector on the way back from a night ambush and returned to base having found no sign of the enemy. 9 Platoon returned from its search to the south-east at 0941hrs, but was sent out again to continue to look for the site from which the rockets had been launched. The platoon returned in the afternoon and still had nothing unusual to report.

At daybreak on 17 August, about 0600hrs, orders were given that dispatched Bravo Company out to the east to try and locate the mortar base plate positions. They took little by way of equipment and rations as they all expected to be back in base the same day. It appeared that the Task Force and battalion intelligence experts had discounted anything other than a minor VC force, maybe a weapons platoon, and were assuming the VC had long gone. They left at 0630hrs and had in fact ordered a late breakfast on their anticipated return at 0930hrs—perhaps a little optimistic given the distances involved. As Harry remembers,

> I heard from the command radio net that they had located mortar and RCL firing areas, along with some blood trails and discarded VC webbing, presumably where some of our artillery counter bombardment had found its mark. With obviously no indicated threat, Bravo Company was ordered to stay overnight on the western edge of the Long Tan rubber plantation, continue looking around on the 18th, to be relieved by another company if later thought necessary. A Charlie Company resupply patrol took rations out to them in the late afternoon, but Bravo Company spent the night there without bedding, not dug in and an ideal target for any large VC force. Imagine the press and news media if an Australian company had been lured out on patrol and wiped out by the VC! They had moved out in reaction to the mortaring, but the VC took no action against them—in what was an ideal ambush area.

Dave Sabben recalls that the day of the 17th was 'a day off' for 12 Platoon. It was company and battalion duties for the day and then spend the night in the lines instead of on an ambush because they were due off on another patrol the next morning.

Late in the day, 8 Platoon was sent out to carry a resupply of rations to Bravo Company. By nightfall on 17 August all Charlie Company platoons were back in base.

For Bob Grandin the days of 16 and 17 August were fairly routine.

> On the 16th I crewed with Kevin Sharpley to do a logistic resupply from 1ALSG, on the back beach of Vung Tau, to the Task Force at Nui Dat. We then flew a reconnaissance to the south of Long Tan and carried out some live firing practice with the M60 machine-guns on the side of the helicopter. Later that day I flew a courier run between Vung Tau and the Task Force. At the end of the day I flew a sortie in which we did an insertion of an SAS patrol into an area to the north-east of the Task Force. This patrol proved to be behind the enemy lines of the ensuing battle on the 18th but they were without radio contact. I arrived back at Vung Tau after dark. We slept comfortably on the night of the 16th in Villa Anna, well away from the mortaring of the Task Force Area.

On the 17th Bob Grandin did a trip with Max Hayes from Vung Tau up to Binh Ba, the site of a South Vietnamese army garrison and hospital some 6,000 metres to the north of Nui Dat, and on to Binh Gia, a township another 4,000 metres north, dropping off army personnel. They returned later in the day to collect them.

On the night of the 17th Alpha Company was just north of the area between the Nui Dat 1 and the Nui Dat 2 features. 9 Platoon, Charlie Company, which had been five hundred metres to the south of Bravo Company, had found nothing and had returned to base. And Bravo Company was camped on the western edge of the Long Tan rubber.

CHAPTER FIVE
OPERATION VENDETTA:
THE BATTLE OF LONG TAN

Major Harry Smith, officer commanding Delta Company, tells how the events of 18 August 1966 unfolded. His story is of well-trained soldiers responding to overwhelming odds. The support of artillery, RAAF helicopters and armoured personnel carriers provided the winning edge. His men overcame fear, uncertainty and doubt to be victorious in a battle that could have spelt disaster for the Australian Task Force.

Dawn of the 18th started as usual with the stand-to: the manning of the perimeter to guard against a dawn attack. It was scheduled as a relaxed day. Delta Company, along with everyone else at Nui Dat, was looking forward to the big event of the day—the first Task Force concert party—with Australian pop stars Col Joye and Little Pattie arriving at the base from Vung Tau about noon. We had not had much time to relax since we arrived back from a company patrol on the 15th. Apart from trying to improve our lot in life in our company base area, 10 Platoon had been detached to secure the APC area and 11 Platoon was 'care-taking' the Alpha Company base area. The concert would be just what the doctor ordered after nearly three months of hard work.

I knew from routine battalion briefings and radio traffic that Alpha Company had been out on patrol for two days since the 16th, to the north-east of the base, having gone out when we came back on the 15th. They had made a few good contacts, killing two VC, and were due back in Nui Dat base later in the day. The other rifle company in base was Brian McFarlane's Charlie Company, although it had platoon patrols south of Long Tan and another on base security duties. I also knew that out at the edge of the Long Tan rubber plantation, Noel Ford's Bravo Company, ill equipped for an overnight stay and probably very hungry, had survived a very quiet night and had seen nothing new. There had been no sign or information from HQ of a VC threat, so much so that Bravo Company's R&C party of 48 had left for their planned break at Vung Tau at daybreak. This left Noel with a small Company HQ group of nine and one under-strength platoon of 23, which was John O'Halloran's 5 Platoon. There was a total group of 32 men, all ranks, out at the edge of the Long Tan rubber plantation.

The other Task Force battalion, 5RAR, was still out to the north of Nui Dat. There was nothing in the air to suggest that the 18th was not going to be just another relatively quiet day—with a great concert! At battalion and company level, we of 6RAR were convinced that local VC had fired their 82 mm mortars and RCLs into Nui Dat early on the morning of the 17th but had then fled from their base plate positions, which had been found by Bravo Company. There was nothing to suggest to us that the VC troops were other than the heavy weapons platoon of the local VC D445 Battalion, probably with another platoon for protection. It appeared they had 'shooted and scooted', leaving the Long Tan area for their own secret base camps well to the east.

At about 0800hrs my command post duty signaller, Corporal Graham Smith, advised me he had received a message that I was to report to the commanding officer at Battalion HQ to receive orders for a company patrol. I recall issuing an informal warning order so that my company would be preparing for action while I was away at the briefing. Having been in Vietnam for a while, it was becoming normal

DANGER CLOSE

SOP (standard operating procedure). All ranks went ahead with drawing rations and ammunition, test-firing weapons and securing their tent lines while awaiting formal orders. 'Pommie' Rencher took care of all my gear for me. I was well aware of the mutterings and rumblings about our company having been given a new task that would preclude a relaxing day at the concert.

My driver, Private Williams, drove me up to Battalion HQ in our company Land Rover and I walked over to report to Colonel Townsend, who met me at the doorway of his tent. After exchanging the usual salutations and cordialities, we discussed the mortaring of the base on the 17th and the evidence found by Bravo Company. I had heard most of the reports sent in by Noel Ford on the 17th and, in the absence of any other intelligence information, I recall agreeing with Colonel Townsend that the VC group was most likely about 30-strong. They had fired their mortars on the night of the 16/17th and by now had long gone. The colonel reiterated that Bravo Company, originally sent out the day before for just a daylight patrol, was only lightly equipped, was short of rations and now down to 32 men at Long Tan.

The CO explained to me, along with commiserations about missing the concert, that there was an urgency to get my company, the only one currently not committed, briefed, kitted up and on the move to relieve the depleted Bravo Company as soon as possible.

At that time on the 18th, there was no current sign of VC at Long Tan nor to the south-east, where Charlie Company's 9 Platoon had patrolled the day before, nor to the north and north-west, from where Alpha Company was returning to Nui Dat.

[At that time we were not aware that 75 mm field artillery had been used by the VC on the night of the 16/17th, indicating a high probability of Main Force VC forces. I had reported what we thought was VC artillery gunfire in a Sitrep at 0400hrs on the 17th, but nothing that would confirm gunfire had been passed back to 6RAR, or on to me. While there was a background

intelligence picture that the VC could mount regimental attacks
in the province, there was no specific information of any large VC
force being in the area. There was no information given to me by
Colonel Townsend that there was any threat from other than
small platoon or company groups of the local D445 unit. Indeed,
in retrospect, it appears little information was given to the Battal-
ion HQ by HQ 1ATF, yet the command element of ATF had
information of the VC HQ 5 Division radio being tracked to near
Nui Dat 2, just north-east of Long Tan.]

My very brief and very informal verbal orders from the
CO were to take Delta Company and go out to the western Long
Tan rubber plantation and relieve Noel Ford's small Bravo
Company group based on the edge of the rubber. I was to have
a look at the evidence and follow up any strong signs with a
view to tracking and locating the 'platoon-sized' VC weapons
group that mortared the Task Force.

[Noel Ford's stated theory, in hindsight, 'well after the event',
was that the aim of the VC mortaring early on the 17th
obviously was to lure our forces out into an ambush. If that had
been the aim, Bravo Company was obviously the first bait to
have been lured into the trap the same day. But no trap was
sprung on them, nor on Alpha Company just to the north, nor
9 Platoon, Charlie Company just to the south, nor when Delta
Company joined Bravo Company on the edge of the rubber just
after noon on the 18th. No trap had in fact been set by the VC.
It is reasonable to suggest the VC were not aware of Bravo
Company and then Delta Company being on the western edge of
the Long Tan rubber.

What I did not know then, but learnt later, was that 275
Regiment, reinforced with a North Vietnamese battalion, along
with D445 and other supporting units, at least some 2,500 VC
soldiers all up, was harboured up in well-dug-in circular areas.
This was not an ambush layout. They were to the north-east of
Long Tan Village, about 2,000 metres to the east of Bravo
Company—waiting—to do what? Attack the base? Were they
hoping that most of the defenders would be out of the base on

*a wild-goose chase, looking for the mortars and leave them an
easy target on the night of the 18th or 19th?*

*Perhaps intelligence from their village network and spies in
the local ARVN camps indicated a concert was planned for the
18th. That night was a very suitable time to catch everyone off-
guard in the base—poorly defended and all relaxed after the
musical interlude and liquid refreshments that afternoon. And
perhaps 274 Regiment was sited over to the north-west to
ambush any reinforcements from the US Army coming down the
highway from Bear Cat. And perhaps all the VC artillery and
heavy mortars were over that way as well, in a position to
support both an attack on the base as well as on the potential
reinforcements.]*

As they arrived back from the Alpha Company lines on
the morning of the 18th, Bob Buick and 11 Platoon received
the news that they would not be attending the concert but
heading off on a three-day patrol. They were disappointed and
angry, thinking that they had once again drawn the short
straw.

It would be just another hard slog through the scrub.
We were going fishing and all we would get was a wet
arse and no fish. Even worse still, we were to miss the
first ever concert party to visit the 1ATF base and the
obvious delights of looking at Little Pattie on stage.
I wondered whether I had really picked the right
army corps for my career. NEVER!

After providing perimeter security for the APC squadron
on the nights of the 16th and 17th, Geoff Kendall and his
platoon returned to Delta Company lines on the morning of the
18th.

We were warned to prepare for a three-day company
patrol to locate and destroy VC mortar and RCL units
that had fired on the Task Force. At no stage was it
suggested that there may have been an enemy

regiment near Long Tan and we rather expected that the VC would be long gone. We were not that ecstatic to be going out for three days as we would miss the concert, but knew better than to whinge. After, all Delta Company was the 'can do' company.

Bob Grandin's first task on the 18th was to do a compass swing on Aircraft 1023.

These are regular checks after servicing to ensure that the compass is reading accurately and to make any necessary corrections to readings. I felt lucky to be one of the crews tasked on this day as we had the privilege of flying Col Joye and Little Pattie to Nui Dat for a concert. We would meet them, be able to have a chat and see what they were like and go to the concert. It needed two choppers to carry them and their band, so Bruce Lane and Cliff Dohle joined Frank Riley and me on the task.

Meanwhile, Alpha Company continued to search for signs of the enemy. Just before midday 2 Platoon, Alpha Company apprehended three women supposedly picking bananas, but because they suspected that the women might have been assisting the enemy, they were escorted back to base. Soon after midday the whole company was ordered back to base.

Just to the south and east of Alpha Company, two Bravo Company section patrols were sent out early in the morning, one to the east about a thousand metres to the rubber-tappers' hut. Private David Thomas of Bravo Company remembers this patrol.

We criss-crossed the area as we moved eastwards towards the rubber plantation. After a while the company stopped and, with Sergeant Harry Keen and two others, I moved further east into the rubber and came upon a small hut at YS 481672. We also found a well some distance from the hut. Close by were a few ammunition boxes and sandals. I noticed the well had recently been used. Water had slopped on the ground leaving that glassy look and indicated it had been used only a short time ago.

It was about this time that he experienced something he had never encountered before or since. Everything went quiet! Not a bird moving or singing! Not even a breeze! No movement of any of the low rubbish bush or leaves on the rubber trees. Most unusual! He decided to slowly slide down on the trunk of a young rubber tree onto the ground, making himself smaller. He noticed the others had done the same, without a whisper from anyone. 'I call it sixth sense or whatever. I was born and raised in the bush,' Private Thomas continues: 'One could feel that something was around, but it was not going to declare itself. I was never a superstitious person by nature, but after that day I developed certain habits I practised as the scout of the section for the rest of my time in Vietnam.'

At the same time the other patrol moved to the south. They located a vacated 75 mm RCL position used on the morning of the 17th. The artillery counter bombardment fire had obviously hit this position. There were empty shell cases plus pieces of bloodstained and discarded clothing.

DELTA COMPANY O GROUP, AT ABOUT 0930HRS

I gathered Delta Company O Group around me, comprising my three platoon commanders, Geoff Kendall, Gordon Sharp and Dave Sabben plus our artillery forward observer, Morrie Stanley. Also, there was my CSM, Warrant Officer Jack Kirby, the mortar fire control sergeant, 'Jack' Thomson, the CHQ Support Section commander, Corporal Denis Spencer, my senior signaller, Corporal Graham Smith and our company 2IC, Captain Iain McLean-Williams. In the background was 'Pommie' Rencher.

I could sense the disappointment of the company at missing the concert. Some incorrectly felt that my strained relationship with the CO and his reputation for giving Delta Company the dirty jobs were the reasons for our selection. I gave my orders for a company patrol operation codenamed Vendetta—revenge for the VC mortaring!

I passed on what information I knew and gave instructions for a prompt departure, single file out through the paddy and long grass, as fast as possible, to rendezvous with Bravo Company as soon as possible. I made 12 Platoon the leading platoon. Our company battle strength, even with the New Zealand artillery party of three only totalled 108. All three platoons were below their normal strength due to some soldiers left in base with minor medical problems, a couple in hospital, others on R&C leave plus other odd detachments, such as the HQ ATF D&E (defence and employment) platoon duty and a language course. 10 Platoon numbered 32, 11 Platoon 28, 12 Platoon 29, with CHQ at 16, which included the Support Section, signallers, plus our medic, Corporal Dobson, and his assistant, stretcher-bearer 'Geordie' Richardson, plus the three New Zealanders. As was usual, the company 2IC and HQ administrative personnel remained in the base.

At about 1000hrs, after everyone had been briefed down at platoon and section level by their commanders, we formed up and left the FDL, heading for the rubber plantation to the west of Long Tan. We moved out of our lines in the rubber and through the gap in our barbed wire into the grassy area, to the accompaniment of the rehearsal music of the concert. We had a trek of 3,000 metres across the hot, overgrown paddy fields to the east, pushing through knife-edged grass near two metres high in places and across the river Suoi Da Bang.

With Dave Sabben's 12 Platoon leading, we set a quick pace in single file. If I wanted good map reading and quick movement I always placed Dave and his platoon up front. He had a natural flair for map reading, unlike one of my other officers who was commanding the company one day when I was away on a duty AAFV (Australian Armed Forces Vietnam) courier trip to Da Nang in I Corps area up north. He navigated by 'following the sun' and gradually went around in a half circle! What was the old saying? 'Blessed are those who run around in circles—for they shall be known as big wheels.'

Dave Sabben remembers Harry Smith returning with new maps and a new, though rather loose, set of orders. 'Get out to Bravo Company and take over the search.' 'We left quickly,' remembers Dave.

It was late morning and 12 Platoon was to lead. The ground between the base and the Long Tan rubber was a gentle slope, but [it was covered by] very thick undergrowth and there were two running creeks to cross. Difficult country to traverse but the compass bearing was constant, so navigation wasn't going to be a problem.

Harry wanted speed, so it was single file through the undergrowth, changing the lead section every fifteen minutes because of the tiring machete work needed to get through the 2-metre-tall grass. The trek out to Long Tan was a slog. After a sleepless night on the 16th, plus little sleep between sentry duties on the 17th, we were all tired and covered in perspiration.

We had to machete this path through the grass for about half the distance. It was stiflingly hot down in the long grass, with no breeze to carry the chaff and insects away. Added to this, there was the pressure from the OC to get to the rendezvous as soon as possible, as the Bravo group needed to return to base before nightfall. Behind us, the rest of the company enjoyed a slower pace and reported hearing the deep throb of the bass and drums plus the distant strains of music as the Task Force's first concert got under way back at base. To a man the diggers were imagining themselves with a coldie in their hands and watching Little Pattie doing the Twist on stage, rather than being where they were, under a 40 kg pack and an unforgiving sun, looking among the long, still grass for the elusive VC who we believed by then would have been long gone. We were glad to reach the relatively cool

shade at the edge of the rubber where the small Bravo
Company group was awaiting our arrival.

We met the Bravo patrol at the RCL position at
the edge of the Long Tan rubber plantation. The OC
Bravo and Harry discussed the task of following up
the VC tracks. The rest of us brewed up and had
lunch. We had only left our FDL a couple of hours ago,
but it had been a hot and tiring day so far. 12 Platoon
had led from the FDL and was exhausted already. But
we knew we would be the rear platoon when we
moved out.

'Delta Company appeared out of the scrub at about 1300hrs,'
remembers Corporal Robin Jones, Bravo Company. 'Those of us
who knew others exchanged greetings as they passed by and went
into all-round defence. We were extremely glad to see Delta
Company as we felt threatened at the time as our situation was very
tenuous due to our small numbers.'

'Delta Company shared their rations with our group,' Second
Lieutenant John O'Halloran remembers.

Major Ford and myself took Harry Smith and others
to the RCL position that was just inside the rubber
from where we were harbouring. During lunch, which
I had with Second Lieutenant Gordon Sharp, a school
and family friend from Tamworth, we could hear the
guitars at the Task Force area from the Col Joye show
that was being held that afternoon. Gordon's last
words to me went something like 'It's all right for you
to be going back to listen to the music while we are to
stay out and face the music'. As it turned out—very
true words.

Morrie Stanley also remembers the meeting with Bravo
Company:

When the companies met, tactical information was
passed on, and I had a chat with Pat Murphy, the NZ

FO with Bravo Company. He explained where we were, spoke of the track system and suggested possible directions for further movement. It was stinking hot in the bright sunshine.

While the company brewed up and had a late lunch from hard rations, I walked around the area with Noel Ford and a small protection group. Noel had been my room-mate at OCS in 1952. He was an academic type, and was soon to leave Vietnam to attend the 1967 Queenscliff Staff College course.

Noel showed me the various mortar base plate and RCL areas, ammunition containers plus pieces of webbing and sandals, some stained by blood from what we assumed were wounds from our artillery counter bombardment fire. I saw signs of several fresh tracks, going east, north and south. Four main tracks led to or from the site. The one from the west appeared to be an entry track, probably from the mortar base plate position less than a thousand metres to our north-west. The one from the north appeared to be both an entry and an exit track. It was only foot traffic and was the clearest of the four. The one heading east showed at least two bullock cart tracks as well as foot traffic and had VC footwear and clothing for the first hundred or so metres, as if the hastily laden and unsecured gear fell off as the cart bumped its way towards the road. This track had been followed by a Bravo Company patrol that morning. They'd lost it after a few hundred metres, so had patrolled to a nearby rubber-sap collection hut in the plantation, found lots of recent track activity in the area and returned to the RCL site. The fourth track, which headed south, was also followed by a Bravo patrol earlier that day and they found that it led to an artillery site about a thousand metres south, from which the exit tracks led east. Neither patrol had seen any VC or any signs less than 24 hours old (remembering that the mortaring had occurred about 35 hours ago).

Noel and I summarised the situation. All had been quiet, nothing had been seen out to the hut a thousand metres to the east that morning and we were happy to agree that the VC

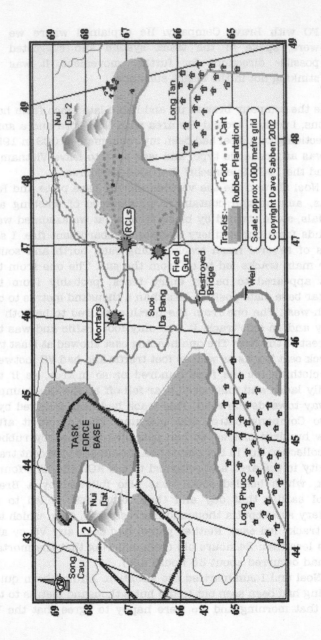

4 Enemy withdrawal tracks

Tracks: —·— Foot ---- Cart

Rubber Plantation

Scale: approx 1000 metre grid

Copyright Dave Sabben 2002

Nui Dat 2

Long Tan

RCLs

Field Gun

Destroyed Bridge

Mortars

Suoi Da Bang

Weir

TASK FORCE BASE

Nui Dat

2

Song Cau

Long Phuoc

DANGER **CLOSE**

mortar and RCL squads who had fired on the Task Force area the previous day had fled in small groups. We recalled that my company had been in this plantation area on the 15th. Alpha Company had been operating to the north and over to Nui Dat 2 on the 16th and on the day before, and at the time were moving back to base, not having seen enemy nearby. The same was the case with 9 Platoon to the south—all was very quiet. Noel was anxious to get back to base before nightfall, so he departed west.

Bravo Company headed back. 'Our pace was fast as we wanted to see the show and then take R&C leave to "Vungers",' recalls John O'Halloran. 'Although 5 Platoon had been at Nui Dat longer than any other platoon, 4 and 6 Platoons had been selected to go on leave first as they had taken the brunt of the fighting and heaviest casualties on Operation Hobart. It would have been easier to think that 5 Platoon stayed on as it was the best platoon, but I believe the other reason to be logical. We kept on moving back towards the base.'

Private David Thomas remembers:

I was lumbered with the task of carrying a VC recoilless rifle anti-tank gun cleaning brush someone had found. Typical army chain of command—give it to the new fellow! As we were moving out to return to Nui Dat I passed a good mate, Frank Topp. We had completed our recruit training together and he was posted to Delta Company. He commented that I was a 'War-y Bastard' because I was carrying the VC brush. I replied, 'If they get hold of you out there, you will be too.' (Poor Frank was killed later that afternoon at Long Tan.)

Corporal Robin Jones recalls:

The platoon set off, happy to be on our way, thinking about something to eat as it had been mid-morning the previous day since we had eaten anything substantial. Leaving the rubber we crossed the Suoi Da

Bang and made our way past the area of an enemy
mortar base plate position. I had at that time no idea
of the events that were to follow!

After Noel left I sat down, had a cuppa made by my batman and
talked with my O Group. I told them the little I knew, what I had
seen and that despite other tracks to the north and south,
I had elected to patrol generally east, towards the jungle well
behind the rubber plantation. My choice of direction was simply
a gut feeling, to go as far away from the base area as possible,
out to maximum artillery range—and that meant further east.
I was aware that Alpha Company had patrolled in the area to
the north and 9 Platoon to the south the day before with nil
contact or sightings. Bravo Company patrols had only been a
little way out to the east that morning. I had no information
from SAS patrols that were supposed to be well out north-east.

*[It was rumoured later that the one and only SAS patrol some
5,000 metres east had found signs of VC moving west. Their
radio had broken down and this information was not revealed
until they returned on the 19th—too late!]*

I said I thought the VC had long gone, as neither Bravo
Company nor Alpha Company had seen or heard anything in
24 hours. I said we would patrol to late afternoon, another
couple of hours, into a company defensive base for the night
and then move around further tomorrow, hoping, but not confident of locating and killing some VC to avenge the mortaring
of the base. While VC had certainly been here on the 17th, it
was now 'all quiet'. Bravo Company had not seen any enemy
around this area over the past thirty hours and thus it seemed
all the VC had gone. As to the enemy threat, based on the available intelligence information given to me, I suggested to my
O Group that the worst case might be a platoon of D445.

*[Had we known of the SAS report, and the ATF intelligence
report of the radio of 275 Regiment 2,500 metres east, I think
I might have been much less enthusiastic about moving east!]*

As it was, we were all tired and in need of a good night's sleep. I preferred jungle to rubber trees for an overnight base. Jungle provided better security from a surprise enemy attack because the thick undergrowth and 'wait-a-while' vines prevented quiet movement at night—and jungle was usually free from the annoying mosquitoes that plagued rubber and grass areas!

Dave Sabben remembers how the O Group was different.

We cleared up from lunch. The OC called an O Group. Our orders were not the usual operation orders. Normally, the patrol was allocated a sector of the TAOR (the area up to five thousand metres out from our base defences) to operate in, and specific entry and exit routes were nominated. This ensured the patrol did not clash with other patrols or with the artillery harassment and interdiction (H&I) fire plan. In our case, however, we'd been given the task of selecting a VC withdrawal route and following it wherever it led us. It was simply up to us to advise base of our location and direction and BHQ would re-route other patrols and change the H&I fire plan to suit our movements. For this reason, it was entirely up to Harry—the commander on the ground—to decide where he would go. Harry did his recce and made his choice. He told us he was going to ignore the main foot trail north and follow the trail of the wounded, heading east.

Although he didn't discuss his selection with us, I suspected that he felt that the foot trail was now 36 hours old and VC on foot would have travelled well beyond our artillery range. Since we would not proceed beyond our own artillery umbrella, that pursuit would have been pointless. Better success might be achieved if we followed the slower moving bullock carts. The trail might well be easier to follow, with less opportunity for ambush (which was always on our minds), and the carts might also be carrying the VC heavy weapons. Whatever his reasoning, his orders were 'We go east'.

At about 1500hrs, I headed Delta Company east in a one-up formation, well spread out in the rubber. 10 Platoon was leading, followed by company HQ, 12 Platoon left rear, and 11 Platoon right rear. After about three hundred metres, we came across a split in the track, with fresh tracks going east and south-east plus some discarded VC webbing. I decided to go east-south-east through the rubber plantation, heading for the cool jungle we knew from the map to be some two thousand metres away, this being the shortest route. This would take us past the hut where 11 Platoon had been a few days earlier and to which Bravo Company had patrolled that morning. There were no signs that indicated enemy remained in the area.

At about 1510hrs I remember calling the CO on the radio and telling him what we had seen. I said that all was quiet and that we were going to 'go east young man', almost as though on the toss of a coin we decided on which track to follow and I would be in touch in due course.

Soon after, once well into the rubber, I gave orders for the advance to continue eastwards through the relatively clean, immature rubber plantation, with neat rows of trees about ten metres high. There was a dense canopy but little undergrowth on the damp ground, giving good visibility.

We weren't more than a couple of hundred metres into the rubber when the very distinct track we were following split into two,' Geoff Kendall remembers. 'One track continued roughly due east while the other broke away north-east toward the edge of the rubber. He [Harry] came and had a look and ordered us to go two-up.'

[Geoff reflects: I have often thought that the old military training that says left before right, low number before high number, is the

DANGER CLOSE

main reason that I am here to write this instead of my good mate, Gordon Sharp.]

I now specified two platoons up to cover a wider frontage, with 10 Platoon on the left, 11 Platoon on the right, Company HQ centre rear, and 12 Platoon in the rearguard reserve position. There were about ten metres between soldiers, which meant that the platoons covered about two hundred metres across. This meant the company was about four hundred metres across by four hundred metres deep. The right front platoon, 11 Platoon, was heading for the old dirt track on the map, shown leading away to the south-east from another old but well-defined dirt road coming in from the north-east and then leading southwards into the derelict village of Long Tan about two thousand metres away.

As expected, the order of movement had Dave Sabben and 12 Platoon at the rear. He recalls:

After our leading role coming out, Harry put 12 as the reserve platoon. We headed just a shade north of due east, following two cart tracks. It was cool in the rubber plantation. Visibility was about five hundred metres up a gentle slope. It was still dry, but the clouds were gathering above us, a little heavier and darker than usual, and we anticipated heavy rain a little later in the afternoon. The two forward platoons were in two-sections-up formation, CHQ and the artillery forward observer (FO) party were located centre rear of them. 12 Platoon was one-section-up, in arrowhead formation, with the other two sections to my left and right rear so that if hit from the rear, I could about-face and present a wide front.

Progress was slow for the first few hundred metres as we were only just moving off from a rest. It is normal for the pace to be slower than usual in order for those following to be able to shake out into their correct spacings before the pace picks up.

Through the trees, we could see 11 Platoon heading up the slight slope towards one of the small rubber-tappers' huts.

The rubber plantation extended about 2000 metres to the east and south. To the north-east, just visible through odd breaks in the tree canopy, was the large jungle and scrub covered hill of Nui Dat 2. To the north-west was virtually impenetrable tall bamboo and thick scrub leading back to the river. The sky was dark and cloudy and the regular afternoon monsoonal rain was imminent as Delta Company moved slowly off south-east at slow patrol pace. Apart from the occasional soft chatter of the radios, with one on each of the battalion, company, mortar and two artillery nets, all was quiet, although initially we could still hear odd sounds of the music from the base concert.

BACK AT THE TASK FORCE AREA

Bravo Company was setting a fast pace back to camp and they could hear the concert under way. Almost everyone was now at the concert. Major Brian McFarlane, OC Charlie Company, remembers that he was alone in his HQ except for a young signaller. 'I was joined by Chaplain Les Thompson,' he recalls, 'the 6RAR Church of England padre. He was doing his routine rounds but could find few soldiers to comfort so joined me in the command post. The junior signaller was too polite and tender a soul for me to terrorise, so I made us all a cup of tea and we chatted on, listening to the radios with half an ear.'

After they arrived at Nui Dat with the concert party, as was usual, Bob Grandin and the other aircrew checked in to the operations tent to inform them of their arrival.

We were given a briefing on activity overnight and informed there weren't any other tasks we would be required to do. We were told that in response to mortar firing into the camp Delta Company, 6RAR were out on a clearing patrol.

It wasn't quite 'just another day' for the APC squadron and Adrian Roberts as they all looked forward to attending the concert that afternoon.

> Much of my 3 Troop's day was given over to track repair of our rather worn-out carriers that we had inherited from 1 Troop after their year with 1RAR in Bien Hoa. As it turned out only seven of my thirteen carriers could be brought to a serviceable state that day, due to lack of track parts.

BACK IN THE LONG TAN RUBBER PLANTATION

'Harry Smith had issued instructions and the platoons advanced to continue the search,' recalls Morrie Stanley.

> It was my role to stay with Harry at all times and no matter where he went, I felt the need to maintain contact with him, so that with the help of my two men I could provide any advice or support that the company commander required. I also needed to be sure of our location, the direction of the platoons and how far away they were from Company HQ. These aspects were of great concern to me, as they are to all gunners who may be required to order fire when friendly troops are in the area.

'11 Platoon was in arrowhead formation,' recalls Bob Buick.

> 5 Section was in front of the Platoon HQ with the other sections left (4 Section) and right rear of the HQ (6 Section). They were in arrowhead formation. It looked like the wakes of three boats in a '>' with each section forming its own '>'. This type of formation is adopted when there is light foliage cover plus the need for dispersal and ability to cover a lot of ground. It allows good control and would be the most

common formation when moving through a plantation or wooded area. The platoon covered an area of some 120 square metres in a triangle formation.

Moving slowly, 5 Section under the command of Corporal Jim Duroux crossed the north–south track. It was a straight track wide enough for one vehicle, designed and used by bullock carts passing through the plantation on a north–south axis. There was a two-strand barbed-wire fence on the western side of the track about half a metre high. Tracks and fences impede progress and are classified as obstacles needing caution and security to negotiate. Consequently, fences and tracks are crossed carefully, as tracks such as this one offered good visibility either way. Where 11 Platoon crossed, the track sloped slightly downhill to the north, our left, and the hill crested some 75 to 100 metres to the right GR (grid reference) 478673. It was a gentle slope, limiting our visual distance to the south and any VC would have experienced the same visibility problems moving north along the track towards us.

I gave hand signals for a quick obstacle crossing, basically putting the forward section on the ground, then passing the next section through to secure the other side of the track. Then the command element started across, Gordon Sharp and Private Vic Grice crossed the track, with Private Barry Meller and myself some twenty metres to their rear. When about ten metres from the fence I suddenly saw two or three VC, casually walking, with their heads down, along the track from the right. They had come over the rise just after Gordon Sharp and Vic Grice had crossed the track and moved into the rubber. The VC had missed seeing them by a few seconds.

I was stunned for a moment or two, not expecting a group of the enemy to be strolling through the centre of the platoon. I recovered quickly, raised my rifle and fired two quick shots at a VC. He dropped as

I had hit him with both rounds. The remainder of the VC took cover and I could not see them. There was confusion in the platoon, with VC in the centre of the platoon formation and I was the only one to have seen them.

Geoff Kendall remembers that:

We were just about to start off again when firing broke out from our right. I moved the platoon away from the track and listened as the 11 Platoon contact moved from patrol contact to section attack to platoon attack.

AT LONG TAN, AT ABOUT 1540HRS: CONTACT ... CONTACT ... CONTACT ...

As Bob Buick remembers it:

They had walked between the last man on the right of the forward 5 Section and the leading man of 6 Section, the right rear section, a gap of 50 metres. This was a one in a thousand chance and probably could never happen again. The VC quickly picked up their wounded or dead comrade and ran to the east. They never returned fire and ran past the right side of 5 Section towards a small hut that was a collection point for the latex that is tapped from the rubber trees.

The silence was broken by small arms fire from my front right, in 11 Platoon area, I recall, at 1540hrs. Gordon Sharp reported to me by radio that a VC patrol, obviously unaware of our presence in the area, had walked nonchalantly, heads down, arses up, chatting away, right into the middle of 11 Platoon, up the track from the south!

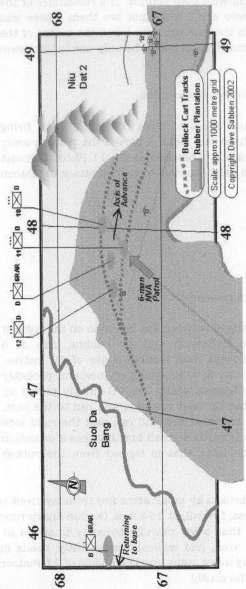

Sharp requested permission to give hot pursuit. I agreed—there were five or six VC, at least one of whom was at least wounded and a platoon should have been well able to handle that task. With 11 Platoon pushing ahead, I ordered 10 Platoon to maintain its direction and rate of advance.

I reported the contact to 6RAR.

AAR 2. 181540 D Coy Contact with 6 to 8 enemy dressed in green at YS478673 possibly wounding 1. Remainder fled east.

'It took us a few minutes to reorganise ourselves,' recalls Bob Buick.

> There was information about the contact to be radioed to Delta Company Headquarters and a search of the area. An AK47, a Russian-designed 7.62 mm assault rifle, was found as well as a large pool of blood on the track. No other enemy equipment was located as the platoon gathered itself together to follow the fleeing Viet Cong.

[These blokes were dressed in greens, had webbing with ammunition pouches, not having the appearance of local VC, D445 Battalion. This fact did not cross my mind at the time and no other member of the Company thought of it either. It should have been like a light on a hill, these were regular troops.]

'Harry Smith told Gordon Sharp to follow the enemy, the normal practice after a contact,' continues Bob.

> The platoon changed formation, 5 Section, commanded by Lance Corporal John Robbins, left, with 4 Section commanded by Corporal Jeff Duroux centre and 6 Section commanded by Corporal Bill 'Bluey' Moore on the right. 11 Platoon Headquarters were following the centre section some fifteen metres from the forward

line. With adrenalin pumping and hearts thumping we moved south-east after the fleeing VC, maybe too fast for the situation. A VC had been hit and this was 11 Platoon's first contact with our enemy: everyone was keen to get into the action.

Noises were heard coming from a small brick hut GR 481672. The platoon slowed and moved cautiously to clear the brick and tin roof latex collection hut. There was no VC or sign that they had been there. The platoon continued pushing to the east in extended line, 5 Section on the left, 4 Section centre and on the right near the east–west track was 6 Section. The distance between the remainder of the company and 11 Platoon widened to about four hundred metres. Despite this being too far apart for safety and normal operational procedures, we continued at a fast walking pace anxious to catch the fleeing enemy.

AAR3. 181555 D Coy recovered one (1) AK carbine at scene of contact.

[Harry reflects: Not being on the lookout for VC Main Force, the penny did not drop at the significance of the green uniform, nor the AK47. It was only afterwards that I realised the significance. The penny did not drop at Battalion HQ either. But apparently, knowing the suspect radio of 275 Regiment was in the area to the east, I later learnt Captain Trevor Richards, OC 547 Signals Troop, one of the few privy to the total intelligence picture, had warned Brigadier Jackson. But that warning did not flow back down the command net to me and we went on pursuing what we thought was just a section patrol from D445—local troops. What we did not know was that the VC patrol had fled well east to 275 Regiment and a large circular dug-in harbouring area. Having been alerted earlier by the firing, they then sent out probably an initial company-sized force to the west to take on what the VC patrol most probably described as about 25 Allied soldiers near the hut—easy prey!]

At about this time, Delta heard the distinctive *pop* of mortars from the south and a few 60 mm or 82 mm bombs landed just to its right. I ordered the company group, less 11 Platoon, to move to the north-west out of the impact area, perhaps three hundred metres, to await the outcome of 11 Platoon's contact and assault on the hut. This further opened the distance between Company Headquarters and 11 Platoon. At the same time Captain Morrie Stanley aided by Sergeant Jack Thomson, the mortar fire controller, worked out compass bearings to the mortar base plate areas and Morrie Stanley ordered counter bombardment fire on the suspected mortar areas to the south.

> As soon as Harry ordered counter bombardment fire, I sent a mortar report (Mortrep) containing only the direction we thought the fire was coming from. With this and other information that my battery commander had in Nui Dat, he engaged the suspected mortar area with US medium (155 mm) gunfire and soon silenced the mortars. Like others, I regarded this VC mortar attack on us as a personal assault and had no difficulty complying with Harry's next instructions for us to move away quickly. He did not need to emphasise or repeat any orders. It was apparent to us after we had moved that the enemy was not observing his mortar fire, because, following our counter fire and move north-west, it became ineffective.

AT ABOUT 1550HRS

Gordon Sharp reported back to me that the hut was clear and they were advancing east beyond the hut. I reported this to Battalion Headquarters. At that time, the rest of the company was about five hundred metres north-west of 11 Platoon. While this proved fortuitous to the eventual survival of the company it was nevertheless of little value in providing any cover fire for 11 Platoon, which was out of sight. But then, we were not aware of any great threat. I recall thinking about the mortars and perhaps a group of D445 down to the south and was thinking about radio orders to move the company into a closer grouping so that we had mutual protection by fire, but events overtook this move.

At the rear Dave Sabben reacted like any soldier keen to be in action.

My assessment of the events that had occurred was along the lines of 'Lucky 11'. The ideal enemy size for a platoon contact was an under-strength enemy section of six to eight, preferably without a machine-gun! The ideal ground for such a contact was an open plantation, so there was little cover for the smaller force to hide in and so visibility was excellent for bringing down artillery fire. The ideal time for such a contact was in daylight, with dry weather and cool conditions. The ideal range was 100 to 150 metres—close enough for accurate fire but not close enough for the enemy to put in a quick assault. Sharp had it all, and he had the light behind him as well. With even the smallest touch of luck, he would have half a dozen VC accounted for, no own-force casualties and a Military Cross on his chest as a Christmas present.

However, those thoughts were still easing around the far reaches of my mind when a great volume of fire erupted from our distant front. Incoming rounds sound entirely different from outgoing and these were incoming! 11 has hit something big. We could hear them firing back, but we could distinctly hear at least two incoming machine-guns, so it was much more than his original contact group.

As they were moving back to base, Bravo Company heard the firing of the first contact and Second Lieutenant John O'Halloran reported their position to Battalion Headquarters. 'We had two radios—one on the battalion net—and we switched the other to Delta Company net. After waiting and listening to the firing and the traffic on the radio we could not understand why we had not been ordered back to assist Delta Company.'

Corporal Jones recalls: 'We settled into all-round defence when we heard the first sounds of small arms fire from the area we had just left, I could hear the radio call sign 4 had contacted six to ten enemy in the vicinity of the hut on the ridge. They had closed with the enemy and were following up. Then a few minutes later, the fire intensified.'

LONG TAN, AT ABOUT 1605HRS

All hell broke loose from 11 Platoon area and Gordon Sharp reported to me that he was being attacked by a large VC force and taking casualties. He called for artillery fire. And about this time the monsoon broke and heavy rain began to fall, reducing visibility to 50 metres and turning the red soil into red mud. I reported to 6RAR:

And then, with further information from 11 Platoon, who were being attacked by increasing numbers of VC, I sent a further report back to 6RAR:

I also called up Noel Ford on the command radio and told him of the increasing enemy attacks. I anticipated I would need all the help I could get and I personally asked him to come back with his platoon to assist. I was under the impression that this would happen, but for some reason HQ did not immediately approve this when Noel asked and thus nothing happened for over an hour, although I was not aware of the reason until later.

For 11 Platoon and Bob Buick things changed dramatically.

Without warning two machine-guns fired from our left front. The enemy opened fire on 5 Section from the scrub and creek line at the southern base of the Nui Dat feature GR 486673. The left man of 5 Section was about 75 metres from the enemy. The fire from two machine-guns cut down nearly all of 5 Section. We were taken completely by surprise and we had never expected this to happen. We had a mind-set that our enemy was local guerrilla forces; the green uniforms of the VC never jolted the brain to identify them as Main Force regular soldiers. This was not expected! The remainder of the platoon immediately took cover as the enemy swept the area with machine-gun and intense rifle fire. In two minutes, most of the blokes in the lead section were cut down in a storm of fire from an estimated platoon.

Gordon Sharp immediately asked for artillery fire to engage the southern slopes of the Nui Dat 2 feature GR 487674. 6 Section was moved to form an L shape to maximise our fire at the enemy near 5 Section. This formation remained static while Sharp was concentrating on adjusting the artillery fire support. The enemy on our left then attacked our left flank 5 Section in about platoon strength of twenty to 30. Those of 5 Section who were capable returned fire and forced the attacking enemy to go to ground. This enemy group then remained in that area, close to

5 Section for the whole battle. I had seen no movement or any fire coming from 5 Section for about ten to fifteen minutes, I feared the worst. I started to move over towards them when a large enemy force, possibly a company of about 80, attacked from the east. We were suddenly in a very difficult predicament. My combat training overcame the fear and uncertainty that I felt. The battle had been going for about fifteen to twenty minutes.

When the attack came from the east I moved to the right, to 6 Section, and directed 'Bluey' Moore to bring his section back to form a reverse L to protect our southern flank. Our deadly machine-gun and rifle fire had stopped the enemy attack from the east. This attacking enemy took heavy casualties from our fire and they too went to ground and started attacking using fire and movement. They were halted about fifty to sixty metres from us. It had started to rain, which proved lucky for us, as the monsoon clouds rolled over the battlefield.

Morrie Stanley swung into action with artillery support.

Harry and I had already agreed on the grid reference of our location. He also approved the request from Gordon Sharp for artillery fire support, which we considered might have been useful even if I directed the fire at some distance from 11 Platoon's known position. Initially, I engaged with my own 161 Battery, but the situation deteriorated rapidly.

Geoff Kendall was keen to join the engagement and help his friend Gordon Sharp.

Radio communications were difficult because naturally the dialogue between 11 Platoon and Company HQ took priority but at one stage I managed to suggest to

Harry that I move forward and see if I could help. I
received a yes and I told the platoon to drop their
packs. We started off, two-up in extended line, towards
the sound of firing. This was a little different to
anything we had done before. It was obvious that
there were more than just the groups of three that
we were expecting to encounter in front of us. Nonetheless, the platoon was great, very determined and
steady despite the bugles that blew intermittently,
obviously part of the NVA command and control
system.

ARTILLERY JOINS THE ACTION

Those still in the artillery lines and not at the concert were carrying
out routine duties. They had just replenished the ammunition that
had been fired the previous night in counter bombardment on the
enemy positions. Then the Kiwi 161 Battery opened up. From the
rate of fire it was obvious that they were onto something and when
'fire mission regiment' for all eighteen guns came over the tannoy
system everyone knew it was bigger than normal.

Everyone could hear the action as, due to a short circuit, which
resulted in an open line from the command post to the guns, the
battle was being broadcast live over the tannoy system. Commands
to 'drop 50' are remembered, and someone else said that the
rounds would be on their heads if this occurred. There were some
choice words being said over the radio as Harry Smith demanded
the fire he wanted. Gun Sergeant Jim King suddenly realised just
how close they were firing in front of their own troops. 'With that in
mind I remember telling my detachment to make sure their laying
and corrections were "spot on" as this was really close. For the rest
of the battle accuracy was paramount in our minds.'

Also at the Task Force area, Bob Grandin and the other helicopter pilots were lazing around near the helicopters, whiling
away the time. 'We could hear the music of the concert, but we
did not like to be too far from our helicopters in case we were
required urgently so had not gone over to the concert area. Our first

recognition of action came when the artillery started firing.'

Adrian Roberts was under the troop shower when a runner arrived from Squadron Headquarters to say, 'The Major wants you with your map.'

This standard message was always the herald of some activity, a call to which I became quite addicted. Hurriedly I dressed and ran over to Squadron Headquarters. Though I didn't keep a record of times that day (but have often wished that I did) it would have been some time after 1600hrs. At Squadron Headquarters, Major Hagerty told me that one of the companies in 6RAR was in trouble and that I should take my troop across to 6RAR Battalion Headquarters for orders. Explaining my vehicle state to him we set about calling up a section from 2 Troop. As I recall there was no degree of notice to move at this time so vehicles and crews had to be hastily assembled for what was an unknown task. My own vehicle was brought back from its Little Pattie task of driving her around the Task Force area. We departed in a hurry with none of the normal preparation such as test-firing of weapons.

The thunder of the field guns of 1st Field Regiment and the mighty roar of the American guns were sending out a message to all that something terribly serious was happening. The guns would not stop their thunder that day and continued well into the night. From all over the Task Force area troops hurried to their action stations, the concert forgotten. Several of the entertainers were taken to safety. Little Pattie and some of the party caught a departing helicopter to Vung Tau. Col Joye was stranded and had to stay as a member of the audience.

All the Charlie Company HQ staff returned to join their OC, Brian McFarlane. They were anxious to know what was happening. They set about quietly preparing their gear and packing rations for the bush, their ears glued to the radio speakers, listening to the voices of their comrades in a mortal fight for life itself. This had individuals thinking about the members of the company whom they knew personally. Preparations to join the battle continued in silence, apart from the thunderous noise and shock waves from the shells as they passed directly over their heads.

Alpha Company was warned to prepare to move as reinforcements for the battle. They had only recently arrived back at the base and were in the process of relaxing, showering, or having a beer. They now had to hurriedly collect new supplies of ammunition, while also trying to grab a quick bite to eat from the glorious barbecue of 'real' meat. However, there was considerable delay before they mounted the APCs.

Meanwhile Second Lieutenant John O'Halloran and the small Bravo Company element waited out near the battle area, expecting to be told to go back and assist Delta Company. They listened to Gordon Sharp and could tell by his voice the trouble the platoon was in.

12 PLATOON WAITS TO GO INTO ACTION

Once again Dave Sabben was thinking about the conditions and the battle raging in front of him as he waited to become engaged with his platoon in the reserve position.

> The heavens opened up with the heaviest monsoon downpour we had ever seen. The rain pelted through the rubber tree canopy and beat into the bare red earth below. Within minutes, the earth had become sticky red mud, staining the greens we wore. As the rain formed puddles on the ground, the force of the heaviest squalls raised a mist of muddy spray almost up to our knees. It was like walking in a thin, wet, red mist. When we went to ground, we were lying in it, with only our heads raised above it. At times, there was lightning, but I don't recall any thunder. Perhaps the dull roar of the rain itself and the almost constant battle noise drowned out the low rumbles of thunder.

There was a lull in the firing. Sharp was on the radio bringing in artillery fire. The first shots landed so far to the east we didn't even hear them. Because they were firing over our heads, the safety factor was 1,000 metres first fall of shot. This was quickly halved and halved again, and within minutes artillery was falling to the east of 11 Platoon and landing within their eyesight. Sharp reported that the enemy 'covered his front' and he could see them moving about and forming assault groups. His startled voice came up on the net: 'They're going to attack *us*!' 12 Platoon closed up on company HQ and formed a screen to company HQ's front. We dropped our packs.

11 PLATOON FIGHTS FOR ITS LIFE

'Gordon Sharp called for additional gunfire to be targeted to the east of us,' recalls Bob Buick.

When the artillery fire did come it was too far away to be effective. Sharp was on his hands and knees looking at the enemy. I had told him to get down or else he would get shot. He continued looking for the artillery fire on the ground, to adjust it closer. As he continued to do this he was shot in the throat and died instantly. There was no confusion within the platoon as we lost our platoon commander. Everyone was under heavy and effective small arms fire, while our own fire control was effective and directed at the assaulting enemy to the north.

Another fifteen or twenty minutes seemed to have passed, each side trying to gain the upper hand. The VC were attacking using fire and movement while we defended grimly. Another enemy group of thirty was seen moving around our southern flank to the west. Private Ron Eglinton, the machine-gunner with

6 Section, saw them outflanking the platoon and opened fire. He inflicted heavy casualties on the group. Ron somehow had become isolated from the rest of his section but hadn't realised it. Mud clogged the ammunition belt and the loading mechanism of the machine-gun. Unfazed, he cleaned the ammunition and continued firing. Although wounded, he overcame the stoppages and at times only fired one round at a time. He kept the VC at bay.

[Ron was to be awarded the Military Medal for his bravery in the field. Although wounded, he remained in position firing his machine-gun.]

The situation had become extremely precarious and Bob, who had now taken over command of 11 Platoon, realised that he might not survive.

When I first realised that there was an excellent chance that I could be killed, I don't remember thinking too much about it. My training overrode any fear that I may have had and what I had been taught over the years took over. There was a job to do. The two enemy groups, one to the north and the other to the east, were being reinforced. The supporting artillery fire was still landing too far away to help us. The incoming small arms fire and rocket-grenades from the enemy was very heavy and accurate. Only 75 metres separated the two sides.

Alongside Bob the 11 Platoon warriors were firing their weapons and stopping the attacking enemy in their tracks. They could see their mates beside them doing the same.

I saw no one falter, each supporting his mate and defending his patch of dirt to the death. I remember Corporal Jeff Duroux coming to the Platoon HQ and I sent him back to his 5 Section. His section was forward of the Headquarters by some fifteen metres. There was only about twelve of the platoon capable of firing. There seemed to be no one alive in 5 Section. 4 Section had a couple dead and some wounded and I had no idea how 6 Section was coping on the right flank. The situation was grim and the artillery fire was still not close enough.

AAR7. 181626 D Coy Estimate enemy now company size.

I sent another Sitrep. I had reported the situation to Battalion HQ. 11 Platoon had taken heavy casualties, including its commander Second Lieutenant Sharp. It was pinned down in danger of being overrun and I said that I required more artillery fire support. We only had one artillery battery in support at that time and Morrie Stanley had apparently been told the other batteries were in support of 5RAR. I recall saying to Colonel Townsend that I wanted the whole of the artillery regiment in support. 'I want the whole regiment—give me every gun they have.' I remember Townsend replying with cryptic words like 'leave the artillery fire to the gunners'. But soon after, I recall Morrie Stanley said he had access to the regiment's eighteen guns. As they were not suitable for close support, the Artillery HQ was dropping the US Army 155 mm shells out the back in the enemy's rear concentration area.

'I upgraded the mission to a regimental fire mission involving 161 Battery Royal New Zealand Artillery, 103 and 105 Batteries Royal Australian Artillery, a total of eighteen 105 mm howitzers,' recalls Morrie Stanley.

The situation for my FO party had been manageable up to this time. We were all together, the weather had been still and clear, we were able to read and mark maps as well as write in notebooks, as there was not much fire coming in our direction. But the situation had deteriorated considerably and Harry Smith appreciated that neither he nor I could perform our functions while we were moving. If we could not perform our roles, then the platoons would be in even more desperate trouble. So it was decided to stop and occupy some firm ground with Company HQ and 12 Platoon, to establish a more secure area in which the wounded could be attended to. An extraordinary storm had started and everything else seemed to be going wrong as well.

At about that time Bob Buick began to relay artillery fire messages to Morrie Stanley. Soon after he reported that 'they were almost surrounded, suffering heavy casualties, could not extricate themselves, and were almost out of ammunition'.

10 PLATOON BECOME ENGAGED WITH THE ENEMY

As though on cue, the skies had opened up and rain was bucketing down. Geoff Kendall believes that unless you have experienced the South-East Asian monsoon you cannot know how heavy rain can be—you actually ingest water by breathing!

Anyway, following Harry's order to do a left flank assault I got the platoon moving forward, we went on probably about 150 metres, strangely not getting any fire directed toward us, although the sound of firing in front of us was enormous. We cleared a little hump and saw a line of troops moving across our right front in what looked like assault formation. I was a little concerned that they could be part of 11 Platoon, so kept the guys going until it was obvious they were enemy. At this stage, the closest of them would only have been twenty-odd metres away but they still hadn't seen us. I ordered my

6 Formation about 1630 hrs

Niu Dat 2

NWA Bn (est)

Suoi Da Bang

B Coy stopped

Rubber Plantation

Scale: approx 1000 metre grid

Copyright Dave Sabben 2002

guys to fire and dropped into a kneeling position that the guys copied.

We knocked over the whole right-hand element; I would estimate about ten to fifteen troops. The others didn't return fire, just turned left and jogged away. There may have been a bugle call but I couldn't guarantee that. We got back up and continued on but moved only a few metres before we were hit with a hail of fire from our left front. Beside me, Brian Hornung, my signaller, was hit with a round through the top of his shoulder. The bullet spun him around and I saw the red patch of blood near his left collarbone. Neil Rankin and the stretcher-bearer treated his wound while Brian, to his credit, tried to help me get the set working. Over in Black Mac's section there were a couple of other guys wounded. We were still under very heavy suppressive fire and it was difficult to get orders to the section commanders because of the noise.

However, they managed to get the wounded together and under the command of the 2IC of one of the sections, John Cash, who was also wounded. Geoff ordered them to crawl out the back and try to get back to CHQ. He told them to tell the boss his radio was out and he would try to advance by fire and movement.

While I was getting this message across to the sections we were hit by mortar or artillery fire. Ten or twelve rounds landed in and around us, including one which looked to me to have landed right on top of my platoon sergeant and stretcher-bearer. We had no idea where this was coming from. Neil later told me that the round actually lifted him off the ground into the air. Somehow we didn't take any casualties from the heavy stuff. We then went forward about forty metres in two leaps of fire and movement—fairly simple stuff—one section fire, the other section go. Another couple of guys got wounded doing this. Our problem was that we could not see targets to fire at, so the people providing fire support were really just firing blindly to our front and not really suppressing the enemy fire. I gave the order to hold where we were at least till we organised the wounded and regrouped.

11 Platoon's radio stopped transmitting and I had to assume the worst, that the platoon had been overrun. 10 Platoon had advanced to attack from the north to try and take the pressure off 11 Platoon, but became obviously embroiled in a heavy fire-fight (exchange of small arms fire) and then their radio went silent, so I had no contact with two-thirds of my company. And no carrier pigeons!

The gravity of the situation was growing rapidly and I spoke personally to the battalion commander on the command radio net, telling him of the worsening situation out at Long Tan and asked for urgent heliborne reinforcements to be flown into the area near where we had met Bravo Company. Colonel Townsend's opinion was that the LZ area might not be safe and that also no ready reaction force was available at that time. I understood from him that plans were in hand to send an APC force out as soon as possible.

Soon after, Private Brian Hornung, although shot through the shoulder, arrived back with the 10 Platoon radio, which had been rendered useless by the same shot that wounded him. I forget what I said and who ordered it, most likely my signaller, Corporal Graham Smith, but my second regimental signaller, Private Yank Akell (in later years to become a major), took off with the spare radio and headed off in the rain into the rubber towards 10 Platoon.

Miraculously, in the gloom and monsoonal rain, he survived enemy fire, killed two VC on the way with his OMC and after calling out 'Mr. Kendall, Mr. Kendall', through the trees, found his way to 10 Platoon and restored communications. Geoff Kendall then advised me he was taking casualties, was pinned down and unable to move forward towards 11 Platoon. I ordered him to withdraw back to the company HQ area to help secure this area and the aid post so that I could send 12 Platoon around to the right and try that way. Geoff spoke with Morrie Stanley, who organised artillery fire to cover his withdrawal.

'Radio communication within the company was all but hopeless,' recalls Bob Buick.

Noise from the loud cracking of small arms bullets passing overhead, the continuous firing of rifle and machine-gun close by, the crashing of exploding artillery and rocket-propelled grenades (RPGs) was deafening. All radio messages needed to be sent a few times, repeated to get the whole message clearly to Delta Company Headquarters. To make radio communications even more difficult, the enemy began to interfere with and jam the radio frequency. Somehow, radio operator Private Vic Grice passed and received the vital information. This included directions for gunfire adjustments, vital intelligence on what the enemy was doing and gathering information for the company. To communicate five metres away we had to shout at the top of our lungs.

The fire from the enemy automatic assault rifles and light machine-guns was so intense that the radio antenna was shot off Bob Buick's 11 Platoon radio.

While Vic Grice was replacing it he noticed a large group of enemy moving towards our rear on our left flank. As soon as he had replaced the antenna I asked for an artillery fire mission in the area. It was during that time, with no communications with Company HQ, that Harry Smith had moved 10 Platoon forward to help us. The shells landed among the VC and probably very close to 10 Platoon.

[Where Geoff Kendall said that he thought they might have been mortared, it could have been this fire.]

There was a time in the battle when the enemy near the hapless 5 Section fired directly into the Platoon HQ. Private Barry Meller, the platoon orderly, and Bob Buick were spotting and indicating the enemy shooting at them. Some of the VC were only about thirty metres, three or four rubber trees away. If one was giving Bob a hard time Ron normally shot him and Bob did the same when Ron was pinned down. 'While indicating a target a VC bullet passed through Ron's open mouth and out his left cheek. Had he had his mouth closed it would have taken his jaw out. We killed the offending VC between us.'

10 Platoon was now withdrawing under cover of artillery fire. Some of their earlier casualties were already back in the makeshift company aid post in a dip in the ground and Corporal 'Doc' Dobson was tending to their wounds.

I heard from the command radio net that the APCs were warned out by ATF HQ to go to 6RAR to collect Alpha Company and move out as their relief force.

AAR8. 181630 A Coy warned for movement.
B Coy told to turn about and move towards D Coy.

[Later I learnt all this was delayed by Brigadier Jackson. Townsend had chosen Alpha Company, who were only an hour back from their own three-day patrol, as there was no other company on 'Task Force Stand-by' as was required by normal operational procedures. But the relief force move had to be approved personally by Brigadier Jackson. It seems the brigadier was most worried about the base. The intelligence reports, which we did not have access to, might have been correct after all, and as well, there might have been another VC regiment on the loose to the north-west!]

I informed Dave Sabben that the battalion CO advised me the reserve company—Alpha—would be put into the APCs and sent to our relief. Dave remembers:

For about half an hour, all 12 could do was lie behind our packs in a thin screen between company HQ and the other two platoons and listen to the firefight and the artillery. To our front, in an arc from half left to half right, there was the constant chatter of small arms fire, now from this direction, now from that, mostly incoming. The rain had dimmed down the light under the rubber canopy and visibility was reduced to three hundred metres or so. Occasionally we saw tracer rounds expend themselves into the mud to our front. The radio traffic was constant, with both 10 and 11 reporting on the tactical situation and adjusting fall of artillery shot. When transmitting, the sound of the small arms fire was loud and sharp. From back some five hundred metres to the rear it had lost its *crack*.

Some quick calculations were made anticipating the arrival of the APCs. Alpha Company and the APCs could be given ten minutes' notice to move, then be mounted and leave the Task Force in, say, another ten minutes. They could cover the four or five thousand metres in, say, thirty more minutes, which included crossing the Suoi Da Bang river at the only known ford. By this calculation, they could reasonably expect to be with Delta Company within an hour. The two platoons out front only had to survive another hour!

The company sited itself in a defensive position. Morrie Stanley and the two other gunners plopped themselves down in the area selected for Company HQ.

We were all to experience a frantic and fearful two hours of battle in that place. It was virtually impossible for me to discuss fire support with Harry Smith because he was devoting all his efforts to assembling what he could of Delta Company to establish a viable defensive position. I had found that Willy Walker and I collapsed more or less into the same hole as he was carrying the radio at that time. Murray Broomhall was temporarily utilised to man a machine-gun and to assist the CSM, especially with the distribution of ammunition. Murray was maybe only ten to twenty metres away, but in those conditions it was a very long distance.

I sent another report, which summed up my opinion of what was happening at Long Tan. It was patently obvious that a much bigger force was attacking us and that it was being reinforced and increasing.

> **AAR9. 181650 D Coy Enemy considered to be battalion at least. 11 Platoon has suffered casualties and being attacked from three sides.**

I heard on the radio net Brigadier Jackson give approval, in principle only, for the APC relief force to move, but Alpha Company and the APCs waited in 6RAR lines for the executive order to move. The tension that I felt under such overwhelming odds caused me to be very frustrated with the apparent failure of the Headquarters groups to be acting for our survival. My anger grew with each passing delay. In one of my conversations with 6RAR I recall being told the APCs were delayed in leaving Nui Dat and I retorted to the CO that 'If they don't hurry up and get out here then they might as well not come at all', or words to that effect.

THE REINFORCEMENTS 'HURRY UP AND WAIT'

The battalion CO and Major Harry Honnor, the NZ Artillery battery commander, were together following developments and preparing for the Alpha Company relief effort. When Adrian Roberts arrived at HQ Major Passey, the operations officer, ordered him to 'Pick up Alpha Company and get to Delta Company and break up the attack'.

[Adrian remembers: Somewhere in this discussion Major Passey said that the CO would be joining us later by helicopter, a remark that has stayed with me over the years because of the ground and battle realities that I was to become aware of later. He subsequently opted to join the APCs with the result that we had for a time a reduced APC/Infantry capability in the field.]

Members of 3 Troop and 2 Section, 2 Troop all remember the frustration as they waited about an hour. Alpha Company soldiers continued to rush around getting ready to go out again, while they were also trying to get a taste of the 'good' food on the barbecue and complete changing their gear and showering after their last patrol. Some of the APC crews also remember preparing a ration-pack evening meal in the back of their carriers while they waited. But the order to move did not come.

[Brigadier Jackson delayed the executive order for Alpha Company to move out with the APCs until 1730hrs. He could have been concerned at denuding the base of too many troops and APCs. He seemed to be worrying about the other VC Regiment— 274, rumoured to be over to the west—now appreciated as a threat to the base. Of course, the delay highlighted the lack of a Task Force reaction force that day—probably due to the concert. 6RAR had three companies out, with the remaining company, Charlie, spread around in other company areas—three platoons defending a battalion frontage. Indeed, as 5RAR had not returned from Bin Ba, it could be said Charlie Company 6RAR was the only infantry in the whole base!]

MEANWHILE BRAVO COMPANY STARTS TO MOVE FORWARD

Noel Ford, OC Bravo Company, asked if they could move towards Delta Company in response to my request to return as soon as possible. The CO told them to stay in their location and await further orders. At this stage they could hear the contact developing into a battle over the radio and heard the artillery missions being fired. Most had never heard anything like this before; to many it was like in the movies, but this was for real. Eventually they received orders to go back to Delta Company but the pace was slower than the pace they had made on the way back to base. The reality of the conflict in front of them had raised the level of fear in each man.

'At some point while we were on flat open ground enemy mortars were fired from the north over our heads,' recalls Second Lieutenant John O'Halloran. 'They were landing 100 metres to the south of us. This slowed us up.'

AAR10. 181655 B Coy Under fire from 60 mm mortar.

[Harry reflects: A few 60 mm mortar bombs landed near Bravo Company well to the south-west, some two thousand metres away, at about 1650hrs. Later it was thought there was a VC group guarding the bridge to the south and had seen Bravo Company in the distance, and gave orders to their mortars. But even if some mortars had fired, most of the vast resources of the VC divisional, regimental and battalion artillery, which included 75 mm field guns, 120 mm mortars, 82 mm mortars, 75 mm RCLs and 60 mm mortars, were not used in the ensuing three-hour battle. Some had been used to shell the Task Force base in the early morning of the 17th, but they were not deployed for fire into the Long Tan area on the 18th. Some fire would be expected if the VC were anticipating establishing an ambush killing ground for the first reaction force, which was Bravo Company. Nor were they deployed for an ambush on Delta Company in the rubber on the 18th. The rubber, obscuring the troops, was not a good killing ground anyway. The gentle inclined grassy area to the west where Bravo Company and Delta Company had arrived was better! The mortars that fell on Delta Company and then, later, on Bravo Company appeared to have been fired from an area to the west of the derelict village of Xa Long Tan, which was some 1,200 metres south of the battle area.]

To this day no one has ever been able to indicate to me where all the guns, RCLs and mortars went after the Task Force shelling. We are talking about a large number of weapons with tremendous firepower which could have decimated Delta Company had they been zeroed in on the Long Tan battle area. I once made a frivolous comment that maybe they had fired on the wrong night, two nights too early, and were sent away for retraining. I personally believe they went to the north-west of the Task Force in readiness to support an attack on the base and ambush any US Army relief force coming down Highway 2 from Bear Cat or Bien Hoa, to the north.

> *[We captured one 60 mm mortar, but saw no signs of 82 mm mortars, although many dead soldiers carried spare bombs of both calibres as reserve ammunition for their battalions' mortar platoons.]*

DELTA COMPANY'S AMMUNITION SUPPLY BECOMES DESPERATELY LOW

With the situation that had developed, it was obvious to me that Delta Company did not have enough ammunition. It would not be possible with our three magazines—we only had 60 rounds per SLR—to continue a defensive fight into the night, perhaps all night, and I called Battalion HQ and ordered an urgent ammunition resupply by helicopter. I anticipated the helicopters could fly out and drop the ammunition down through the trees, with our location being given to them by throwing coloured smoke, which should drift up through the canopy. This process was nothing new, but I knew it was going to be difficult in the heavy rain and with the choppers perhaps being heard and fired at, even if not seen through the trees. The other downside was that I would have to cut the artillery fire support while the choppers were inbound and overhead.

AAR11. 181700 D Coy Request ammunition be dropped through the trees.

DANGER CLOSE

Bob Grandin remembers that 'It was mid-afternoon, just after the music began, when the artillery barrage commenced'.

It startled everyone as it was not expected and one thought that there would not be any routine firing during the concert. When another salvo was fired, the ever-impatient Frank Riley decided he would go to Operations and check what was happening. I decided to follow. As we approached the tent it was obvious this was not some minor interdiction, but that Delta Company had made contact. The rate of firing increased quickly, the number of guns involved increased and the tension conveyed over the radios rapidly increased. They had made contact with a very large force moving through the Long Tan rubber towards the Task Force Headquarters.

When Harry Smith called for an ammunition resupply by helicopter, Group Captain Raw recognised the difficulty of tasking 9 Squadron helicopters into an unsafe area in contravention of the Air Staff directives. It was suggested that Canberra would need to be contacted to give approval. As the issue of command and control over the helicopters had already become a contentious issue with Brigadier Jackson, this discussion made him furious. He wanted aircraft in the field immediately to help his men. He turned to the US liaison but was told that he could not get immediate support, but that US Army helicopters could be up from Vung Tau in about twenty minutes. At this stage the battle became more furious. Artillery was firing what appeared to be continuously, Harry Smith was making desperate pleas for the fire to be brought closer and closer to his position, in fact he appeared to be asking for it to be brought down on his position.

Frank, who was always frustrated by red tape, stepped forward and said he would go in with his helicopter. He argued that he was commander of the aircraft in the field and had the right to make tactical decisions about what he could and couldn't do. If he weren't in the Operations tent he wouldn't be asking anyone for permission. He would go, on his own if necessary. As a transferee from the helicopter support flight in Butterworth, Malaya, he was always flying around alone, he said, and didn't need anyone else. Part of this retort was in response to my suggesting that we hadn't thought out how we could actually do this task. How could we find them? Why wouldn't we just be shot out of the air by this superior force? How could we land? What could we actually do that would help? This was all too logical for Frank, we would just go and see.

Jackson was pleased to see some guts from the air force, and he turned to Raw to see his response. The Group Captain was keen to help, but worried about his responsibility; however, he was willing to accede to Frank that he had the right to make decisions about his aircraft and he would not stand in his way. Someone suggested at this stage that we could drop ammunition through the trees. 'Let's do it,' was the cry. At this stage there was a discussion as to who was going to go with Frank. I suggested that this was like a suicide mission. Frank just responded, 'You don't have to come, volunteers only.' Bruce quickly said he was with him, then the rest of us said we would go, although I can remember continuing to discuss it as we moved down to the choppers. Things like, how are we going to do this and come back? We rushed over to the 6RAR pad and waited.

The crew of the first helicopter was Flight Lieutenant Frank Riley, with Bob Grandin as co-pilot and gunners Leading Aircraftsmen 'Bluey' Collins and George Stirling. In the second helicopter Flight Lieutenants Cliff Dohle and Bruce Lane were the pilots and Leading Aircraftsmen Bill Harrington and Brian Hill the gunners.

DANGER CLOSE

At the same time, Major Owen O'Brien, officer commanding 6RAR's Administrative Company, remembers that when the battle began to get under way he was at the concert. As the artillery fire began to intensify it was apparent that something serious was happening and he looked around for his signaller and driver. They both appeared immediately, having the same thoughts as him. On the way back to the battalion lines, O'Brien radioed the commanding officer and was ordered to stand by to coordinate an ammunition resupply for Delta Company.

The order to prepare ammunition for delivery by helicopter came soon after 1700hrs. O'Brien proceeded to the 6RAR 'Eagle Farm' helipad. RSM George Chinn arrived there at about the same time, it being a prime function of the RSM to arrange ammunition in battle. Soldiers came from everywhere to help. The two helicopters arrived. By this time, it was raining and darkness was not far away. There was some doubt and radio discussion about the ability of the choppers to fly the mission successfully. The helicopter crews were absolutely determined to go and Chinn and O'Brien simply assumed that the job had to be done regardless of risk. Riley and his aircrew did everything asked of them, willingly and without question, and every one worked unstintingly and very fast to prepare the ammunition for delivery.

Major O'Brien gave the order to wrap the ammunition in blankets, these being for the wounded, and directed that various types of ammunition be mixed in bundles for ease of distribution at the other end. Moreover, they decided to break some (perhaps not enough) of the boxes open, and to package some machine-gun ammunition belts in sandbags, to make it easier for Delta Company to distribute under fire. Because the administrative elements of the battalion were under his command it was not hard to arrange blankets from the Q store (and nearby beds) and for a number of shell dressings to be included for the wounded.

[In retrospect Major O'Brien believes they should have had an ammunition resupply already packaged for quick delivery. That omission was rectified soon after Long Tan when he arranged for two company second line resupplies to be packaged in magazines, which he thinks became standard procedure in all battalions.]

The crews had discussed how to deliver the ammunition and it was decided to use the same technique as was used with SAS insertions and extractions, remembers Bob Grandin.

The lead helicopter, with Frank and I on board, was to take a lighter load and go out at height (about six hundred metres), to locate the target zone and make contact. The other helicopter, with Bruce and Cliff on board, would fly at low level and we would direct it into the drop zone. As it departed we were to dive down and drop our load. This was designed to improve our safety, as at height the probability of being hit by small arms fire was greatly reduced and at treetop level the time of sighting was so small that it was difficult to fire an accurate shot.

Major O'Brien discussed with Riley the need to suspend artillery fire during the resupply (of which he was acutely aware) and radioed both Battalion HQ and the Fire Support Coordination Centre (FSCC) on this. He told Riley and Cliff Dohle that they would have to do the drop in perhaps one minute over target, so critical was the need to sustain artillery fire for a rifle company in close contact with a large enemy force. They were under no illusion about the fact that Delta Company needed not only small arms ammunition but also continuous artillery support for survival.

As the aircraft were loaded (and it all happened very quickly, with no time for careful analysis or management by committee) it became apparent that some soldiers would be needed in the helicopters to heave out the ammunition. The on-board door machine-gunners could not leave their guns. Several of the soldiers asked to go aboard and Major O'Brien told RSM Chinn to select some and that he would make the final decision.

Chinn told O'Brien he intended to go himself in one aircraft. It was pointed out that RSMs are responsible for *organising* ammunition, not *delivering* it. He forcefully and almost insubordinately told the major he was going, come what may. O'Brien had known Chinn for twelve years, from the time he joined the army, and had served with him in the SAS. So he said, 'Bugger you, George, I'm coming too.' Later the commanding officer asked why a company commander and the regimental sergeant major had gone on a dodgy resupply mission instead of staying at Nui Dat doing what they were paid for. They could only say that it seemed like a good idea at the time and the commanding officer said, 'Bloody silly thing to do, but well done.'

A CHALLENGE FOR THE ARTILLERY

The artillery faced numerous problems on the gun line, which would become a real test of character and professionalism. The first of these problems was the torrential rain, the like of which they had never encountered before. It was soon after the engagement commenced that the sky just opened up and it poured, with lightning everywhere. A bolt of lightning cut the lines to the tannoy system used to pass orders to the guns. This resulted in orders having to be shouted in relays to the gun platforms until the damage was repaired. Another bolt of lightning struck the lines, which caused Gunner Deacon, the Kiwi switchboard operator, to be thrown across the exchange, and a member of a gun detachment was similarly stunned by yet another bolt of lightning.

A second problem they faced was the gun aiming points (GAPs) and sights, made even more difficult by the rain. The gun sights were aimed using direction to a post with a mark or light attached to it and the angle of elevation was indicated by a spirit bubble in the gun sight. The rain was so heavy that all guns 'lost' their GAPs during the battle. A smoky haze caused by the cordite fumes not dispersing from the gun position compounded the problem. To keep firing many crews finished up using a bicycle torch fixed to a star picket as a GAP.

In the eleven months 105 Battery had been in Vietnam they had had continual problems with condensation fogging up their gun sights. (The battery had previously been with 1RAR at Bien Hoa.) Each gun had three sights, one in use, one as a spare, while the other sight was in a local pattern humidity box to dry out.

During the battle all sights were used on the gun position including the spare sights, normally kept in the Q store. Sights were placed in metal ammunition boxes with small petrol stoves to help them dry out quickly.

To compound the problem further, the battery had received new Canadian sights two months before the battle that required different 'drills' to the Italian sights they also used. Both types were in use during the battle and it was only through the experience and skill of the gunners that no mistakes were made.

The third problem was ammunition. The ammunition issued by the US Army was unreliable. If firing different 'lot numbers' at the same time, the fall of shot could have a depth of 400 metres. 105 Battery had adopted the policy of having two different types of ammunition—'close target', where the one batch of a lot number was used by all guns when firing in support of our own troops, and 'H&I', which were small batches of lot numbers and different weighted projectiles. These were used to harass 'Charlie' by firing at irregular intervals to keep him wondering where the next round was going to fall. It was fortunate the battery had adhered to a routine of maintaining stocks of ammunition on the gun line. They had replenished the ammunition used the previous night and each gun had 100 rounds of 'close target' ammunition when 'fire mission regiment' was called.

It was quickly realised that with the number of 'ten rounds fire for effect' and the periods of 'continuous fire' that went for ten to twelve minutes at a time, they would soon run out of ammunition. This was reported to the command post and a massive ammunition resupply from the ammunition dump was put into effect. Cooks, clerks, medics, Q store staff, technicians from the RAEME workshops and members of 131 Divisional Locating Battery assisted in resupplying the gun line.

Normally 105 mm ammunition has the fuse attached when received. But at that time the target lot number which could be used for close target ammunition at the ammunition dump was 'plugged', that is, without a fuse. This meant that the ammunition had to be unboxed, the projectiles removed from their canisters and the plugs removed. At the same time, boxes of fuses were opened and the fuses screwed into the cavity of the projectile left by the removal of the plug. The 'helpers' excelled themselves, ensuring this was done as quickly as possible under the guidance of the battery sergeant major.

Other volunteers were loaded with as many rounds as they could carry and raced to the guns in the teeming rain hoping to God they were not going to be struck by a bolt of lightning or slip in the red mud. Some members had to run up to 100 metres to reach different guns. This was a feat in itself. At no time during the next three hours did a gun have to stop firing because of a shortage of ammunition. A Chinook helicopter arrived with a slung load, which boosted the ammunition supply, although it then had to be manhandled from the helicopter to the ammunition dump.

The crews also had to contend with toxic gas. Although there was torrential rain, there was no wind and the gases from the cordite took its toll on some members on the gun line. A clerk assisting in an ammunition bunker on one gun was overcome by the fumes and passed out. One gun sergeant had to hand over to his bombardier and others were just plain sick. The cordite fumes, by not dispersing, developed a smoky haze around the gun position, which made it difficult to breathe, and as already stated, made it hard for the gun layers to find their aiming posts.

Lastly, they had to contend with the problem of fatigue. A gun detachment comprised seven men, yet it was rare to have a full detachment on a gun. During the Battle of Long Tan, the standing patrol of section strength had to move out under the command of a gun sergeant. The strong points also had to be manned, which further reduced the numbers on the gun line.

Considering most of the members on the gun line had been awake since the mortar attack on the night of 16/17 August, by 0700hrs on the morning of the 19th most were suffering extreme fatigue.

It is interesting to note that while the 105 batteries fired over four thousand rounds; 'Eure's Battery', the US 155s, only fired 300 rounds of 95 lb 155 mm howitzer high explosive. This under-utilisation was a disappointment for their commanding officer.

> **AAR12. 181702 D Coy Request air strike area YS487669 to YS487672.**

I requested an air strike with napalm, rockets and bombs across the front of 11 Platoon in the hope of persuading the VC to back off. As with the choppers, I knew we would have to stop the artillery fire while the planes attacked, but that was a risk that I had to take. I knew air support would have a devastating effect on the VC, if we could get the airborne fire controller (FAC) onto the target in the bad conditions, as well as indicating our positions with coloured smoke.

The operations officer at 6RAR told me that there were US Air Force attack aircraft overhead in response to my earlier request for air support and I requested they drop napalm 200 metres across the front of 11 Platoon guided by coloured smoke. I was told to stand by to give radio directions to the FAC overhead. I was also told the guns had been stopped to facilitate the air strike.

After many calls on the radio, I could not make radio contact with the airborne FAC. In the end, knowing I could not hold the VC off without the artillery support, I had to tell Battalion HQ to send them all away as I wanted the artillery fire back urgently. Buick and Stanley then immediately went on with the artillery fire in front of 11 Platoon.

[The aircraft later dropped their bombs and napalm in suspected enemy rear areas specified by Battalion or Task Force Headquarters.]

I was desperate to find a way to get 11 Platoon out. I thought that a platoon attack from our right might take the pressure off 11 Platoon for a short time. The VC had halted 10 Platoon's attack on the left. We could now try the right flank. I called David Sabben into Company HQ and told him 12 Platoon with Company HQ group in tow would move out to the right, the south, to try and get to 11 Platoon from their rear. 10 Platoon, which was withdrawing to the company area, would secure the area of the aid post.

We formed up, 12 Platoon leading, and started to move off, but then following a series of radio messages on artillery and command radio nets I realised that command and map reference work was not possible on the move. The FOO and I had to stay put. As 10 Platoon was not back yet, I had to tell David Sabben to leave his 9 Section to help protect the company aid post and HQ area. He then moved off with only two sections, just twenty men all up, less than two-thirds of a full platoon.

'I heard on the company net Harry order 10 to withdraw and 11 to remain in place and await our arrival,' remembers Dave Sabben.

> He called me over to him. Squatting in the rain, trying to protect his map and chinagraph markings from the rain, he told me 12 Platoon and CHQ were going to advance to 11's rear to support their withdrawal. My orders were to put two sections in front of Company HQ and one behind, and to start an advance towards 11 Platoon. The withdrawing 10 Platoon would meet up with us en route. I was told to hurry.
>
> I called in the nearest two section commanders: 'Drinky' Drinkwater and 'Chico' Miller. Drinky's 7 Section would lead out, the Platoon HQ group would follow, then Chico's 8 Section, followed by Company HQ. Mac McCulloch's 9 Section would bring up the rear. Both 7 and 8 Sections got up and formed into arrowhead, ready to move out. I had directed them slightly east of south, towards the hut that 11 Platoon passed on their pursuit. There, I would turn east and come in directly behind 11 to avoid running into any VC that may be attempting to outflank them in wide encircling movements. I ensured that Company HQ was behind Chico, then took my place behind 7 Section, and we

set off, leaving our backpacks where they lay. CSM Kirby was to form up my third section behind Company HQ.

Almost immediately, 10 Platoon came up on the radio advising that they were withdrawing with their dead and wounded, that they were down to about half strength and would need a firm base to treat their casualties. Unknown to me, the FO, Morrie Stanley, had also advised Harry that constant artillery corrections couldn't easily be made on the move. Harry had to stop and form a firm base. On the radio, Harry advised that he was keeping my third section (Mac's 9 Section) and ordered me to proceed with the other two sections to the relief of 11 Platoon. There were just twenty of us. Drinky's 7 Section, Chico's 8 Section (each of eight men) and a small Platoon HQ, comprising Graeme Davis, my platoon medic, Alf Bartlett, my radio operator, Paddy Todd, my platoon sergeant, and myself. We headed first south to within sight of the hut, then turned east.

Bob Buick and 11 Platoon were just trying to stay alive.

I had no idea where the rest of the company were or what they were doing. I was concentrating on what was needed and adjusting the gunfire. I kept on yelling out that the company was coming to help us and that the battalion in APCs was on the way out. Of course, I did not have a clue what was happening 100 metres away let alone 1,000 metres away. It did give me hope and I'm sure it helped our morale. There were dozens and dozens of enemy to our front and too bloody close for comfort. Among my most vivid memories are those of the diggers of the platoon calling out to each other. They were supporting themselves and their mates by calling out names. The courage, tenacity, skill and endurance displayed by the young men that day would live with me forever.

Only eleven months had passed since these blokes had marched into the Training Company at Enoggera. They had arrived in September 1965 to be trained as infantrymen. Now they were in action performing and producing the results as well as any Australian digger had ever done before.

We were lying down, hidden in the mist, the VC were moving around trying to find us to attack, we could see them, but were hidden from their view. However, 11 Platoon was in very serious trouble. We were being fired on from three sides by about 150 to 200 VC. However, the poor visibility caused by the rain was on our side. But we were unable to withdraw due to our heavy number of casualties. The supporting gunfire was not providing a pathway for us to retreat through. Individuals were unable to move around the platoon as all movement attracted concentrated enemy fire.

I sent our position and asked for a fire mission at that location. I had resigned myself to the fact that with twelve of us remaining, three of them wounded, we had no place to hide or move to. But Morrie Stanley would not fire on our position, it was not the thing to do. It must have helped Morrie, me sending our position, because he adjusted the gunfire closer and closer until it was landing about 50 to 100 metres across our front and right flank where the most enemy were. Our situation appeared hopeless, but we hung on.

Morrie Stanley remembers the exchange.

Bob Buick requested artillery fire on his own position. I decided to discuss the matter with him on the company radio. There have been several reports and opinions about our radio conversation, but I must emphasise that neither of us bears any ill feeling about the matter. We have spoken about it several times since. Bob had assessed that with about ten men left fit to fight out of 28, they could not survive more than another ten to fifteen minutes. I reminded him of the danger and advised him that unless his troops were dug in and had overhead protection, I was not prepared to adjust the fire onto his position. Certainly he insisted, strongly. Whether I replied and declined or failed to reply, I am uncertain. I did not, however, deliberately adjust fire as a result of his request. He reported later that the fall of shot continued to be 50–100 metres from him and among the enemy.

'There is nothing as spectacular or frightening as being close to artillery gun-fire,' recalls Bob Buick.

Each projectile weighs about fifteen kilograms of high explosive and steel. When it hits a tree or the ground hundreds of steel splinters fly everywhere, most of it being projected in the direction of the shell's path. That helped us, as the guns were firing directly over our heads and towards the enemy. The first six shells landed right among the largest concentration of Viet Cong. They shredded 40 men to pieces within the first few seconds, an awesome sight. I seem to remember asking for five or six repeats with small adjustments. All told, 30 to 36 shells spread along our eastern front and around to the south.

Visibility had been reduced so much it was difficult to distinguish the trees 100 metres away. With the lightning flashing continually and the thunder booming directly overhead, seemly enveloping the entire battlefield, it could be mistaken for Armageddon. It was looking more and more hopeless to me as there seemed little that could be done. I was unable to move from the position and I was very reluctant to leave so many of our blokes. We had sustained too many casualties, over half the platoon were killed or wounded. I didn't even miss having a smoke for two hours. I didn't miss seeing the air full of tracer rounds passing around our heads and seemingly moving in slow motion. It became entrancing looking at the tracer fire, like a child's fascinations with fireworks. There was usually one tracer to five normal rounds and the tracer was like a swarm of bush flies around us. You could not put your hand up without getting your fingers shot off.

At 1715 hours Harry Smith sent a Sitrep to Battalion:

AAR13. 181715 D Company Reported 11 Platoon appears to be surrounded, 12 Platoon attempting to reach 11 Platoon but is pinned down.

By this time, 12 Platoon had been able to advance about half the distance to where Dave Sabben believed 11 Platoon to be before they were spotted and fired upon by VC to their north.

They were attempting to follow up 10's withdrawal or to encircle 11 Platoon. We went to ground and returned fire. It was a small group of VC and they were more than 150 metres away—almost at the limit of visual distance in the conditions. We saw some fall and the others go to ground and withdraw.

AAR 14. 181730 A Coy Ordered to move ASAP.

About an hour had passed since the APCs had arrived at Alpha Company lines. Finally the CO called Adrian Roberts and Charles Mollison into a briefing. There was still only a speculative concept of what was happening in the rubber plantation and the strength of the enemy. After discussing actions for the infantry, the route out offered by Roberts was accepted and the commanders raced off to brief their troops.

In Alpha Company lines Lieutenant Peter Dinham remembers that soon after his platoon had returned to base, a warning order came through to prepare to move out. They were still changing out of their wet, dirty clothing and looking forward to partaking of a buffet-style fresh meal in the vicinity of Company HQ. Fresh food was a welcome break from the normal hard rations consumed during operations and patrol activity. About 1730hrs the platoon commanders were all called to the company commander's tent for an urgent O Group. They were advised that Delta Company was under sustained attack by at least an enemy battalion and that Gordon Sharp's platoon was cut off. They were now on fifteen minutes' notice to move and the task would be to move to Delta Company's location in APCs to relieve that company. Peter Dinham dashed back to the 2 Platoon tent lines, briefed the section commanders and they all undertook rapid preparations with the CSM, Warrant Officer Class 2, Jack Roughly, reissuing fresh ammunition.

AAR15. 181735 D Company Reported all Platoons and Company Headquarters under attack from East and South.

Dave Sabben was approaching 11 Platoon from the west with his group of 12 Platoon.

> Our fire had attracted the attention of another group of VC to our south. This was a bigger group and they had a medium machine-gun (MMG), which opened up on us. Its fire was somewhat erratic, sweeping the plantation as if to draw our fire so they could follow our tracer back to our position. We waited silently as the MMG rounds burst through the rubber trees above our heads. Leaves and twigs showered on us and the white latex of the wounded trees splattered us during the near misses.
>
> A group was forming up alongside the MMG and was preparing to advance in our direction, but not

exactly towards us. We watched as it moved off and it became obvious that they were a group trying to outflank 11 Platoon from the south. We waited until they were well within range—eighty metres or so—and they still didn't appear to know we were there, despite the MMG fire. We opened up, hitting the group who immediately went to ground. There were signs of confusion in their group with movement in all directions, then they withdrew, dragging their casualties. I think they were trying to close the door on 11 Platoon and were confused when fired upon from their left flank.

With the withdrawal of the group, I once more tried to advance towards 11 Platoon, but was able to move no more than a few metres when the MMG opened up again, this time with more accurate and sustained fire. 12 Platoon went to ground again. This was the position in which we were to remain for almost another hour.

11 PLATOON RUNS OUT OF AMMUNITION AND DECIDES TO MAKE A RUN FOR IT

Bob Buick was still isolated with 11 Platoon and starting to develop a desperate plan.

I decided to get what remained of the platoon out, go back and take as many survivors as I could. I knew that some, maybe even myself, could become further casualties, but to stay was madness. It was getting dark earlier than normal due to the storm and visibility was less than a hundred metres. We had no ammunition left for the rifles and machine-guns, even though the platoon's fire discipline had been magnificent. We had carried 600 rounds per machine-gun and 60 rounds per rifle. The warriors of 11 Platoon, after more than two hours, with no ammunition, were lying in the mud, hand grenades ready. A couple of diggers I

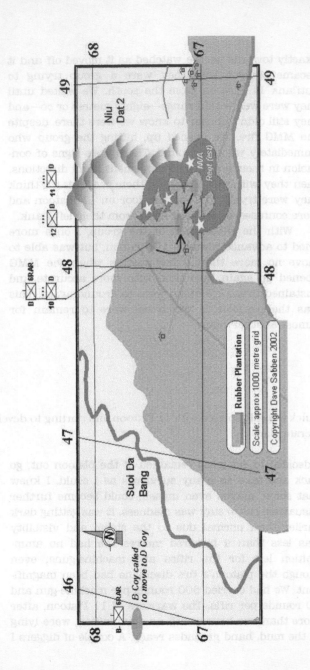

saw had an entrenching shovel and machete in hand for the final assault. The final defiant stand, hand-to-hand combat with the enemy.

Three issues were foremost in Bob's mind.

Firstly, because of the heavy enemy fire and the continuing attacks I was unable to move. With so many casualties I was faced with a difficult choice. Whether to remain in location and wait until the company could support us in such a way as to permit 11 Platoon to withdraw with our dead and wounded, or retreat with those that could move. Secondly, the artillery supporting fire had been initially ineffective in close support to the platoon. When it was adjusted very close to us, it destroyed the enemy to our front. This knocked the effectiveness out of the enemy such that there was very little fire coming from them. The guns destroyed and neutralised the enemy allowing me the opportunity to consider the options, including to retreat. Thirdly, the weather and time of day were becoming a factor. The monsoonal rain, low clouds and lateness of the day reduced visibility to about 75 to 100 metres. This was to our advantage, increasing our chances of successfully making a clean break and moving out of the area.

How to get out of here and move to a safe place with as many of the platoon as I could? To stay was to achieve nothing. We could not survive another VC attack. Crazy plans raced through my head. Should we try breaking out to the east straight through the attacking enemy or go back to the west? Behind us was the only place there was no VC, so the company must still be behind us. I decided to go back to the west. If I could not find any friendly forces I would take the remnant of 11 Platoon to the Suoi Da Bang. This was a small river on the western side of the rubber, between the Long Tan rubber and our base at

Nui Dat. Near the river we could hide overnight, then in daylight, next day, make for the Task Force base.

While Dave Sabben was pinned down in his position he received radio messages telling him that 10 Platoon and Company HQ were receiving probes on their position by VC who had followed up 10 Platoon's withdrawal.

From time to time 12 Platoon could see movement to our north, where the VC were moving towards Company [HQ], but mostly it was too far away to fire at. On two occasions, the VC to our north undertook a flanking move on Company [HQ] that brought them towards us and to within firing range, so we opened up on them. This caused great confusion both times and resulted in one instance of them changing direction towards us in a feeble attempt at an assault. The group was small—some ten or twelve men—and they were easily beaten off, leaving behind half their number dead. The main danger for 12 Platoon was from the south, where we began to experience probes and then small assaults on our position. The VC had worked out that there were now troops to the west of 11 Platoon and were in the process of trying to flank us from the west. If this were bad news for 12 Platoon, it would have been welcome to 11 Platoon had they known it. By maintaining our position, we were able to stop the Viet Cong from closing the back door on 11 Platoon. All we needed was for 11 Platoon to appreciate that the Viet Cong hadn't been able to encircle them and work out that someone was holding the door open. Their radio had gone out again some time earlier, so they couldn't be advised or told to move west.

Bob Buick yelled out his orders. When the word was given everyone was to go back about 150 metres and regroup. 'A few minutes later I called out "GO". I looked around me and the blokes were getting off the ground and running back. I took off after them.'

Back with 12 Platoon, Dave Sabben was still receiving unwelcome attention from the south that now included some sporadic light mortar fire—small 60 mm bombs, or RPG rounds—which often exploded harmlessly in the trees around them. When they got through the canopy, the mortar bombs buried themselves in the mud before exploding, again severely limiting their range of damage. In fact, the mortars claimed only one casualty from 12 Platoon.

Paddy Todd was lying behind me facing north, his legs spread apart a few yards from mine as I lay facing south. A 60 mm mortar bomb or RPG dropped through the canopy and buried itself between his ankles before going off. Paddy said it felt like both ankles had been hit by a baseball bat, but we couldn't see any wound. In fact, tiny shrapnel fragments had peppered both ankles, but we couldn't see the puncture marks in the boots for the mud. He said he was not in pain—his feet were numb, so we put it down to concussion.

AAR16. 181740 Air strike unable to be effected due to low cloud. Aircraft dropped bombs and napalm in areas YS4967.
AAR17. 181740 Delta Company Will try to extract casualties and concentrate at YS477673.

During this time Geoff Kendall and 10 Platoon were withdrawing towards Company HQ.

We achieved this by a couple of backward fire and movement leaps. This got us out of the area being blanketed by enemy fire and must have been out of their sight because we were able to get back to Harry's location without further casualties. On arrival the OC ordered me to put my platoon down in defence facing toward the 11 Platoon firefight area. I

put Black Mac McDonald's section left forward, Buddy
Lea's section right forward, with Doug Moggs' section
behind Platoon HQ and me. 12 Platoon had moved off
toward 11 and for a while, at least, we seemed to have
a lull in the battle. It was still possible to see enemy
moving to the east although in most cases they were
too far away to make it worthwhile firing. Whether
they knew where we were, or what they were
planning was a mystery to us and left us uncertain of
what would happen next.

**AAR18. 181745 A Company Departed Base area in Armoured Personnel
Carriers of 3 Troop 1 Armoured Personnel Carrier Squadron.**

Adrian Roberts was aware that within the 1ATF boundaries
there were only a few places that APCs could enter and exit. So they
made for the Engineer Wire, which lay to the east and allowed
access to the Water Point.

Arriving at the Engineer Wire I was horrified to
discover that the gap had been changed and the new
gap so well concealed that I had to send a runner to
the engineers, who were at their evening meal, to get
someone to open the gap for us. I didn't keep time of
these events but my recall is that it took about ten
minutes, which would put us leaving the Task Force
perimeter at about 1800 or 1810hrs. I knew from
my time with 173 Airborne Brigade, on Operation
Hardihood, that I could get across the Suoi Da Bang
at a crossing place used by bullock carts in the dry
season. It lay south of the road between Xa Long
Phuoc ruins and the ruins of the Long Tan village.
The crossing place was immediately upstream from
a concrete dam that I reasoned would prevent us
being swept downstream in the event of difficulties
with currents. I knew from the results of a 2 Troop

reconnaissance some weeks earlier that entry and exit further north was simply not possible.

During this delay I was informed through 1APC Squadron that the CO of 6RAR now wished to move with the APCs to Delta Company. I was aware that Delta Company was in dire straits. What to do? I opted to send back two carriers, my troop officer, Second Lieutenant Ian Savage, and Corporal Jock Fottrill, to provide some limited tactical grouping [carriers normally operated in threes] while I pushed on to the river crossing at the Suoi Da Bang with the other eight carriers. I believed that Savage would catch up with me at that point.

Adrian Roberts, with only the eight carriers left, moved through the wire following a route around the northern edge of the destroyed village of Xa Long Phuoc.

During this move it poured with rain, a tropical downpour which only those who have seen monsoon rains can appreciate. The rain slowed us down as we wallowed through the red mud, but the rain also served to mask to some degree the noise of the APCs, which might have helped us surprise the enemy. At some time along the march to the river crossing Ian Savage, at CO 6RAR's direction, requested that we halt to allow them to catch up. I opted to push on to the crossing where I knew we would be naturally delayed and they could join us at that point.

On reaching the crossing site it was clear that, because of the rain, the current was flowing well over the 3.5 kph allowed for APC swimming—but there was nothing for it but to press on in view of Delta Company's dangerous situation. This was 3 Troop's first crossing of a river as an assault and the first in an uncontrolled situation, that is, outside peacetime rules. Adrian Roberts was also concerned.

The 3 Troop carriers lacked pivot steering brakes and track shrouds so had a terrible time in the water. At least two went in circles, bumping their way across against the dam wall. I remember looking back into the cargo hatch opening at the then seated infantry, their pale and anxious faces looking up as I attempted to reassure them as my turn came to cross. The infantry had to be seated inside to balance the vehicle. I got a section of carriers across the river to secure our hold on the far bank. The three carriers fanned out to form a perimeter. I followed and then the remaining section. The 2 Section carriers from 2 Troop were newer vehicles having arrived in SVN in June and consequently had less difficulty crossing the Suoi Da Bang. However, the latter lacked gunshields and intercommunication facilities between crew. Further, the radios were compatible with those in 3 Troop to the degree that we could only talk with 'squelch on'. This meant 2 Section 2 Troop had to endure maddening high-pitched squeals in their ears when we communicated.

Adrian Roberts had seven carriers across the river and there was no sign of the CO 6RAR.

I decided to leave one carrier commanded by Lance Corporal 'Tiny' O'Shea to secure the crossing place and to join Second Lieutenant Savage on his return with the Battalion HQ party. This provided him with the minimum tactical unit necessary once he crossed the river. At this point my carrier strength was down to seven and effectively a platoon was now lost to Alpha Company until the CO 6RAR and the three APCs caught up with us. The crossing took about fifteen minutes and was complete at about 1830hrs. Again the CO 6RAR, through Second Lieutenant Ian Savage, requested that I halt. I shouted this down to Charles Mollison, the Alpha Company commander, together with the intention to press on. (I could hear on the monitor-only facility that Delta Company seemed about to be overrun.) He agreed with a hand gesture and I moved off. Shortly after this Charles requested our location from me. I gave him a location just south of the Xa Long Phuoc–Long Tan road at the junction of the road running north-east through the rubber plantation.

In the immediate vicinity of the Suoi Da Bang were small terraced rice fields which gradually gave way to banana stands before reaching the road which runs west to Long Phuoc and east to Long Tan village ruins. North of this road was a rubber plant-ation. Adrian Roberts continues:

I placed Sergeant Ron Richards' APC section on the east (my right) reasoning that his gun shields and communication facilities were better on the side of the most likely enemy threat. With myself immediately west of the sunken road and in the centre, and Sergeant Blue O'Reilly's 2 Troop APC section west of the road (on my left), I ordered two-up formation so that both O'Reilly and Richards had two carriers forward left and right of each of them. This meant that O'Reilly, myself and Richards were in line behind. The balance of the carrier force, when it finally arrived, could move in line behind, thereby forming the depth and reserve. This was the standard APC assault formation we had practised so often in Puckapunyal, unfortunately, until now, never with infantry.

AMMUNITION RESUPPLY HELICOPTERS TAKE OFF

Aircrew spent some time sitting on the pad waiting for a clearance to go. Through this period the level of anxiety grew through not being in contact with what was going on and the apparent danger of the operation. Contact had to be made with Delta Company and timing

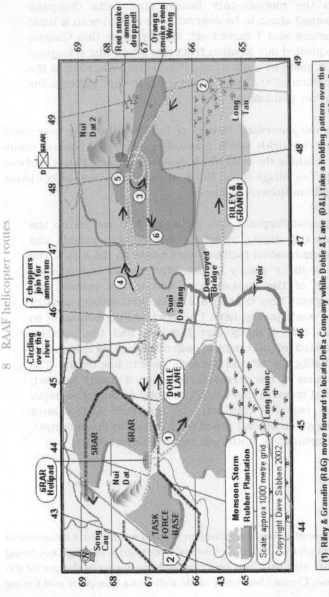

8 RAAF helicopter routes

Red smoke – ammo dropped!

Orange smoke seen - Wrong

Nui Dat 2

Long Tan

RILEY & GRANDIN

2 choppers join for ammo run

Circling over the river

Suoi Da Bang

Destroyed Bridge

Weir

DOHLE & LANE

Long Phuoc

6RAR Helipad

5RAR

6RAR

Nui Dat

TASK FORCE BASE

Song Cau

5RAR

Monsoon Storm
Rubber Plantation

Scale: approx x 1000 metre grid

Copyright Dave Sabben 2002

(1) Riley & Grandin (R&G) move forward to locate Delta Company while Dohle & Lane (D&L) take a holding pattern over the river. (2) R&G overfly Long Tan village, turn north west towards the battlefield. (3) R&G call for smoke - see "Orange". "Incorrect". Circle anti-clockwise and see "Red". "Correct". (4) Rejoin with D&L and guide them to Delta Company position. (5) Ammo drop made "...right into the CSM's lap...". (6) Both helicopters return to Task Force helipad.

DANGER CLOSE

for the drop arranged. The artillery barrage had to be stopped. Finally, when they were told to go, it was shortly before 1800hrs.

Bob Grandin recalls:

> The RSM and another soldier jumped in to push the cargo out when we arrived. Beauty, two more to go up when our load of ammunition exploded with a hit from the ground! As we lifted off the pad and reached the top of the trees another surprise awaited us. To the east was a large thunderstorm with intense rain falling over Long Tan. So much for flying high. I was reading the map and using the radio as Frank flew into the storm. He had to slow down to maintain some visibility. We were back to twenty knots! I was concerned that we were sitting ducks. I remember drawing myself back into the armour-plated seat trying to make a small exposed target. It was extremely difficult to see anything, in front, to the sides, or even down.

Sometime, just after 1745hrs, Harry Smith received the good news.

> I was advised the helicopters were headed our way, and shortly after, we had to stop the artillery fire. I advised everyone to stand by for the throwing of coloured smoke when the choppers were overhead. We waited for the desperately needed ammunition to arrive. I checked my signallers to ensure they were on the ball with the radio frequencies needed for the Albatross net if they did not use our own channels. As was usual, Signaller Graham Smith was way ahead of me with the radios and already had everything set up. I advised my platoon commanders that we would lose the guns when the choppers were near and that they should be prepared for any VC action they might launch when we were more vulnerable.

Up in the helicopter Bob Grandin got a visual sighting of the ground.

Suddenly I saw the bend in the road from east to south at Long Tan. We were behind the enemy position! I yelled to Frank to turn around and head west. I radioed '91 throw smoke'. An orange puff of smoke appeared through the rubber trees, I called 'I see orange smoke'. To which the reply came 'Wrong, wrong'. We broke away sharply heading south. Our instant thoughts were that Charlie (VC) was listening and trying to lure us to his position. Our instinct, however, told us that it had been the right position, so I called for smoke again. From the same position a plume of red smoke appeared. I called 'Red smoke' and was relieved to hear 'Roger that'. 'Stand by for delivery' I responded and we headed west to find the other chopper which was circling over near the Task Force area. I called 'Albatross 2, we have contact, head east'. We couldn't see much, so we asked them to turn on a light. Through the rain we saw the red anti-collision light flashing on the top of the helicopter and heading towards us. Frank gave them left and right turning instructions as they headed towards the drop zone. I called 91 to prepare for the first drop. Frank called 'Roll now' and the chopper rolled onto its side with the boxes of ammunition raining down on the position.

As Cliff's helicopter disappeared west into the rain, we dived towards the position, rolled onto our side, pushed the boxes of ammunition so they would slide out and turned west, all in what seemed to be one motion. As the boxes disappeared into the trees a call came on the radio, 'Beauty, right on'. We returned to Nui Dat and joined the others. Another aircraft had been tasked to come and take the entertainers to safety. We returned to the Operations Tent and reported that we had not seen anything to report during the mission. As the squadron commander, Wing Commander Ray Scott, was on his way we were sent back to the helipad to wait further orders.

Major O'Brien and RSM Chinn both saw members of D Company below as the helicopters came in at treetop height to make the drop. Although they could see no figures they could identify as enemy, they did see tracer rounds arcing into the air from obviously unfriendly weapons some distance away. They marvelled later that both helicopters survived and that they had picked up heavy bundles of ammunition as though they were matchboxes and hurled them out of the aircraft. Fear gives strength to the arm.

AAR19. 181800 9 Sqn RAAF Dropped ammunition to D Coy.

I was relieved when the two RAAF helicopters arrived overhead and made a successful ammunition drop in very difficult flying conditions. They flew just above the heavy enemy ground fire, dropping the ammunition boxes through the rubber trees right into our lap at the Company HQ area as had been indicated by coloured smoke and confirmed by radio. The CSM and others had to cut open the metal bands on the boxes and then distribute the ammunition. It was difficult and very slow for the guys to load slippery rounds into SLR and Armalite magazines. I wished that I had had the foresight to request ammunition in magazines, but that would have delayed the drop, which was more important to us. Luckily we were not embroiled in a firefight right then. I made a mental note to recommend ammo in magazines for our SOPs.

> *[These thoughts went into my brainbox data bank along with lots of other things that I would raise if we got out of this—like how come the Task Force was not aware of the large VC force close the base? How come I have already lost most of a platoon? Like how come there were no reinforcements on stand-by for a situation like this? All these things went around in my mind, while I desperately hoped that 12 Platoon would not get pinned down and that somehow, we would see them, and the 11 Platoon survivors, back into our HQ area soon.]*

Bob Buick and 11 Platoon were moving back.

This was no planned phased withdrawal. There was no fire and movement, covering each other as we had trained and the way it was expected to be done. It was run like hell for about twenty metres, go to ground, then do it all over again. It was crucial that we made a clean break, this was the only way we could do it. I ran back ducking and weaving. I zigged, Private Ron Carne zagged, we ran into each other. Down we went. A heap of arms and legs sliding in the mud as heavy machine-guns fired around us, their bullets cracking into the mud. The bullets tore at our clothes and Ron had a large piece of flesh removed from a cheek of his bum where a 12.7 mm (50 calibre) bullet hit him. We got up during a lull in the VC firing and kept going, catching up to four or five others.

The radio call from Company HQ triggered a break in the stalemate for Dave Sabben.

They advised that the choppers were overhead and that Company HQ was throwing a red smoke grenade to identify to the chopper where they wanted the ammo dropped. The throwing of a smoke grenade triggered a thought in my mind. Once the chopper was clear, if 12 Platoon threw a yellow smoke grenade towards the 11 position, perhaps the 11 Platoon survivors would see it in the advancing gloom of the plantation and realise that there must be Aussie soldiers where the smoke was coming from. This we did, throwing a yellow smoke grenade about 50 metres eastwards. There was an immediate reaction from the VC. A blizzard of tracer rounds was directed into the area where the smoke grenade landed. Fire was directed into the area from both north and south, so I hoped that each was receiving the other's overshoots. The VC firing quickly died down when it attracted no response.

A ricochet from that bout of firing found another of my diggers: Private Terry Ryan. A bullet, which had lost most of its velocity, lodged in his forearm near the elbow. More in shock and disbelief than in pain he plucked it out and handed it to me. 'Keep this for me, Skipper. I wanna get the bugger that sent it,' he said, as he returned to his firing position.

Drinky crawled up to me and pointed out movement to our direct east—the direction from which we expected any 11 Platoon survivors to come. I told him to hold fire until we could identify them—and he looked at me as if that was the most superfluous piece of advice he had ever been given—which it probably was! In recognition of that fact, he didn't even relay it to his section.

While regrouping, catching their breath and looking around for others, Bob Buick saw a yellow smoke grenade. 'We had found our mates! Private Vic Grice was killed during the withdrawal and another couple of diggers were wounded. Some of the platoon had been separated during the withdrawal, so there were six to eight out of the initial 28 with me. We were still in deep strife.'

'We recognised the Aussie troops and covered them as they came in,' recalls Dave Sabben.

Some shouts and waves and they made their way to us in ones and twos. When Buick arrived, I directed him to Paddy lying a few yards away and shouted to Paddy to get some ammo redistribution going. As they made their way in, the enemy followed them. We fired to their flanks as best we could to suppress the VC fire. We saw one of the 11 Platoon guys hit just short of reaching us, but his mates dragged him in. In the same burst of VC fire, Private Webb, who'd only joined the platoon as a reinforcement recently, was also hit. Lying on his stomach, the bullet entered through the base of his neck and remained in his chest. But he was still alive. How it missed everything vital, I'll never know. I caught a glance as 'Doc' Davis, my medic, opened Webb's shirt. There was blood everywhere.

As the last of the 11 Platoon diggers came in Drinky turned to me with the air of someone mightily pissed off with his circumstances and said, 'D'ya think we're gonna get outta this one, Skip?' I flashed him a glance and looked around. We had been in heavy contact for about two hours. Artillery had been falling to our front for ninety minutes, had been landing as close as 100 metres from 11 Platoon and was now landing 200 metres from us and was even then being brought in closer. We had called for APC reinforcements more than an hour before and then we were told that they had only just left the base. We couldn't get air support because of the monsoon rain we were under. All our training told us we would have a tough time locating the enemy and here we were trying not to be located by them! Half of 11 Platoon was down, a section of 10 Platoon was down an hour before, and they had been in heavy contact since then. I had three wounded from 12 Platoon and the VC now knew where we were, so I could expect to lose more before I got back to Company [HQ]. If not at 50 per cent casualties yet, the company was heading that way fast. It was a casualty rate certainly not included in the planning manuals. I could see VC dead to our north, south-east, south and near the hut, and *still* they were coming at us. I turned back to him and said, 'I don't think so, Drinky. I don't think so.' His nod was mostly in the eyes and he made his way back to his section to face the VC following up the 11 Platoon withdrawal.

The 11 Platoon survivors were now in the 12 Platoon position. Most had brought their weapons, even though they had no rounds—a sure sign of an unbeaten soldier, no matter how tired or stressed. Dave Sabben's medic, 'Doc' Davis, was treating each of 11 Platoon's wounded as well as the wounded that 12 had sustained in the last hour. In the course of his duties, he himself was wounded. Bending over a wounded digger, Davis was hit with what was assumed to be a tracer round. It passed through his upper arm and into his chest, cauterising the wounds as it passed. There was little blood and no exit wound, but Davis was in pain and another digger picked up the medical kit and took over.

At this time, 12 Platoon was being continually attacked by about fifty VC. Dave Sabben advised Harry Smith that 11 Platoon was with him and was told to withdraw back to the Company HQ. Meanwhile Sergeant Jim 'Paddy' Todd, the 12 Platoon sergeant, and Bob Buick had got together and over a smoke discussed the day's work. Bob recalls.

> I think Paddy was the oldest soldier in the company at the time. A veteran of Korea, Malaya and Borneo. He had been around the parade ground a few times, a good partner to Dave Sabben. Wounded during the battle, he was calm and I remember making this comment to him as we lay in the mud. With the rain streaming down our faces and bullets cracking past our heads, I said, 'Paddy, you're getting too f—ing old for this crap!' He smiled and sucked on the wet cigarette.

Paddy Todd had been wounded in Korea in the early 1950s. There he lost part of a finger. In a rubber plantation in South Vietnam he had been hit again. He couldn't walk and he looked for signs of wounds, but there were no signs like blood or torn clothing. He had felt no pain and only knew he couldn't walk. He then did something that was completely unselfish. Knowing it would take one fit digger to assist him back to the company aid post, he quietly crawled away, into the darkness, to find his way back by himself. (When they removed his boots in hospital, mortar shrapnel had passed through both boots and ankles and the blood had filled his boots.)

Having verified from Buick that all the known 11 Platoon survivors had been accounted for, Dave Sabben made plans for 12 Platoon's withdrawal to Company HQ.

I looked around for Paddy to get him to organise the evacuation of the wounded first, but Paddy was not there. He was gone. With Paddy gone, I asked Buick to take over the administration of the move—wounded first, one able man per one wounded, account for all weapons and kit. I pointed out the direction and the first group moved off. Company HQ was about 250 metres back in a straight line, bypassing the dogleg we had taken to get to our current position. As I returned to the sections, 'Bushy' Forsythe passed me to join the wounded. He had copped a light wound but it didn't appear to be too serious as he still had his rifle and webbing.

As the first group of the worst wounded moved off, my attention was called to a VC force forming up to our south-west. Again, incredible as it seemed, they didn't appear to know we were there and appeared to be forming up to move due north to assault the company position. I supposed that they had seen us, but had assumed we were other VC forces, with our dark, wet uniforms, floppy hats and basic webbing. I re-sited my two working machine-guns along two avenues of the rubber trees and waited for this VC group to cross our front. A few minutes later, they moved off, in three ranks of about twenty each. In less than a minute, their slow, steady pace had them passing us less than 50 metres away. I waited for the first rank to pass through the gun sights and opened fire on the second and third ranks. The devastation of aimed machine-gun fire along a rank of soldiers was terrible. The second and third ranks simply collapsed. The startled first rank then turned and ran back the way they'd come—right into our two fire-lanes. Few made it.

The almost total destruction of the assault group drew a storm of fire from their reserve element—close and accurate the fire was, too. They knew where we were and they were firing low, correcting their earlier tendency to fire high. Private Kevin Graham, Chico's 8 Section machine-gunner, was hit in the chest and rolled away from the gun. His gun number two took over the gun and the next digger along took over the belt-feeding duty. It all looked so like a rehearsed manoeuvre that I just stared for a moment, not comprehending that Kev had indeed been wounded. Buick sent a man to collect him and he was evacuated with the second group of wounded. A thought flashed through my mind that he was my sixth casualty out of twenty men—fortunately, all wounded, no dead. Fourteen left!

I needed to be heading off now as our numbers were low and the enemy appeared to be re-forming. Besides, we too were running low on ammo. As soon as the firing died down, after we had picked up the remaining kit and weapons, the group began back to Company HQ. I was last out of our little position and the empty bullet shells, glistening wet and scattered in the mud in the fading daylight, made a lasting impression. I looked around to ensure that all soldiers and weapons had been taken. I was surprised to see the pure white rubber latex bleeding out of the numerous bullet wounds in the tree trunks around our small position. Later, it took on all sorts of surreal levels of meaning for me. Were the trees bearing the wounds to protect the soldiers from their fate? But, at the time I simply noted the fact as a sight I'd never seen before. Fortunately, we made it back to Company HQ without further incident.

Just after the helicopters had flown away, out of the gloom came 12 Platoon and the remnants of 11 Platoon to join me. I was relieved by their return. While I was very glad to see them, I was saddened by the number of 11 Platoon missing, along with the wounded in 12 Platoon. We were also concerned about Paddy Todd and hoped he was alive. But I could not dwell on all that. I was thankful the right flank move by 12 Platoon to aid the 11 Platoon withdrawal had fortuitously succeeded, but now we had to get on with the battle. After speaking with the platoon commanders, and getting their casualty figures and allocating their areas for defence, I reported to 6RAR by radio:

AAR20. 181810 D Coy now concentrated (except for 15 dead and missing from 11 Platoon). (At YS477673)

During this time Adrian Roberts and the APCs were continuing their advance towards Delta Company.

Moving across the Long Phuoc–Long Tan Village road into assault formation we came into young rubber, low and crowned at crew commander head height, which made visibility difficult. I remember that there was some undergrowth. The sunken road north-north-east provided a good axis for our advance to Delta Company. As we came out of the young rubber into older trees the crowns were well above us. It was then that we saw the enemy.

AAR21. 181810 A Coy contacted support elements of D445 Battalion at YS476667. 2 Platoon dismounted and assaulted enemy who withdrew east. *[Ed: This appears to be reported at too early a time as the Radio Log indicates 1830 hrs for this event.]*

I remember a formation that stretched across my front moving resolutely from east to west. The men were grouped so that it looked like some sort of arrowhead formation. In the rain the green bush hats and clothes momentarily caused me to think it was Delta Company. In that second I saw the un-Australian back camouflage and Corporal Gross, Ron Richards' right-hand crew commander, at the east of our front called, 'Enemy contact' and opened fire. The enemy formation stretched across our entire front. At 40 metres between carriers our front was about 240 metres. We had come onto his flank and he was clearly surprised. I estimate the enemy strength was about a company [approximately 100]. We opened fire and the enemy to our front began to fall back using fire and movement to cover their withdrawal. They moved north-east in good order. I saw enemy soldiers dragging their wounded by the ankles covered by the fire from their fellow soldiers, throughout the engagement they seemed to fire high (thank heavens). I will never forget the effect of our .50 calibre machine-gun fire. A man struck by such fire is thrown away, his body arched like a bow. Throughout the assault I continually ordered 'Check fire' and 'Fire low' because I knew that somewhere up ahead was Delta Company and the prospect of hitting our people with overshoots really concerned me.

Sergeant Frank Alcorta, 2 Platoon, rolled off the top of Sergeant Richard's carrier immediately the action commenced. The APC crew commander of the extreme right carrier, Corporal Goss, had opened with a long burst from his .50 calibre machine-gun. They were heavily outnumbered by well-equipped, clearly well-organised and disciplined troops who stood between Delta Company and the relief force.

Peter Dinham, 2 Platoon commander, was now faced with an enemy force to the north and Frank Alcorta outside the APC. Frank gave every appearance of taking on the VC by himself. As a result of yelling into Sergeant Richards' ear, with Corporal Lou Stephens also adding his voice, this being the only method of effective communication, Dinham eventually had the rear ramp of the APC lowered. Meanwhile Ron Brett had jumped off the APC and joined Frank Alcorta, both of them moving about twenty metres to the right and slightly forward of the APC and engaging the enemy force in front of them. This was a dangerous situation, because once forward of the carriers they masked the APC fire and risked their lives from that fire. Similarly, when another infantry soldier decided to engage the enemy from on top of the APC, he created an extremely dangerous situation and in fact his M16 discharge came from behind the crew commander, Ron Richards, hitting his gunshield.

The remainder of those within the APC, consisting of Platoon HQ plus Corporal Lou Stephens and his section, debussed and formed up in an extended line on the right (eastern side) of the APC joining Frank Alcorta and Ron Brett. They then engaged the enemy force to their front. In this brief encounter, seconds seemed like minutes. The images of the prelude and fire fight are still clear today. Lieutenant Dinham remembers:

> As we approached the rubber, the noise from mortar, artillery and small arms fire, interspersed with the noise from a tropical thunderstorm, increased to a crescendo. About 200 metres into the plantation we suddenly encountered an armed body, dressed in khaki and black, some with pith helmets and most with camouflage nets hanging from their packs. They were moving from east to west in front of us. It quickly became evident that they were VC, as our own troops had white tape wound around the headband of our bush hats for identification and did not use camouflage. The noise of battle, the tropical downpour and the poor visibility had obviously masked our approach.
>
> To our astonishment, the APCs stopped just as at least a hundred, probably more, camouflaged enemy troops emerged from the scrub and undergrowth. Just beyond, in the rubber, artillery rounds were smashing everywhere. Between them and the rubber were the VC, well armed, uniformed and confused. The rain and gloomy cloud cover only compounded a scene from hell.
>
> A burst of enemy fire passed somewhere to my left. The angry crack of some near misses was unmistakable, even with all of the other noise.
>
> I ordered the APC section commander to open

fire, but he was initially reluctant to do so because of uncertainty regarding Delta Company's location and concern about the possibility of accidentally engaging Delta Company. My machine gunner Ron Brett opened fire and the APC .50 calibre machine guns then joined in and caught the enemy by surprise.

As the ramp was now down, those of us remaining with the APC debussed. Each soldier carried out his routine in a disciplined and orderly fashion, even though there were enemy soldiers in the immediate area. It was the first time they had been in battle and I was proud of the way they carried out their drills.

I stood slightly behind and to the left of Lou Stephens where I could observe the deployed elements of the platoon. I was next to a rubber tree, using it as a support while I opened fire on a number of enemy to my front, watching them drop as they were hit. After several moments something flicked at my face, sufficient to distract me. I looked up to see two fresh bullet holes at about eye level.

I immediately adopted a lower profile.

In this brief exchange I fired sixteen shots, the only shots I fired in anger throughout my time in Vietnam.

We estimated later that we had caused about 40 casualties, though only eight bodies were found in the area next day. The enemy broke contact and withdrew to the east. It is hard to believe that twelve of us, supported by the APC .50 cal machine-gun took on a numerically superior force and caused it to flee, helping to save Delta Company. Frank Alcorta and Ron Brett deserved to be commended for the valour both demonstrated that day.

Adrian Roberts was unhappy that some infantry were out of the carriers. He tried to find out from the company commander, Charles Mollison, who had ordered the movement. It quickly became obvious that it had not been ordered.

The difficulty of communicating by shouting over the engine noise and the firing, and hearing answers while ears are covered by headsets is enormous. It was during this initial contact that an infantry soldier standing up in the cargo hatch to my immediate right received a bullet graze across his temple and began discharging his weapon in the air. I remember shouting back words to the effect 'Take his weapon before he kills someone'. Jock McCormick remembers forcibly removing the dazed soldier's weapon.

In response to Adrian Roberts' command, the APC section commander used hand signals to indicate that the infantry were to remount. Accordingly, Dinham ordered the platoon to remount. The troop then continued north. Sergeant O'Reilly's section continued to engage the enemy all the while. His carrier on Adrian Robert's left front, commanded by a National Serviceman, Trooper Smith, suffered a jammed round in the .50 calibre barrel. In the midst of the heavy fighting Trooper Smith's driver stood up in his seat, unscrewed the barrel, replaced it and sat down while Smith carried out the required checks before resuming firing. Incredibly, they believed that if they did not look at the enemy he would not shoot them!

BRAVO COMPANY HAD BEEN MOVING BACK TOWARDS DELTA FROM ABOUT 1730HRS

Bravo moved back across the paddy, forded the Suoi Da Bang, which was beginning to rise, and followed their tracks back to the rubber's edge. Visibility was poor. The rain was torrential. By this time they all appeared black in the shadow of the rubber as they entered near the previously located RCL enemy position. They had the grid reference of Delta Company location, though they didn't need it due to the volume of small arms fire coming from that general direction. Once in the rubber they spread out; Company HQ led the way and Corporal Jones was on the right flank. The

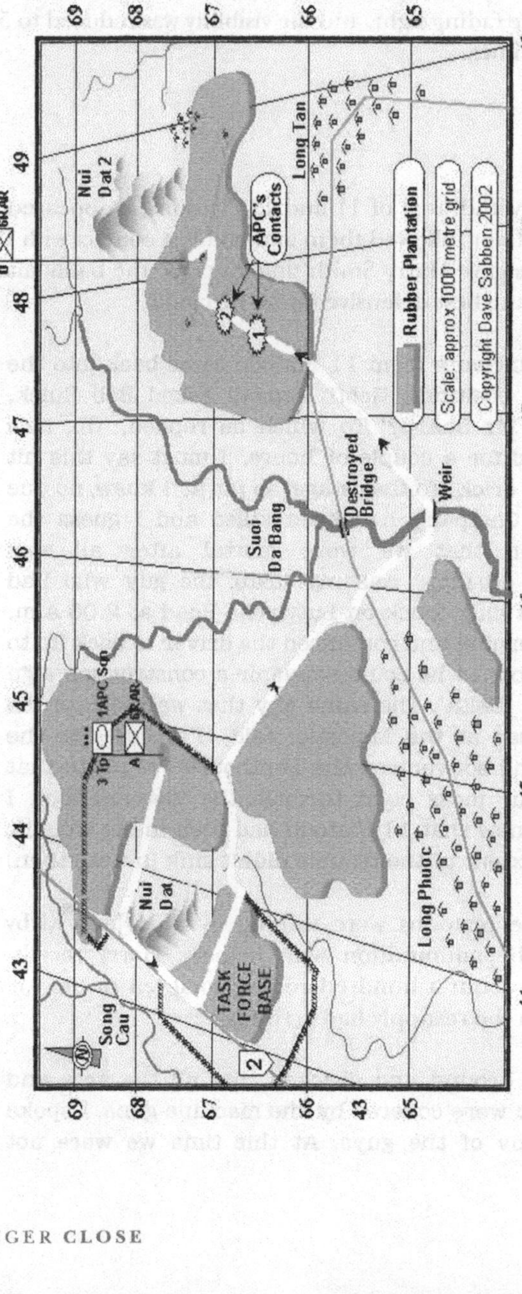

9 APC relief force route

Nui Dat 2

Long Tan

APC's Contacts

Rubber Plantation

Scale: approx x 1000 metre grid

Copyright Dave Sabben 2002

Suoi Da Bang

Destroyed Bridge

Weir

1 APC Sqn

3 Tp   1 RAR

A   6 RAR

Nui Dat

Long Phuoc

Song Cau

TASK FORCE BASE

6 RAR

pace of the advance was relatively fast. The rain now became even heavier with the fading light, and the visibility was reduced to 50 or 100 metres at times.

DELTA COMPANY REGROUPS IN A DEFENSIVE POSITION

Following the withdrawal of 11 and 12 Platoons, it appeared that the enemy had not followed them and had lost contact with Delta Company. This gave Harry Smith time to place the badly mauled company into the best defensive layout he could.

> As the survivors from 11 Platoon came back into the company positions, Geoff Kendall asked Bob Buick, 'Where's Mr Sharp?' To which he replied, 'Oh, he's been dead for a couple of hours.' I must say this hit me like a brick. To that stage, as far as I knew, no one in Delta Company had been killed and I guess the realisation that we were mortal after all was salutary. 'Sharpy' was my mate, the guy who had stopped a milk truck on Lutwyche Road at 2.00 a.m. in the morning and convinced the driver to back up to a lamp post so he could souvenir a construction sign that said 'Delta'. The same guy that walked into the private bar at the Majestic, said, 'I'm here for the photo,' and souvenired the Penthouse Pet photo that graced our mess right through the Vietnam tour. I guess I knew that 11 Platoon had been in big trouble, but the extent of the trouble didn't sink in until then.

While the platoons were settling in CSM Jack Kirby distributed all the ammunition with helpers. Harry recalls that they had only about a hundred rounds total left in the forward platoons when the resupply had arrived.

> I walked around and checked that all the arcs and fire fields were covered by the machine-guns. I spoke with many of the guys. At this time we were not

under fire, although we knew the VC would be re-organising to take us on. They were no fools and by then their scouts would have worked out where we were. It was obvious that we were up against uniformed and well-equipped regular Main Force VC, rather than the black pyjama-clad local forces. I had no doubt we were in for a tough fight. I knew we could not withdraw and leave our casualties. That was not an option. So we were here to the end. I hoped that reinforcements would eventually get here, as the bottom line was that we were obviously outnumbered. But on the plus side, we had our company team spirit, we had the guts and will to survive, we had plenty of ammo, we had the artillery and so far the VC had not mortared us.

Apart from the fifteen missing of 11 Platoon and Paddy Todd from 12 Platoon, we had everyone else back in the area, an area about a hundred metres across and the same in depth. I had positioned 11 Platoon covering the north west, the company's back door. In the eastern sector, where I expected enemy attacks, I had 10 Platoon covering the east to the south, 12 Platoon the north to the east. The remaining Headquarters personnel, those not in the command group, filled in the gap from the south to the west. This was the company's final defensive position. There was no withdrawal from here and the next thirty minutes would tell the story.

In the lull, I was able to walk around often and coordinate the defence with platoon commanders and talk with some of my soldiers. I recall one of my soldiers, Shorty Brown I think, asking me, 'Do you think we'll get out of this, boss?' I just knowingly winked back at him, confidently indicating I thought we would. I had dismissed any other thought from my mind. It had not occurred to me we might not survive. It was only after the battle I became fearful and frightened by what might have happened. I guess

I was too busy to worry, exploring every past experience to seek guidance in what we might do to repel the enemy. I would have given quids for a few Vickers machine-guns—far better in defence than M60s, plus some of the M60s were having feeding problems with the muddy soil on the ammo belts. We had these US versions of the German-designed Spandau gun, but without their integral round ammo magazines. Our ammo belts were carried around the neck and when the gunners went down onto wet ground the rounds were covered in mud. Our Second World War-type Owen guns, great in close jungle, were of little use in the rubber where engagement ranges were 50 to 75 metres. Our hand-me-down Armalites from 1RAR, issued a year earlier at Bien Hoa, also had problems. But we had to make the best of what we had and where it was possible, we changed some weapons around so that the best ones were up front. Even though the fire had temporarily ceased, I knew the VC were no doubt probing to locate our position and that they would continue their attack.

Bob Buick led the seven remaining unhurt of 11 Platoon to their position.

We received an ammunition supply as we passed through the Headquarters. I noticed the command group, Harry Smith and Morrie Stanley with the radio operators, quietly going about the task of fighting the battle. There was an air of calmness about the place that made me confident and calm. This was a holiday in comparison to what 11 Platoon had witnessed over the last couple of hours. Quiet, reassuring and businesslike, the apprehensiveness I had had previously passed.

Positioned on the back or reverse side of the slight rise in a small hollow was the company aid post. Our company medic, Phil 'Doc' Dobson, was moving around attending to the

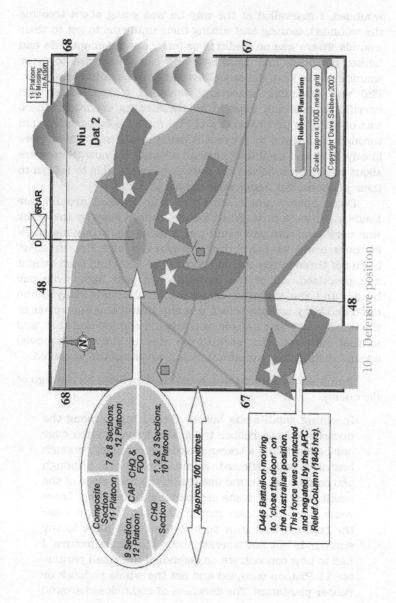

11 Platoon:
15 Missing
in Action

Niu
Dat 2

6RAR

D

Rubber Plantation

Scale: approx 1000 metre grid

Copyright Dave Sabben 2002

N

Composite
Section
11 Platoon

7 & 8 Sections,
12 Platoon

CAP CHQ &
FOO

1, 2 & 3 Sections,
10 Platoon

9 Section,
12 Platoon

CHQ
Section

Approx. 100 metres

D445 Battalion moving
to 'close the door' on
the Australian position.
This force was contacted
and negated by the APC
Relief Column (1845 hrs).

10. Defensive position

wounded. I marvelled at the way he was going about treating the wounded, tearing and cutting their uniforms to get to their wounds. There was no medicine or fancy arrangements. He had limited morphine and dressings, very basic resources to cover wounds and to keep the casualties comfortable until evacuation. Phil was attending to several wounded blokes, some with horrific wounds and most in life-threatening condition. There was one digger unconscious and Phil forced a large safety pin through his tongue to prevent it being swallowed. There were bloody field and shell dressings all around. By now there were about twelve or so in the aid post. Some were able to return to their platoons, but many were unable to stand.

Some enemy small arms fire still cracked around our heads, none were close. When a bullet passed close by the *crack* was very loud and you could feel it going past. Our machine-gunners could be heard firing controlled aim fire in short bursts of three to five rounds. Exactly as they had been taught and practised. All of the incoming fire was high, over our heads, and the visibility decreased all the time. Maybe the mind and body accepted what was happening and regardless of the uncertainty and danger, you just did the job and that was all that mattered. That seemed the case as individuals moved around distributing ammunition and assisting the wounded.

Bob Buick sat looking out, scanning the gloom for any sign of the enemy.

Incoming small arms bullets flicked high among the branches of the rubber trees, about five metres over our heads. When a tracer round struck a large enough branch it was deflected, spinning in an arc. Although you could walk around upright on the back slope of the small rise, I saw some crouching and crawling. Later some joked that they moved like that for days after the battle. I was in a sort of daze, still alert to my surrounds but not worried about the whole picture. I had to now concentrate on defending the small perimeter 11 Platoon occupied and not the whole paddock or rubber plantation. The darkness of night closed around us like a foreboding blanket. I sat staring, scanning the perimeter, and thought for the first time, 'This would really be a shit of a way to die!' Was there a relief force? Could they get to us? I had no idea. It was very gloomy under the canopy of the trees and visibility was diminishing quickly. The enemy was starting to give 10 and 12 Platoons a hard time.

At one stage a large group of maybe 50 soldiers moved across Geoff Kendall's left front, that is, south to north.

I was concerned they might be the missing Bravo Company element and tried urgently by radio to establish if anyone knew where Bravo Company was. Eventually this group of enemy got into our discarded packs and started opening them. I ordered my guys to fire and again inflicted casualties. The next day we found only one had been taken and we recovered that after a contact some weeks later.

All but one of 12 Platoon was now inside the company perimeter with Dave Sabben.

The missing one was none other than Paddy Todd. He'd left us before we'd left the last platoon position, but had not yet turned up at Company HQ. Suddenly, there's a singular yell from the southern perimeter and two diggers race out front and bring back Paddy. It appears that he had crawled back the way we'd come, first to the west, then heading north, whereas I had directed the rest of us to cut the dogleg and return in a more direct manner. I never got to tell Paddy about the last VC group we'd hit on their way to assault the company. Paddy must have been directly in front of them when we hit them. Had Paddy looked over his shoulder and seen 60 or so VC bearing down on him, I reckon he'd have sprinted back to Company HQ, two broken ankles or not!

Throughout much of the battle, especially after the defensive position had been established, Morrie Stanley had ordered almost continuous artillery fire in a series of fresh regimental fire missions with adjustments.

A lot of that fire was probably hundreds of metres away from our infantrymen because, at the time, I was very conscious of the need to play safe with so much firepower. I was actually advised on one occasion that the artillery fire was too close, and as a result I screamed 'Stop! Stop! Stop!' several times on the artillery radio. I know I yelled, but the noise was so intense where I was that I could not hear the radio response from the gun area at Nui Dat. The guns simply had to stop and they did. From after action reports it seems that we may have gained some benefit from that fire in depth by demoralising and disorganising the VC in their attempts to locate and destroy us.

I was able to take advantage of the rain and intense gunfire that caused the area to be shrouded in smoke, steam and fog. This helped me because my judgement of distance was assisted by the observation (or lack of it) of flash against this screen. The enemy and some of our own boys were also silhouetted to us. One effect of all this gunfire was the noise. From the time fire commenced at about 1600hrs until about 1900hrs when the battle proper ceased, the tremendous din gave the effect of a continuous violent thunderstorm. As a result of all the noise, my observation of hundreds of 105 mm shells falling reasonably close to us plus the periodic suspension of fire from Nui Dat for air clearance purposes, I became somewhat unsettled. I reported on the artillery radio 'The situation is too confused to use the guns.' I might as well have said to my battery commander 'Help'.

[Many years afterwards my regular operator, Chris Cooper, told me that he had been lying naked in the sick bay in the battery

area at Nui Dat trying to recover from the serious infection he had, when all hell let loose from the guns. He dashed, still naked, from the sick bay to help those on the gun line by breaking 105 mm ammunition out of boxes.]

My call for help was answered by Harry Honnor, who suggested a safe grid reference at which I could re-commence firing and adjust as necessary. I will be forever thankful for the way he restored my confidence. Harry Honnor had been authorised by the CO of 1 Field Regiment to manage the artillery battle from Battalion HQ at Nui Dat. That he did. I could sense his influence because at times I could hear the guns firing when I had not ordered fire and at other times, when I had ordered fire, I suspected it had been moved or suspended. I couldn't really hear most of the stations on the artillery radio net, and may not have gone through the usual procedural formalities. Quite frankly, I developed a selective hearing problem and only wanted to speak with Harry Honnor at call sign 39.

At one stage I decided to remove one battery from the regimental fire mission and apply that battery to the south-western area to deter any assaults from behind us. My M16 had been lying in the mud all the time because I was concentrating on my map and chinagraph pencil, brushing away the muddy water so that I could see details on the map. After a while there were few marks on the map. I had to keep re-marking the blob on the spot that marked our position, plus I had to keep the map oriented so that I did not make errors with the grid-lines. When Willy Walker decided that I should keep my M16 handy and thrust it towards me, I again carefully placed it in the mud. He had devoted all his efforts to maintaining radio communications and even erected an antenna in the rubber tree behind which we were lying. For much of the time, neither Willy nor I was able to maintain any records of fire orders. I have been asked whether

I thought of utilising Murray Broomhall or Willy Walker by sending them forward to observe the fall of shot, or indeed whether I should have moved forward myself. I did not actually consider those options at the time, but my response now is that, in effect, we were forward and any attempt to move further would almost certainly have been fatal. Small arms and MG fire was raking the area from about a metre above the ground and shrapnel was falling about the place. So much so, that Willy pushed me down when I considered that a kneeling position might provide a better view. Certainly we can all do things better, but I really did not want to upset what little stability we had in our position or the effectiveness of our communications with the guns.

[Looking back on the event, I know that I made a number of procedural errors in the area of fire control orders. The one best known, and which later became cause for a bit of a laugh, was when, in my excitement, I deviated from the then current procedure and ordered 'gunfire'. That order was from the superseded British protocol and was given instinctively. As far as I was concerned, it was an order to all three 105 mm batteries to maintain fire, which I would adjust or which would later be cancelled by a fresh order. I did not hear the following radio conversation and even if I had, it probably would not have raised a laugh at the time. Apparently, a gun position officer had asked me to verify the order for gunfire, expecting perhaps that the order would be changed to 'fire for effect'. Instead of a reply from me, he received a blast on the radio from the CO of the regiment who has been quoted as saying, 'When he asks for gunfire you give him bloody gunfire!']

Generally, the situation was very frightening with the rain, sound and shock of shell and small arms fire. I think the incessant violence and confusion caused us to draw mainly on instincts that we had developed from training and previous experience. I heard a

DANGER CLOSE

young man near me saying to himself 'Steady, aim, fire'. That was his job and that's how he kept control of himself. Many of my decisions were also made instinctively, sometimes when little information was available and there was no time for lengthy consideration. That is why it becomes difficult after many years to focus on one's own experience and to know that events can become so real from later reports that a person can truly believe that other people's experiences were theirs too. Most of all, I know that Willy and I were lying together in the mud for a long time, he with the radio and I with a map and chinagraph pencil, although I did grab the radio handset a couple of times, sending orders and reports myself during some particularly tense periods. No doubt I was wet, cold and scared, but I do not recall having the feeling that we were about to be overrun. I cannot explain why, except that most likely concentration on the job in hand did not leave much room for such thoughts.

Murray Broomhall was helping the CSM with ammunition distribution. I still recall when the CSM, Jack Kirby, came to me and said, 'Excuse me sir, could I have your spare ammunition?' The way he did that was so typical of the man. Anyway, I told him to help himself from the small pack I had on my back, and he may have taken four M16 magazines, leaving me with the one on my rifle. When I was directing a regimental fire mission, roughly covering the company front, I saw a couple of VC to the left wandering about with what looked like a heavy tripod. There were also a few groups of between ten and twenty VC in the area, which may have been about 50 metres from us. Jack Kirby yelled out words to the effect of 'What are those two up to?'. That immediate threat was removed by small arms fire.

In this relatively quiet period, I made sure that everyone had the ammunition ready for the next onslaught. CSM Jack Kirby was outstanding in his work to get the ammo out and around to all and to give words of encouragement to the soldiers. He inspired us all by the way he went about his business. Soon after, heavy VC fire started to pour across our position. We hit the dirt. They had pinpointed us!

I sent another report to 6RAR.

AAR22. 181820 D Coy Enemy appear to be regrouping to attack. Under heavy MG fire mainly from the East and South East.

The enemy had started to sweep our position with virtually continuous machine-gun fire with an enormous number of tracer rounds, which lit up the dark rubber like fireflies going past in a hurry. With the artillery bombardment the noise was horrendous—no wonder most of us have industrial deafness! I reported to Battalion HQ: 'Enemy could be reorganising to attack. Two platoons 75 per cent effective and one platoon almost completely destroyed. Organised for all-round defence.'

The first of the major assaults was forming up. Morrie Stanley had been walking the artillery in from all sides, carefully avoiding the original 11 Platoon position. The artillery was closed in to 100 metres. We could see the shells land. We could feel the concussion through the sodden earth and we smelt the explosive. Best for us, we could see the damage it was doing as it protected us from the VC masses.

Dave Sabben could see the way in which the enemy was operating.

We saw them forming up and moving around down the avenues. Their officers and NCOs were doing exactly what we would be doing. The formations were the same, the spacings, the rate of movement—it was all so familiar from our own training. Then we would hear a bugle or a whistle and they would move off. They had the fearsome prospect of moving through the area where they knew artillery was landing from time to time and in many instances that was their last living thought. Time after time a bracket of artillery landed within lethal distance and holes were blown in their ranks. But not every time. Many ranks and individuals made it through the line of high explosive. When those remaining went to ground, a bugle would sound and another line of VC would rise and charge forward. Those remaining would drop down beside those compatriots that had made it through the first time. Then the bugle would blow again and another line charge forward. This was repeated time and time again. The major assaults came about five minutes apart. First, one from the south-east, then one from the north-east, then another from the south, and so on. They were uncoordinated, coming at us in small groups and with lulls of up to several minutes between assaults. These lulls gave us the chance to spread the ammo resupply and reload a few rounds into our magazines. But each time we wondered if one of these assaults would overrun our position.

Geoff Kendall also recalls:

The enemy seemed at this stage to finally get a grip on how large a force we were because the suppressive fire which they seemed so good at started in earnest. They seemed to have identified our width on the ground and they absolutely poured it in on us. There was a lot of tracer so you could identify about how high the fire was off the ground (less than one metre) and there wasn't much we could do but hug the ground. The rain had eased a bit and we could see them forming up for each big assault. Their tactics seemed pretty much the same as ours, a reasonably spaced assault wave at a fast walk with a reserve about 40 or 50 metres behind them. Our artillery was devastating, particularly on the reserve line. They were flattened like a pack of cards while the assault wave was still just a bit outside the area where we would start firing. I must say that no orders would, or could, be given to our guys as to when to fire. They seemed instinctively to know to wait until the enemy was about 40 metres out before firing. The next day there was an area about 30 metres in front of the forward two sections of 10 Platoon where there were 44 enemy bodies, literally three deep.

Unfortunately, the enemy not actually hit when the assault petered out went to ground where they were and started sniping between assaults. I believe that the three guys killed in 10 Platoon were all killed by enemy in this situation. Rick Aldersea was the machine-gunner in the left section. He moved his position to get a better field of fire and was killed immediately. Max Wales, his 2IC on the gun, went to get the gun and was also killed. At one stage between assaults Yank Akell, who was on the other side of a rubber tree to me, killed an enemy who was working through between my two forward sections. Jack Jewry was killed some time between the two major assaults. Jack was 2IC of the right forward section and shortly after, Buddy Lea, his section commander, was badly wounded. I moved Black Mac to Buddy's section to take over.

The second major assault on Geoff Kendall's 10 Platoon seemed very much like the first, but by this stage the situation looked much worse.

It was rapidly getting dark and if they had kept coming in the dark they probably would have been able to get in among us. We would then have had to fight hand to hand and sheer numbers might have been a problem. I probably didn't consciously think that at the time but I did realise that the situation wasn't good. I was using Brian Hornung's SLR, my AR15 [Armalite] having given up the ghost with a separated cartridge case early in the piece. I had about half a magazine left and suspected some of the riflemen may have had even fewer rounds. I thought for the first time that perhaps we weren't going to get out of it. I thought of my wife about to give birth to our first child and the lousy deal it would be for a kid to be born after its father was dead.

The company had had no time to dig in and I realised that in any case diggings would have soon been filled with red mud and rain from the monsoonal downpour. Some protection came from lying in small folds in the muddy ground and hiding behind the thin trees, which was purely psychological, as the bullets went right through them, shattering the bark on the way. I vividly remember seeing bullets tear through the trees just above the MFC (mortar fire controller) Sergeant Jack Thomson's head and the white rubber latex fluid oozing out of the holes. He was lying just in front of me and, like me, wishing he had had his six 81 mm mortars in range to add to the artillery fire. They could have filled in gaps between gunfire salvos and Jack could have put them into vital areas quickly. But the mortars were back at Nui Dat! That was about 800 metres outside maximum range. Another thought went through my mind: what happened to the Second World War tactic of man-packing Vickers guns and mortars so that they were always in range? And why didn't we have 60 mm mortars like the VC? I could have used all the extra firepower.

Fortunately, the position at which we had chosen to stop was on a slight reverse slope and therefore the enemy machine-gun fire mostly went just above our heads, with only the fire of the upright VC assaulting waves getting right into our area. That was a plus for us, as we could cut most of them down before they could actually see us and they had to fire from an upright position on the move. The odd VC got up a tree and fired into us, but most of them were spotted and either got shot down by the forward sections or were blown down by artillery shell bursts which took out the whole tree.

Given the weight of enemy firepower over the next half-hour or so, the small number of casualties was quite amazing.

At least one of these was caused by artillery fire that I had requested be brought in closer to our lines at one stage to stem a heavy VC assault. I saw this large VC assault coming in from the east. We had to stop them and needed the artillery in closer. I told the FO to bring the guns in, almost on top of us, realising that we might take the odd shell burst in our own perimeter and maybe kill someone, but we had to stop the VC from getting into our position. When he ordered 'drop 50' he was told by Artillery HQ that they considered it unsafe. In my usual manner I was intolerant of people telling me what to do when they weren't there, irrespective of rank. I picked up the radio mike and told 6RAR HQ to tell the gunners to fire the bloody guns where I wanted them to fire or they would lose the lot of us. Morrie was then given the OK to fire on his net, and we stopped the bastards.

We only lost four killed in the final company defensive area—albeit not dug in—thanks to the gunners and their accurate artillery fire, and to the courage, tenacity and resilience of my own company in giving the VC back as much as we were receiving. My soldiers just kept up a steady and accurate volume of small arms fire into the assaulting VC, who were surging forward over the bodies of their fallen comrades. Thank heavens we had ample ammunition. Although not a religious person, I recall thanking God for the RAAF choppers and the gunners. Morrie Stanley and his crew were outstanding. Although Morrie was later to place much of the praise on his battery commander, let me make it very clear Morrie was the man on the spot and he called the tune of the song we wanted to hear to the guns back at base.

The VC continued to launch assault waves on the 10 and 12 Platoon area. Machine-gun fire poured in from out near the slopes of Nui Dat 2. Warrant Officer Jack Kirby saw a heavy machine-gun post being set up about 50 metres out and personally went forward a little and silenced the crew. Preceded by bugle and whistle calls and odd drumbeats muffled by or lost in the noise of gunfire, the enemy assault waves continued relentlessly, the sky ablaze with tracer rounds. They did this without a lot of radios. But, with our own fire and the artillery gunfire, we repelled wave after wave as they continued to assault with a seemingly endless supply of troops.

These assaults on Delta continued and we sustained a further ten or twelve casualties. As they were moved to the company aid post I had to shrink our perimeter. Beyond, the artillery had been brought in even closer and we could now feel the concussion of the exploding shells through the air as well as through the ground. The din was horrific. VC tracer rounds danced towards us in apparent slow motion, at the last minute seeming to speed up and pass overhead.

David Sabben recalls:

The VC were still generally firing too high, as they had done much of the time. One VC bullet was, unfortunately, not quite high enough. Private Paul Large was shot in the forehead and died instantly. Privates Noel Grimes and Neil Bextram, one either side of him, dragged him back to the CAP and then returned to their firing positions.

The rain was easing off now, but it was getting noticeably darker. On the perimeter my men could no longer see the distant VC in silhouette as they could before. The force with which the assaults were being pressed on us appeared to be slackening off. The VC appeared to be less enthusiastic about their advances. As I could well imagine, as the number of their own dead that they had to pass to get to us kept growing. This continued for another half-hour until the APCs arrived. We could see camouflaged troops moving around to the south to get behind us and when we realised that it was not Bravo Company arriving back, we engaged them. They carried tree branches to disguise their figures when they stopped. I ordered Company HQ Support Section to engage them and I even got in the act with my own Armalite, firing into the VC about 60 metres away down the rubber tree lanes. I don't know what effect we had, but suffice to say we were not attacked from that direction. I think this was probably the northern flank of the VC which was eventually intercepted by the APCs on their way in. The VC were travelling back east and it was probably the noise or the knowledge that the APCs were coming up from the south, rather than CHQ fire, that caused them to turn back.

AAR24. 181850 A Coy Contacted estimated two companies of enemy YS478670. The enemy were moving to the west with the obvious intention of attacking the rear of D Coy. A mounted assault caused heavy casualties among the enemy who broke contact and withdrew east.

'With the infantry recovered we edged forward,' remembers Adrian Roberts.

My recall is that the enemy seemed to have withdrawn. However, only a short distance on we came to seemingly more groups of enemy, this time all withdrawing at speed to the north-east. The enemy numbers were probably another company in size (100). Again they spread across the troop front. I should say here that I had an excellent view across my front because I had chosen to sit up on a board across the crew commander's hatch. Although this exposed me, it enabled me to see and hence control my troop. That view from the beginning, together with radio communications, gave me a sound overall control of my troop throughout the action. I don't remember feeling vulnerable except for subsequent passage through the artillery fire.

This second group of enemy gave Adrian Roberts and the APCs problems.

To my right front, across the sunken road, I saw an explosion in front of the carrier commanded by Corporal John Carter and a rubber tree came down. At the same time enemy small arms fire cut down

Carter's radio antenna, which I saw fly off the vehicle. Ahead of the carrier I saw an enemy soldier with what turned out to be a 57 mm RCL on his shoulder, another enemy soldier reloading the weapon followed by its firing and a second explosion, luckily into the fallen rubber tree. With that Carter leapt from his .50 cal MG (which I learned later had jammed) and commenced to kill the RCL crew with Owen gun fire. Carter's driver tossed him replacement magazines as he emptied the weapon into the unfortunate enemy gun crew.

Now we had a problem. Every Armoured Corps soldier is taught that anti-tank guns operated in pairs. We had knocked out one. Where was the other gun? The troop paused momentarily. On the left Sergeant O'Reilly's section had even more problems. His far-left carrier crew commander, Corporal Peter Clements, had been hit, mortally as it turned out. Two infantry soldiers had tried to take over his gun and had also been wounded. Luckily the APC driver managed to silence the MG by rolling over its operator. O'Reilly was also off the air, having been knocked down by a bullet graze. I was calling him when Charles Mollison, OC Alpha Company, from the troop compartment of the carrier demanded to know why we had stopped. He was clearly agitated. I shouted to him that we were looking for the second anti-tank gun and that O'Reilly's far carrier had lost its crew commander. Captain Mollison grabbed Trooper McCormick, saying, 'Send him to the Carrier.' I said, 'No, I'll send Sergeant Lowes.' I also made it clear that I ran my troop. It was impossible to communicate without shouting because of the noise from the engines, gunfire and the artillery bursts, as well as the barrier of my earphones. Sergeant Lowes grabbed his gear and without hesitation left the APC via the rear door and ran across from carrier to carrier to Clements' APC. He was almost shot by an infantry soldier on that APC who mistook him for an enemy soldier until he realised that Lowes wore a black beret. Sergeant Lowes reported back to me that Clements was dying and that two infantry soldiers had been wounded.

Sergeant Noel Lowes was a very brave man and his run between carriers across the battlefield deserved to be remembered. Unfortunately his effort has been clouded by the fact that I ordered Lowes to take the carrier and its wounded back to 1ATF. I accept that my concern for the wounded prompted me to send the carrier back with a Platoon HQ on board. That was a mistake; compassion overcame military judgement, but it carried no consequences except for criticism of me. It was no worse than the platoon's worth of infantry we didn't have for most of the battle because three carriers were tied up in bringing the CO 6RAR to join Delta Company. With Sergeant O'Reilly recovered, I pushed on with his two carriers to join Ron Richards, who had launched forward during my distraction.

Sergeant Richards had actually driven through falling artillery, reached the south-west of Delta Company, realised we weren't with him, had done an about-face and driven back to meet us. What that manoeuvre did for enemy intelligence on the battle I cannot imagine!

For Geoff Kendall the arrival of Ron Richard's APCs was also a surprise.

Suddenly, up to the right there was a roaring sound and three APCs charged through the rubber, firing their machine-guns; they then turned around and went back the way they had come. It was the quintessential psychological moment and right across our front enemy started to get up and withdraw to the east, with us still firing at them as they left. I looked around and everybody had the same look, no smiles, just sort of stunned.

Adrian Roberts and the APCs reformed and pushed on.

I recall seeing artillery bursts bring down trees in black oily bursts of smoke. Strangely I felt little. I remember feeling numbness—I reached across and took my steel helmet outer and jammed it over my beret as we came through the artillery bursts. Sergeant Richards and I had hardly linked up when the CO 6RAR and my remaining three carriers arrived in the rear. At this point we were still a little way south of Delta Company. The CO requested, through my Troop Officer Ian Savage, that the troop assault to the east.

I swung the troop to the east just below the line of a track that runs east through the rubber. I am told, though I don't really remember, that I ordered headlights on to blind the enemy during the assault. We assaulted in a two-up formation, with Savage's three carriers in the rear reserve position carrying CO 6RAR. The enemy fire that came back at us was some of the heaviest I saw in two tours in Vietnam, very heavy, but high. I remember that something they fired hit the trees and exploded in little puffs of smoke. (Maybe it was the rubber tree sap being sprayed by the bullets as they hit.) Their fire seemed to stop and CO 6RAR asked that we cease the assault and withdraw to Delta Company, which I did, swinging the troop diagonally back to the north-west until we met the company.

BRAVO COMPANY CROSSES PATHS WITH THE APCs AND ARRIVES AT DELTA COMPANY POSITION

Bravo Company had come under enemy small arms fire and some eerie green 20 mm tracer fire seemed to be searching them out. They passed an enemy group forming up in a gully/re-entrant some three or four hundred metres from Delta Company. 'I now believe they thought we were also the enemy,' recalls Corporal Jones.

As we were heading in the same direction and our wet clothes would have appeared black to them, they allowed us to pass calling out and yelling, waving. At this time the machine-gunner and myself were almost among them. Suddenly, they started to fire at us and my legs have never moved faster, but luckily that fire was high. We had a job keeping contact with the rest of the company. I couldn't see Buttegieg's section. It was still raining but not as heavy. However, it was making distinguishing people, friend or foe, very difficult. About this time we came up to the crest or a slight rise, in front of us I could see others climbing over a barbed-wire fence. This fence proved to be a bloody nuisance.

The enemy seemed more concerned with the arrival of the APCs and only took a fleeting interest in Bravo's presence. The APCs were constantly changing direction but were moving towards them as the VC were now running across their front in numbers. Small arms fire was received in Bravo's direction. One of the soldiers in Jock Smith's section was wounded. The APCs roared past them straight into the direction of the enemy group they had just passed through earlier.

It was within minutes of crossing the APCs' line of advance that Bravo was in the Delta Company location. Private Thomas remembers: 'I was still on the left flank and not sure how far Delta extended when two figures appeared out of a pile of broken branches and trees. Thankfully I did not blaze away. The look of stunned relief was something I will never forget.'

For Corporal Jones their arrival remains an indelible memory.

On arrival at Delta Company HQ location I was moving directly towards the wounded of the company, located in a small depression in the ground. I cannot describe the emotion that I felt at that time. The wounded were in this depression, about some twenty of them. Those who were able, yelled out 'Thank God Bravo Company's here' or 'We're saved'. The CSM Jack Kirby was helping to put us in a defensive position facing to the north-west boundary of the rubber. I knew Jack Kirby from my days in 3RAR. He was walking around giving orders and encouragement to many; his actions placed his life at risk as I watched. 'Get down you big bastard,' I thought.

AAR 25. 181900 B Coy (-) Arrived in location with D Coy and deployed to cover the west. *(The Bravo Company strength at this time was 32, Ed.)*

There was a lull in VC fire when Major Noel Ford and his platoon arrived. In retrospect, I believe the VC had started to withdraw east about this time as they obviously became aware of the APCs coming up from the south. They had had a belting from the guns. (And as we saw next morning—they had had enough.) I was able to stand up and walk around with Noel, briefing him on our situation. Noel told me they had some close rounds from VC 60 mm mortars earlier, had seen some VC in the distance and had been fired on by an APC as they came back to the battle area. I was glad to see him and quickly briefed him, asking him to place his group to defend to the south-west to western area as we had seen VC trying to get around there. I told him Company HQ had fired on them in the gloom, that they had been worried that they might be Bravo Company returning, but as they were well camouflaged with branches and moving from left to right, we assumed they were VC.

ALPHA COMPANY ENTERS THE DELTA COMPANY AREA

Adrian Roberts formed a line, just east of the Delta Company position, facing east towards the enemy as requested by the CO 6RAR. Alpha Company dismounted to positions between the carriers. Darkness was just falling.

Harry Smith and his company heard the roar of the APC engines and some .50 calibre heavy MG firing. Then they saw them, some with headlights flashing, coming in through the rubber from their right: the south.

Any remaining enemy in front of us fled east. The noise of the battle ceased, replaced by noises of moaning wounded out to the front and then the jubilant talking among the company at having survived what seemed an impossible situation. My gut instinct was that we had to be prepared for the VC to reorganise and counter attack, but as minutes went by, it became obvious nothing was going to happen immediately, as they would have attacked before we were all reorganised. I felt the worst was over, and with the APCs, Alpha Company, Bravo Company, and the artillery, we could hold out easily all night now. As the rain had also stopped, I knew we could get air support if needed, airborne flareships and all the goodies the Yanks offered.

The VC had failed to overrun us. Thank God for the artillery, the APCs, the RAAF, and the courage and tenacity of my own men.

> AAR26. 181910 A Coy Moved into D Coy Area. Dismounted and secured area east of D Coy.

Bob Buick can still see and hear the APCs coming through the lanes of trees towards them.

> They had no idea where individual soldiers were and had already been in contact with the enemy. They were more alert looking for the enemy than us. Some of us jumped up waving our arms. It was very much like the cavalry rescuing the victims from the Indians as seen in a Western movie. In our case the cavalry were metal boxes growling through the mud, weaving among the trees and occasionally firing a machine-gun. A flood of relief passed over me. It was just dark

and with the and with the extra firepower and soldiers on the ground the Viet Cong would not have a chance. The badly needed ammunition and other supplies on board the APCs were passed around. A new vigour seemed to have passed through members of Delta Company as there was no way we could lose this battle now.

Dave Sabben remembers that it was now darker and the VC had given up their assaults and they were now only receiving sporadic incoming fire by individuals, probably as they covered each other withdrawing.

There was a final fall of artillery and then silence. As if an order was given to both sides, the artillery and all small arms firing ceased. And finally, in the distance, but getting louder by the second, the low growl of the APCs approaching, changing gear and direction, speeding up and slowing down, glimpses at first, growing into the full reality of eight or nine APCs threading their way towards us. There were a few feeble cheers from somewhere over on the other side of the company and the APCs were circling us. They ground to a halt and turned to face outwards. The rear ramps came down and the Alpha troops tumbled out and went to ground between the carriers, facing outwards. They wouldn't know the firing had stopped, having been trapped within the noisy vehicles on the way in, but as the last of the troops slid into position, an almost solid silence clamped down on the scene. This silence, broken only by the now gentle rain and the *clicks* of the APC engines as they cooled down, lasted for the few minutes it took for the last remaining light to fade. It was full dark before whispered voices led to some of the APC internal lights being turned on and the reorganisation began.

The arrival of the APCs was also a relief for Morrie Stanley.

Whether the artillery fire ceased before the APCs and Alpha Company arrived, or vice versa, I am not really sure, but I am sure of the feeling of relief when a couple of APCs came through the smoke into our area and members of Alpha Company could be recognised. I reported this on the radio and I think Harry Honnor stopped the artillery firing for me and the relative quiet that followed was very strange. Actually, I was very concerned about our security when we were all hanging around the APCs in the dark because it was hard to believe that the VC had broken contact and that the end of the battle had come so abruptly. Willy and I grasped hands and did a few vigorous push/pull exercises to get our circulation going because I felt freezing cold plus the wet skin on my hands seemed to be rubbing off. However, lighting a smoke was the thing to do and I had no difficulty in doing that, while the wounded accepted my offer of a soggy smoke whether or not they were smokers.

AAR27. 181915– A,B,D Coy Reorganised after action. A Company continued east.

Colonel Townsend and his HQ party alighted from a carrier and after talking with Harry to get a feel of where the company area was Townsend took command of the battle area. He gave orders to Alpha and Bravo Company commanders to secure and patrol the area in case of a VC counter attack, but all remained quiet. The VC had by now obviously had enough and gone, no doubt dragging and carrying many dead and wounded and their weapons with them.

A YANK JOINS THE 'ACTION'

An interesting aside occurred with the arrival of the CO. An American gunnery sergeant, Frank Beltier, had managed to jump aboard the carrier while it was in the Task Force area. He had grabbed his gear and gone to find 'some action'. His presence was discovered on the way out and it was reported to his superior, who immediately threatened to court-martial him, if he survived. Several stories circulated about how he became disoriented and was then discovered by members of Alpha Company, who nearly shot him as an enemy soldier. However, Lieutenant Steinbrook arrived the next morning to thank those who had cared for him, and in his relief at finding that he was all right, decided not to punish him.

LATER IN THE EVENING

There had been a constant buzz of quiet activity behind Dave Sabben as the force consolidated and restored order to the chaos of the last few hours.

Alpha Company had formed an outer perimeter around us, utilising many of the able-bodied Delta diggers. The CSM had several groups organised: one group of NCOs was supervising the distribution of ammo and water bottles, another was supervising the loading of our dead and wounded onto the APCs. Yet another group appeared to be collecting all the unclaimed and damaged weapons, plus other kit lying about and loading them into another APC. The two sergeants and Mac were taking a roll call, and consolidating a list of missing and casualties.

The CO and the three company commanders met in one of the APCs to decide what they were going to do next. Dave Sabben met up with Geoff Kendall, who was talking to one of the Alpha platoon commanders.

We more or less just sat and stared. Currently, we were 'ministers without portfolio'. Our troops, NCOs and senior officers were all busy and there was nothing for us to do. I don't remember much of this stage of the night except for drinking a lot of water. The activity at the company position slowly came to a halt as tasks were completed and the next decisions were made.

On the perimeter there was some activity. Lieutenant Peter Dinham remembers that 'During this time, movement and moaning could be heard to the east and three separate attempts were made to locate the source, hopeful that it might have been some of our own wounded'. The first attempt was by the Alpha Company sergeant major, Warrant Officer Class 2 Jack Roughly, the second by Corporal Ross Smith from 3 Platoon and the third by Corporal Smith accompanied by two others. All attempts involved crawling forward of the company perimeter with a radio, towards the sounds. None of the attempts were successful as the sounds ceased when the source was approached. These were acts of heroism that were never fully recognised.

Corporals Smith and Peter Bennett went on one of these excursions. Smith recalls (extracted from *Duty First*, vol. 2, no. 4):

I crawled out into the night towards the sound of moaning. I was armed with an Owen machine carbine and Peter had a self-loading rifle. We used a night compass bearing to maintain direction and to be sure we knew the correct route back. As we got closer we yelled out Australianisms: 'Anyone from Sydney?', 'Who won the rugby league grand final?' and so on. There was no answer. We moved on a bit further and did some more yelling. The moaning stopped but again, no answer. Then there was a brilliant flash of lightning. Peter grabbed my leg. 'Did you see that?' I had seen it all right; there were a number of enemy soldiers moving about to our front. I took a back bearing with the compass and indicated to Peter the way home. He felt my arm. 'When I start shooting, go in that direction,' I whispered. But there was no more lightning and the enemy obviously had not seen us. So we made our way back and reported what we had seen and done.

Peter Bennett also recalls:

As we crawled out into the night through the mud and
slush, I was thinking about those missing, about what
it would be like lying out there wounded, perhaps not
able to move. Not knowing whether our fellows or the
enemy would get there first. The only time we could
see anything was in the lightning flashes and they
made the following darkness seem even blacker. It
became obvious we were not just going to find our
fellows as we called out, time and again. When we
did, the moaning stopped. I was convinced that the
moaning and screaming we had heard was from our
blokes, but then, in a brilliant flash of lightning, I
could see enemy soldiers moving about. It was only
then that I realised the screaming was from enemy
wounded being dragged off the battlefield. After a
while we returned to our platoon location, empty
handed and dejected.

It was my greatest concern that the VC might search the
battlefield that night and mutilate the bodies of my missing
[men] as I had heard this was the enemy's habit up in I
Corps in the Da Nang area. I was not happy when Colonel
Townsend ordered a withdrawal of everyone back to the edge
of the rubber to evacuate casualties by helicopter dustoff. I
argued heatedly with the CO that I wanted to stay and sweep
through the area to where 11 Platoon had been in APCs at
first light. Alpha Company commander, Charles Mollison,
supported me in this plan. I argued that we could quickly
make an LZ where we were by pushing the young rubber
trees over with APCs, chopping others, and take the wounded
out from there, saving them the trauma of having to be
moved in APCs.

Also, with Bravo's group, I argued we had the best part of
two full companies plus the APCs. There was well over a
regiment of artillery zeroed in and we could have US Air Force
aircraft, helicopter gunships and air strike aircraft overhead

on immediate call. Further, we would be ready to move forward at first light and even if they didn't attack, our presence would have held the VC well away from the missing and hopefully countered their moves to clear the battlefield. Also, I felt a hurried withdrawal in the dark might make us vulnerable to any VC ambush in the rear. One of the basic principles of war was to have a secure base—and we had that—why leave it and go off into the never-never?

Additionally, I felt that once out of the area there would be a natural reluctance by the Task Force to let us get back in quickly at first light—and I was proved right! I didn't win the argument. So we had to get on with the withdrawal instead of getting organised where we were! I don't know whether Townsend made the decisions or whether he bent to the overtures of Jackson.

BACK AT NUI DAT 9 SQUADRON GATHERED

The whole squadron had arrived from Vung Tau and was sitting on the pad, waiting, recalls Bob Grandin.

> I remember contemplating what would happen if 'Charlie' dropped a few mortar rounds into the area at this time. So much for the air staff directive, we would lose the entire contingent at once! As dark fell we were given some dinner. We were told that we were going to do an evacuation of the wounded, but the APCs had to make contact, withdraw to a secured location and then we could go in. It was decided to only send Cliff and Frank's aircraft in if absolutely necessary, and so we were tasked to go in last.

THE WITHDRAWAL TO DUSTOFF LZ

When the Australians recovered their composure a little and accounted for all the casualties, missing and survivors, they eventually withdrew. They left the battle area at 2245hrs in APCs with the dead and wounded, except for the fifteen of 11 Platoon who were missing. This left Alpha and Bravo Companies to cover the withdrawal and walk out on foot through the very dark plantation about 45 minutes later. Behind them the artillery harassing fire, still controlled by Morrie Stanley, kept clear of the 11 Platoon area but it started to fall in and around the area. This was on likely escape routes to the east in the hope of keeping the VC out of the area and perhaps catching some of them leaving.

Adrian Roberts remembers that they had loaded the dead into Second Lieutenant Savage's APC.

> Savage, because of his position, could avoid the diff-
> iculties of too much movement in among our own
> infantry in the darkness. He led the column out to the
> west and down the rubber's edge to the LZ site, which
> appeared to be a cleared area on the pictograph map.
> We set off and made the move without incident. I had
> ordered the troop to stop, turn outward in herring-
> bone formation and fire if we ran into any enemy. We
> moved out with convoy lights on and the leading
> vehicle using headlights.

Eventually word moved down through the darkness for everyone else to pack up and move across country (in pitch darkness) to secure a landing zone which would enable the dustoff helicopters to lift out the wounded and dead. Corporal Robin Jones of Bravo Company remembers being given the responsibility to lead this withdrawal.

> I received a message to report to Major Ford. When I
> arrived I was briefed to set my compass on a bearing
> and the bearing was checked by the OC. I was to lead
> Alpha and Bravo Companies back to the area of the
> evacuations. This was a case of blind navigation, as
> you couldn't see your hand in front of your face. We
> stopped numerous times after falling over or running
> into a tree. Obstacles were numerous. We made the

rubber's edge about an hour or so later. I never liked night navigation ever again.

Peter Dinham, Alpha Company platoon commander recalls:

We moved out in single file, in pitch-black conditions, effectively maintaining contact with the man in front by hanging onto his webbing. My platoon was the last to depart the battlefield with the Commanding Officer's Tactical Party moving just in front of my platoon HQ and behind my leading two sections. My one remaining section followed behind platoon HQ, constituting the rear guard. It took what seemed an eternity to move a relatively short distance, approximately 1000 metres.

At some point during the move Adrian Roberts told Harry Smith about an idea he had in the event of needing helicopter night evacuation. He would form a square with the carriers and with the cargo hatches open leave their internal lights on to indicate the LZ.

At the LZ we did just that, formed a hollow square with the carriers spread out and infantry in positions between each vehicle. Harry asked me to control the LZ, so together with my radio operator, Trooper McCormick, I stood out at the head of the square. Armed with two torches we sought to guide the helicopters in and to keep them away from the rubber and the area of Delta Company's battle.

182355 3 Tp 1 APC to hold east and south flanks, B Coy the west.
D Coy collected casualties and loaded them into APCs.
D Coy/APC Secured LZ YS 473675. A and B Coys withdrew to LZ. LZ marked by APC with internal lights on and hatches open

---

Bob Grandin remembers that the night was dark and stormy.

It was not good conditions for flying. Air support had not been possible and only a few medium-level bombing sorties had been applied to the back fringes of the enemy position. The noise of the artillery continued. Chinook helicopters were coming and going as they provided resupply missions to the artillery. Tension was high as each crew member contemplated the task ahead within the unknown situation of enemy movements. Was this a multiple-pronged attack, were more troops going to appear from the west, had the enemy just retreated from Long Tan and were they now re-forming to the north? Suddenly there was movement. The CO, 'Scotty', called us to a briefing.

The APCs had made contact, they were clearing an area for us to collect the wounded. Scotty was going to go in first, check the situation, collect a load and then call the next aircraft off the pad. Although it appeared quiet in the area the exact movements of the enemy were unknown, so no lights. He disappeared into the night. We waited for what appeared to be a long time. The position was only a couple of clicks outside the wire. Finally, Squadron Leader 'Laddie' Hindley, the flight commander and 2IC, called us to a briefing. He gave us an order in which we were to go into the position which would be lit by the lights of an APC; it was small with surrounding trees. 'Take your time,' he said, 'don't rush it.' Each aircraft allowed the one in front to take off and then started up. Radios were switched on to listen to the events as they unfolded. Some were having no trouble descending into the dark position, while others were going close to trees and having to pull back and try again. Finally it was our turn to go.

It was the blackest of nights. The clouds had completely blocked out the sky. We moved to the holding position and circled waiting for the aircraft before us to pull out. There was a hold-up as one pilot was having some problems with his approach. Then it was our turn. Frank and I had decided to share responsibilities. I would look outside and talk him down, watching obstacles and rate of descent. He would keep a close eye on the instruments, making a form of ground-controlled approach. We slid smoothly into the position. Someone ran forward and said that there were no more wounded. We could go, or maybe take some bodies out! Frank said we would take the bodies and about four were tossed into the back.

We slowly climbed up into the black night, being careful of the trees. As we reached the top of the trees, a huge fireball erupted in front of us. I called on the radio, 'Stop the artillery, we are still in the area.' A response came that there was no firing. Scotty was on his way back from Vung Tau and called on the radio, 'Frank, are you all right?' We said 'Roger' to that and then we were informed that a medium-level bomber had dropped a load on the hill just to the north of our position. It had been listed as a free drop zone! We flew back to the hospital at Vung Tau and dropped off our load. Then we returned to our pad at the air base and headed back to Villa Anna. It was now well past midnight but the cooks had stayed up and prepared a meal of steak and chips which we ate ravenously, washed down by a Fosters.

Finally we climbed into bed, exhausted by the day's events, but curious as to what had really happened that day. Why were we back, where had the enemy been, how come they hadn't shot us down, how are all the guys on the ground? We would look forward to seeing them soon and talking about it all over a beer.

AAR28. 182355– US DUSTOFF
190045 9 Sqn RAAF Evacuation of casualties.
1 sortie by US DUSTOFF, 6 by RAAF Iroquois.

While RAAF aircrew relaxed in their quarters at Vung Tau (one of the areas that caused problems between the RAAF and ATF), Harry Smith and Delta Company spent the rest of the night in the cabins of cold APCs.

I sat with Townsend, still anxious to be allowed to go back in at daybreak in the APCs, but this was not permitted. The company, in a state of shock and unable to believe they had escaped what seemed an inevitable end back in the rubber, were wondering about the fate of those missing. They huddled around in the carriers, listening to the distant sounds of artillery falling around the battlefield. Somewhere around 1.00 a.m. on the 19th, Townsend told me the Task Force commander had issued orders for what was now going to be a Task Force operation in the morning, which entailed the return to the battlefield, with more APCs, Charlie Company and a company of 5RAR. I remember Townsend was most unhappy that the Task Force was getting in the act, taking kudos away from 6RAR.

[This was just what Townsend was to do with Delta Company: downplay its role at Long Tan, in favour of a battalion operation. In the 1990s 6RAR was promoting Long Tan as a battalion operation which started on the morning of the 17th with the VC mortaring of the Nui Dat base. And Delta Company's stand became the vehicle for the Task Force commander and the Battalion commander to be awarded gallantry DSOs. Townsend recommended Delta Company, through me, for the DSO, but although appalling, that was downgraded to MC by General Mackay in Saigon, and thus my platoons went from recommended MCs down to MID.]

Adrian Roberts remembers that the remainder of the night was spent 'standing to' as they waited for the enemy to come again, but he did not. 'Curiously, the CO 6RAR came and sat in silence in my carrier for most of the remaining night until dawn. We did not speak.'

With the departure of the choppers, the hatches closed and silent routine took over again. I called together my officers and senior NCOs for the first time since the O Group that afternoon. In a lit but sealed APC we tried to put together the list and sequence of events. I needed their assessments of VC numbers and casualties inflicted for a report to the Task Force commander who would fly into the APC harbour at first light.

'The rest of the night and early morning were a blur,' recalls Dave Sabben.

> After putting the events of the previous twelve hours into some sequence and perspective, I had some food and a brew whilst trying to answer the questions of the Alpha and APC guys. Then, well into the wee hours of the morning, I found some uncomfortable and fitful sleep.

Morrie Stanley didn't remember moving out of the rubber to where they assembled with the APCs and spent that night. He does remember that 'the sound of dustoff choppers coming in to extract the wounded was very reassuring'.

> To me, this seemed like a good time to collapse somewhere for the night, but Harry Honnor had other ideas. On the radio he, correctly, suggested that I should prepare a fire plan to continue for most of the night to harass enemy who may still have been lurking around the battlefield and to keep them away from the diggers who had not returned. An APC made a comfortable enough place for me to prepare the small fire plan and after sending it by radio to Nui Dat, I probably sat there and fell asleep. The guns fired during the night at a more leisurely pace and that was virtually the end of my fire support duties at Long Tan.

I didn't think anyone slept during the rest of the night. So ended Delta Company's Operation Vendetta. Certainly we had found much more than the platoon of VC we had expected. We knew we had fifteen missing, four dead and some twenty wounded, and we wondered just what we had done to the VC. I think we all knew they had lost many more than us, even from what we had seen close in, let alone the artillery fire, but would the evidence be taken away during the night? I hoped ATF would organise a US Army block to the east of the Long Tan area to cut off the withdrawing enemy, but as later discovered, this did not happen. Like the return to the battlefield on the 19th, nothing was to happen quickly.

CHAPTER SIX
THE AFTERMATH:
OPERATION SMITHFIELD

Over the following days the grim task of returning to the battlefield and 'cleaning up' occurred. This was a traumatic event for all, especially for Bob Buick as he returned to the site of 11 Platoon's bloody battle and his dead mates. There was some joy as two diggers survived through the night alone in the rubber. Harry Smith guides us through these events.

I spent the rest of the night, very tired, wet and cold, and worried about the missing, in the cabin of Adrian Robert's APC with Colonel Townsend. I was anxious to be allowed to go back in at daybreak in the APCs, which was not permitted. Colonel Townsend drew up plans and orders for the return into the battle area after receiving advice from Brigadier Jackson that elements of 5RAR would reinforce 6RAR. The operation was given the codename of Smithfield at about 2300hrs on the 18th and advised to me about 0400hrs on the morning of the 19th. It was a Task Force operation to follow up the battle. I remember Colonel Townsend resenting the intrusion of a 5RAR company and that it had thereby become a Task Force event.

[Smithfield was named about midnight on the 18th and actually commenced on the morning of the 19th or it could have been

*made retrospective to the night of the 18th when Townsend
assumed command. But it has conveniently been used by 6RAR
and then ATF to manipulate the facts so that it appeared that the
Battle of Long Tan was a battalion operation from the start.
Some reports indicate that it commenced on the morning of the
17th, after the mortaring of the Task Force.*

*My personal company After Action Report, headed Opera-
tion Vendetta, was re-typed to exclude diagrams of VC tactics, re-
headed Operation Smithfield, and attached to the battalion after
action report without discussion. In the conclusion written by
Townsend it said, 'The performance of D Coy was admirable and
overall command and control was good' and finished with
'6RAR has achieved a great victory'.*

*There is no doubt in my mind that, from the 19th, when a
possible defeat was turned into a legend by D Company, there was
no way that 6RAR would permit the accolades, proper recognition and fitting awards to be showered onto my company. Not
when it had always been accused of elevating itself above others,
through its commander's insistence on very high standards of
fitness, discipline and training.*

*With that in mind, as we discuss in Chapter 8, it is not
difficult to understand why the awards for Delta Company were
downgraded as the 6th Battalion and the Task Force jumped on
the victory bandwagon.]*

Apart from the fact that they were following the practice of
calling operations after town names, Smithfield was a nice choice
since it at least incorporated the name of the commander of the
battlefield the day before.

At some time during the night it was suggested to me by
Colonel Townsend that Delta Company should return to base
at first light to 'lick its wounds' and rest up prior to reorganising, but I insisted on getting back into the battle area—first.
After all, the missing were from my company and there was
no way my company was going to walk away from the battlefield without seeing what had happened to our missing and
what damage we had inflicted on the enemy. I was convinced

in my own mind that between the small arms fire of my company and the enormous amount of artillery fire, together with the contacts by the APCs on the way in, we had taken a heavy toll of the enemy. But would there be any evidence left by the VC, given their traditional tactic of clearing the battlefield and taking away all their own casualties and weapons? And had they taken any of my missing as prisoners, or worse?

All these things weighed heavily on my mind and I was very anxious to get back in there. There had been no enemy counter attack or any sign of action during the night and it was fairly obvious that the VC had left the area when the armoured personnel carriers had arrived. Of course, they could have set an ambush awaiting our return into the area. But that was unlikely given their losses and the problems of trying to reorganise their ranks during the night. Moreover, they had to face a larger force with more armour in the morning, with all our artillery still in range. There was also offensive air support on call and no afternoon monsoon rain to reduce visibility.

Instead of moving back into the area at daybreak (about 0600hrs) I remember the cautious return advance did not commence until 0845hrs. Reinforcements from 5RAR arrived by US Army helicopter and other 6RAR forces were in APCs extracted from the squadron during the night. It was three hours after first light when we moved out.

So it was mid-morning of 19 August 1966 before Colonel Townsend gave his orders for the move back onto the battlefield of the day before. Delta Company alone, with no rubbernecks along to violate its privacy, was to return to recover its dead. Alpha Company went back to where it and 3 Troop had fought through the two companies of D445 Battalion. Delta Company, 5RAR moved in APCs to the exposed eastern flank of Delta Company for protection and the other companies followed on in support and to assess what had to be done. Considering the large number of enemy troops possibly in the area and as they would know that we would return to search the battlefield, it was far from clear what we would find and what nasty surprises could have been planned for us.

The CO ordered his OC admin coy, Major O'Brien, to fly to the battlefield early on 19 August, presumably for instructions on administrative support matters. However, upon his arrival, the CO blithely instructed him to fly eastwards in a tiny army observation helicopter (armed with only a rifle), to look for enemy and/or their tracks. 'The pilot was as nervous as I was,' remembers O'Brien. 'We flew alternately either very high or at treetop level, neither very comforting.' They did wide arcs to the east, north and south (to Bin Gia, Xuyen Moc and the coast) looking for signs of a force preparing for a counter attack or retreating in disarray. They saw nothing of consequence, perhaps something to be expected with such a cursory investigation.

The sound of approaching choppers woke Dave Sabben.

Delta Company of 5RAR was being flown in. I saw a group of 12 Platoon diggers, and went over to them. There was a pile of ration packs and full water bottles on the ground with brewing kits and they were all preparing breakfast. I remembered that our ration packs and kit were still in our backpacks, which were still out on the battlefield where we left them, so I joined in. They were all tired and drawn, probably not having had any more sleep than I, but they were reasonably chirpy, all things considered. They asked a few questions about the events of yesterday, but they appeared to be more interested in 'What next?' I couldn't answer then, but Harry had an O Group planned for 0800hrs and the orders for the day would be given there and then.

I caught up with Mac, who had got the platoon roll from Paddy and was now acting platoon sergeant. We went through the list of casualties and decided we would retain a three-section structure, even though two of the sections would now be at half strength. Some of 12 Platoon's nine casualties were light and we could expect their return to the platoon within a few days.

At about 0700hrs a single Sioux chopper brought in the Task Force commander and following him in two Hueys some of his staff and the Task Force photographer.

At the O Group I advised everybody of the orders of the day. The events of yesterday had triggered a combined US, ARVN and Australian operation across the whole province, with forces converging on the area in the hope of trapping the withdrawing VC before they could regain their sanctuary areas in the Nui May Tao hills to the far north-east. Our role was to retrieve our own missing, then search for and gather any intelligence available on the battlefield (including any VC bodies, personnel and equipment).

While the O Group was in progress, the Task Force commander and several of the Task Force officers came over and interrupted. They congratulated us on what appeared already to be a great victory, despite our losses. The Task Force photographer was snapping anything and everything.

After the O Group, I kept the officers back and filled them in on some of the activities going on behind the scenes. I informed them how I hadn't wanted to leave the battlefield the previous night, but had been overruled by the CO. How I wanted Delta to be first back in the morning and again the CO had overruled me. I was straining at the bit to be onto the APCs and into the battlefield to recover our own casualties, but was being held back by what I saw as excessive caution on the part of the CO and maybe the brigadier as well.

Adrian Roberts remembers that they stood to and then seemed to wait for an incredible time while elements of the Task Force arrived before going back into the battle area. '3 Troop was given the task of carrying Delta Company back into the battle area. I carried Harry Smith and his HQ personnel in my APC.'

As Geoff Kendall and Delta moved back into the rubber he recalls thinking,

> Christ, we must be the only company in the battalion. Notwithstanding, it turned out well. The fact that we got to see first hand, on the spot, what kind of

damage we had done to Charlie the day before has probably kept most of us reasonably sane. Commanders throughout the centuries have commented on the sight and feel of a battlefield the day after. My feeling was a sort of disbelief. Did this really happen yesterday afternoon?

Bob Buick has vivid memories of that morning.

The dawn seemed to come very slowly on the 19th. Birds were singing and as I stood on top of an APC, I saw a circle of APCs with a lot of diggers crammed into the perimeter of a small clearing used by the choppers earlier. This day was to be a test for all of us. I was one of many who didn't want to go back into the rubber. I thought that the VC were still there and had no pressing desire to get into another firefight; 11 Platoon had been decimated enough, for the moment. Let Alpha and Bravo Companies go in. Let them take on the VC. 11 Platoon and I had done our bit, as had the rest of Delta Company. I guess it was after what seemed like an eternal night, in which my mind had been playing tricks. Now as the acting 'Skipper', I felt I had bigger responsibilities.

In the back of my mind I knew we had to get our mates and clear the battlefield. That is what being an Aussie digger is all about. Tense and twitchy, we advanced back through the area towards the place for which we had fought so long and hard on the previous day. My apprehension increased as I moved through the battle area. This feeling was soon to change as I was confronted with the awful sight of the battlefield.

To me, the battlefield was worse than a hurricane disaster area. Most of the trees in the area of heavy contact had been blown apart by artillery shells and cut by machine-gun fire. There were no leaves left on most of the rubber trees and there was white rubber latex running out of bullet holes. Then we started to find VC bodies and weapons and equipment everywhere.

'I felt so small as I moved back to where the platoon missing lay dead,' remembers Bob Buick.

The landscape and vegetation looked like a giant had walked through the forest and flattened trees with his footsteps. There were areas about a hundred metres square with all the trees smashed and broken. Latex sap poured down the trunks. There were branches and crowns blasted from trees with the impact of high explosive shells and rocket-propelled grenades. The stench of death from the bodies wafted through the air. Weary, but alert, the diggers carefully looked around and under the smashed vegetation expecting to be fired on at any second. A signal that it was on again. There was the odd rifle shot. Fired by a digger who saw a dead Viet Cong lying in the firing position with a weapon in his hands. This was not a time to take chances.

I was feeling good until I arrived at the place my platoon had so valiantly defended, then I cracked up. The 11 Platoon dead were face down, holding their rifles, killed firing their weapons. Private Vic Grice was sitting with a grin on his face and looked so peaceful. The radio on his back was still working. This showed that the VC had not been in the platoon area. The rain had washed the battle field clean but the bodies were beginning to swell and that sweet sickly pungent smell of rotting human flesh permeated through the still morning air.

The VC never penetrated the 11 Platoon perimeter during the battle and the scene of the piles of bodies to the east and south was horrific. It was a charnel house. There were whole bodies, bits and pieces of bodies and piles of rotting flesh maybe attached to an arm or leg. For me there was only one joyous moment among the carnage and mayhem. A voice calling my name. It was Private Jim Richmond from our left 5 Section. I dashed over calling for a medic and assistance. He had been shot twice through the chest, had shrapnel in his lungs and was lying face down in the mud. Jim Richmond and Private Barry Meller were the only two survivors from the ill-fated 5 Section. Barry, shot through the mouth and one leg, had been found as we moved back into the area leaning against a rubber tree and had exclaimed to those that found him that he felt we had taken our time in getting back—or words to that effect. He had managed to get some way back towards the Delta HQ position but had finally rested against a tree. I wasn't expecting to see any of the missing fifteen men alive. Jim and Barry had beaten the odds twice.

All of Bob Buick's emotions welled up inside of him.

I became very emotional and wept. I also became violent towards an officer, 'a tourist', who had flown out for a 'look around'. I punched a major after he made what I considered undignified and unwarranted remarks about my dead soldiers. I cannot remember his words today but at the time his words caused me to explode in anger. Had it not been for the RSM, WO1 George Chinn, I would have been in deep trouble. In another incident, Jack Kirby hung a newspaper guy up in a rubber tree by the collar of his shirt. I was going to shoot him if he did not piss off and leave me alone. The last thing we needed were the wankers from the base areas, be they officers or news journalists, coming for a stickybeak, to write a story, commenting on what they saw without any apparent empathy or compassion.

After the incident with the newspaper guy Bob Buick was sent off to count the dead VC.

Grabbing Private Peter Dettman, a machine-gunner from 12 Platoon, we went to the area in front of and to the south of 11 Platoon's last stand. As we moved through and over the bodies I counted and placed a branch on each body counted. This was to eliminate a double count. Peter was nearby carrying his machine-gun should an enemy lying doggo decide to have a go. After counting about 130 and an hour of walking through and on mangled bodies we had to give it away. It became sickening after a while and neither of us was in the mood to do this. I counted whole torsos, the main part of the body. It would have been impossible to count the arms and legs plus try to match them with bodies.

We did come across a young soldier from North Vietnam. He had been shot in the left groin and not recovered by his comrades when they withdrew. He was only a boy in his mid-teens and was terrified of us. I am 183 centimetres tall while Peter is well over 200; he carried the machine-gun in one hand like Rambo. We towered over the wounded teenager. Dettman was resting the muzzle of the M60 on his forehead while we called for a medic. The poor brave young fella, fighting for a cause, an ideal, just like us. A medic arrived with a couple of others in a very short time, to look at a live VC I suppose. A bottle of iodine was poured into the wound, it brought tears to our eyes watching, but the tough little bugger never flinched. The medic then picked the dead maggots out of the wound and dressed the wound. I have often wondered whether that young man is alive today. I would be interested in meeting him again, have a yarn and swap stories. I hope he is still alive.

We came across the bodies of 11 Platoon soldiers lying where they were killed. There were also the two wounded, Private Jim Richmond and Private Barry Meller. Both were evacuated to Vung Tau hospital and we recovered thirteen bodies, thus accounting for everyone. The VC had not touched them or their weapons. An Armalite was reported missing, but I believe that was 'purloined' and later taken back to Australia by a soldier who shall remain nameless. In fact the only missing item was one of the packs dropped by 10 Platoon when they went in to help 11 Platoon and I recall that was recovered from a VC casualty on a patrol some weeks later.

As he moved back into the area they had been on the previous day, Dave Sabben saw how the young rubber trees, which had been in neat and orderly rows, were now a mess and one couldn't see more than a hundred metres in some directions due to branch-falls. The tree-burst artillery—especially around the company's final position—had shredded the branches and the red soil was now totally covered with leaves and branches.

Passing through our final position, we approached the closest artillery impact zones and entered a world of mangled weapons, webbing, equipment plus bodies. We passed through. Further on, we found our backpacks that we'd had to abandon early in the battle. They appeared to be intact, but we retrieved them carefully, in case of booby traps. Of note was the extraordinary quiet of the area. It was as if we were walking in an empty cathedral and everyone was constrained to talk only when they had to, then only in whispers.

12 Platoon was then detached to retrace its steps to its position of the previous day. Delta 5RAR and Alpha 6RAR had cleared the whole area earlier that morning, but they had only swept for possible resistance—they had not attended to VC casualties. At one stage I crouched down beside a rubber tree, facing a wheeled medium machine-gun, its crew lying dead beside it. The PR photographer snapped off a few

photos, the noise of the shutter unnaturally loud in the stillness of the place.

From an area where several large branches had fallen, we heard a shallow whimper, as if a small cat was meowing. We approached carefully and found a wounded VC under the foliage. We covered him with our rifles and removed the branches, but he was not dangerous any more. He had a hideous wound that had opened up his entire abdomen. His gut was plainly visible, looking like plastic in the dappled sunlight. Even as we looked, we could see maggots moving around his intestines. He put two fingers to his mouth in the international appeal for a cigarette and someone obliged. We called the Doc forward, and he administered a painkiller, but the guy had already passed the pain threshold. I didn't know if he could survive, but I called for a stretcher and we moved on.

On returning to the battle area Morrie Stanley, like others, was stunned by the eerie silence that pervaded the scene of utter devastation.

We were not stunned out of action, but tired and shocked. I had no feeling of disgust or fear when viewing scenes of human destruction and the damage done by the artillery. We just felt tired, but the infantrymen did not cease performing their duties. They silently cleared the area of enemy weapons and equipment. CSM Jack Kirby asked me if I had any objection to my two operators assisting in recovering the dead diggers.

As Adrian Roberts entered the rubber he saw three prone figures side by side.

I remember the anger on the carrier when it was assumed these green-clad figures were our men whose boots had been removed. Closer, we realised that they were an enemy 60 mm mortar crew, killed by artillery fire. The rain had a curious effect—it seemed to wash the bodies into merging with the ground.

While Major Brian McFarlane, OC Charlie Company, received orders to fly by helicopter to join the colonel in the field at first light, his troops under command of Captain Harris departed in APCs at 0645hrs to join the force at Long Tan. The remainder of Battalion HQ and some platoons of Support Company moved by APC as well. Brian McFarlane was one of the first to arrive at Long Tan that morning and remembers meeting Harry there. Brian recalls:

> Our association in combat operations went back ten years to Charlie Company, 2RAR in Malaya and now I was so proud of him and his company that for the first time in my life I was speechless. I could only stand there like a dodo and shake his hand. I hoped that no hint of a tear would well up and invade my eyes to display my emotions. Speech would not come. I let go the poor fellow's hand and went off without a word to seek out the colonel and receive my orders.

By the end of the day Dave Sabben remembers that the whole area of all the Delta contacts had been cleared and they had collected the weapons plus other hardware into one spot.

> We counted the VC bodies and searched them where possible looking for documents, but without many found.
> We found three VC still alive, one of whom appeared not to have been wounded. The two wounded VC were evacuated. The third was under guard. The battalion intelligence officer (IO) questioned him that afternoon.

Two of the bodies collected from the battlefield were remarkable for their differences—they were dressed in a better cut of uniform, with boots instead of Ho Chi Minh sandals. They wore a pistol belt with an empty holster and a small pouch that contained cleaning gear and some spare pistol ammo. The bodies were taller and paler than the average VC dead, leading us to wonder if these were Chinese or some other nationality of adviser to the NVA.

The pile of VC weapons and equipment included a heavy wheeled machine-gun, a 60 mm mortar, two recoilless rifles, four rocket launchers, 33 AK47 assault rifles plus assorted US carbines and garrands. There were 1200 rounds of ammunition, 300 grenades, 100 mortar bombs and several rockets. The US Army rifles and assorted odd weapons were the trademark of the local VC, while the others were Main Force weapons and equipment.

I personally relieved a dead NVA officer of his 7.62 mm Tokarev pistol in a nice leather holster on a leather belt with a red star in a brass buckle. I regarded this souvenir as fair game and did not hand the pistol in, wearing it around the base area instead of my issue Browning for some weeks until eventually I was ordered to hand it in to Battalion HQ. I 'heard' there were other pistols, rifles, binoculars, compasses, bugles and sundry items that were also souvenired during the battlefield clearance that day. I think it is fair to say that there were many more weapons found on the battlefield than are recorded in after action reports. I was lucky enough to have the Tokarev pistol returned to me at a later date and have since presented it to the Australian War Memorial.

On the day following the battle Bob Grandin flew a mission with Bob McIntosh in which they distributed leaflets over a wide area to the north and east of the Task Force area, possibly along the route of the retreating enemy. 'Dropping leaflets was a regular task. The leaflets were designed to encourage people in the area to pass on information about the enemy and offered rewards for those that participated.'

In the late afternoon Geoff Kendall, Dave Sabben, CSM Jack Kirby and I flew out of the battlefield and back to base, leaving the rest of the company under command of Alpha Company to continue the clean up. We had a hurried shower, changed our clothes and were once more on a chopper, this time to the US 36 Medevac hospital to see the wounded. The meeting was only an hour—just enough to meet our guys at their bedsides and bring them up to date with events since they were flown out. All the patients knew of the battle and they all wanted to hear our reports. Most of our guys were in reasonably good spirits, but we found it hard to handle the amputees in the wards. Two of the lightly wounded were discharged then and there, returning with us.

At the hospital, also visiting the guys, were the Delta diggers currently attending the language course in Vung Tau. There was mixed feelings among them at having missed the action, but they all agreed that being at the course was better than being in the hospital.

Back at the company lines we found that the company quartermaster sergeant, Staff Sergeant Gildersleeve, had already taken the casualty list and removed the bedding, kit and personal effects of the guys who would not be coming back to the company. Whether killed in action (KIA) or returned to Australia (RTA), their kit was gone from the diggers' lines and the empty spaces in the tents stood out like beacons. We stayed overnight in base before once more putting on the red-stained greens and returning to the battlefield.

Adrian Roberts coordinated the activity of his APCs.

Sometime during that morning Second Lieutenant Ian Savage and I followed field telephone lines east for about two hundred metres to a huge circular emplacement made up of well over two hundred weapon pits. Later in the morning Savage with Corporals Carter and Fottrill took an infantry section from Alpha Company back to the area of 3 Troop and Alpha Company's fighting on the 18th and undertook the grim business of battlefield clearance in that area. All of the troops involved were both exhausted from lack of sleep and still in shock from the combat on the previous evening. Every enemy body was a potential booby trap and there was always the possibility that a determined wounded enemy could make a 'suicide' effort to kill our soldiers. It was a very stressful and distressing time for all concerned.

Corporal Fottrill took one wounded enemy prisoner. A 57 mm RCL and a quantity of small arms, light machine-guns as well as grenades and ammunition were recovered. A small number of enemy dead were also removed for central burial back at the area of the Delta Company stand. I spent that afternoon at the ruins of Long Tan Village recovering one of Ron Richards' carriers, which had run into an old, overgrown trench system and tipped on its side during a reconnaissance of possible mortar sites.

Bob Buick had an unexpected visitor late in the afternoon on 20 August, Sergeant Jim 'Snow' Curtis, a mate of many years.

We had been together since 1959, from recruit days at Kapooka. In the same company with 2RAR from 1959 to 1965 and now in different companies of 6RAR. He was with Alpha Company. Due to the training requirements in Australia and operational requirements we had not seen each other for months. We sat on a fallen rubber tree trunk in that foul-smelling, decimated rubber plantation, had a smoke and coffee, quietly talking about the battle. He said, 'There is something dead around here!' I laughed and thought he was joking. Having been away with his company searching to the east of the battle area he had not become accustomed to the smell, the 'perfumed garden' of rotting bodies. We had cleared the area of bodies and whatever bits we could find in the particular location we lived in. Surrounding us were many bodies still to be buried. I had missed the four bodies under the foliage of the tree we sat on. The horror on his face must have prompted some smart remark from me because Snow did not stay too long afterwards. He went back to his company muttering, 'Buick, you're bloody mad'.

Back at 9 Squadron, Bob Grandin was tasked to do the courier run between Vung Tau and Nui Dat with Frank Riley. Later in the day they did a troop support mission as the radio command helicopter over Long Tan.

Now back with the company, I found that the grisly task of collection and burial was well under way. Although a bulldozer was requested it could not be transported to the area and did not arrive. All non-metal remains were put into graves, which were dug by hand. The metal was collected into piles and an APC drove around collecting the piles. The diggers were tired beyond belief and wanted to see the end of the rubber plantation, but equally, wanted to finish the job.

News in from the large sweep was that more and more treatment stations and shallow graves had been located, but no live VC or equipment caches. This was disappointing, since all the signs told of a rout and a disorganised withdrawal back to the north-east. Webbing and clothing were littered about along the main withdrawal routes, but the VC had been careful not to leave behind any weapons, ammo or documentation. The battlefield had a mild stench about it—not yet vile, but becoming so. The main focus was to get the dead buried and this would be achieved by the end of the day. The cool weather and the afternoon drenching had helped keep the flies down, but maggots were a worry on every corpse.

There was some criticism that the body count was overstated. Unfortunately, all I can say is that we had to dig by hand graves for about a hundred VC dead in one small area alone, near where 11 Platoon fought. There were independent reports of bodies found and buried by other units around the battle area, from the final company position to the APC contact area. All these were collated by Battalion HQ and added up to 245. These did include bodies found some five hundred metres behind where 11 Platoon had fought and it could be assumed they were from artillery or air strikes in depth, or were seriously wounded who died when they were withdrawing east. There were several bodies of VC found later in a large trench area well to the east who could have been killed in that area or dragged there by the retreating VC.

I was told by HQ 6RAR that the diary of the VC commander at Long Tan, captured by US Army forces some time later, showed his admitted losses to be in the order of five hundred dead and near a thousand wounded. Later, I learned the body count from graves and other information in VC documents discovered after Long Tan, particularly by 6RAR on Operation Marsden in the huge Nui May Tao hospital complex during their second tour in 1969, eventually amounted to 850 KIA and 1800 WIA. All were attributed to Long Tan. These figures are quite realistic, especially given the large number of deaths from wounds that could be expected from the less than adequate hospital facilities in 1966. In any case, whatever the figures, they were obviously horrific losses for the VC, most sustained from a battle with a rifle company utilising all the artillery support it could muster.

Bob Buick discusses the grim nature of the battlefield-clearing task.

Training takes over from feelings but we were not trained for what we had done. There was something about a battlefield, with all the dead and mangled bodies, that the strongest of people still found revolting and unacceptable. Today, I can still see the battlefield, smell and taste the air; the flyblown and maggoty bodies that fell apart when dragged into a hole. In the beginning individual graves were dug as a rectangular hole. The problem with this was the bodies were stiff with rigor mortis, limbs were broken or cut to suit the hole. This quickly became sickening so the holes were then dug to suit the shape of the body, much more humane. One body was buried face up and during that night an arm rose out of the ground. In the morning of the 20th, there it was, this arm, sticking upright out of the ground. Nobody took any notice of it. Nobody was going to stick it back in the ground so it was left. Later that day a sign was hanging off the hand on which was scrawled 'THE CLAW'. Australian digger humour, at its best or worst?

By stand-to the task of burying the dead had been completed. Most of the graves had been shallow and the afternoon monsoon rain had re-exposed the odd arm or leg here and there. We reburied where possible, but it was all pretty temporary.

Overnight, we heard noises in the plantation and stood to again, but nothing eventuated and the noises ebbed and flowed for the rest of the night. We were spooked by the noises, as we could not identify them, but it was unlikely that there were VC out there searching the battlefield for survivors after two days. In the morning, it was revealed that the noise was caused by pigs digging up the graves. They had exposed some of the limbs, so these needed further burying. By late morning, the battlefield was declared 'cleared' and everyone began to return to base.

By the night of 20 August, Adrian Roberts and 3 Troop began to feel like zombies, they were so tired.

Somehow we got through the routine of sentry watch that night and on 21 August returned to 1 APC Squadron in the ATF base. I remember Harry Smith made us honorary members of Delta Company mess. I do remember feeling very proud of the troop and myself, believing that we had done something special.

During the day, the engineers left and Alpha Company departed. In the early afternoon, Delta climbed wearily aboard the APCs and left. I guessed it was fitting: we were first in, so we should be last out. This concluded Operation Smithfield, the three-day Task Force follow-up operation after the Delta Company battle at Long Tan—the culmination of Operation Vendetta.

Plans for the rest of the day were just to get back to the lines, shower, change and settle back in. The diggers had been in the same greens for three days already and had been living out of ration packs heated up on hexamine stoves. The APCs had brought in a beer ration the day before, but that's not the same as a shower, a shave, a change of greens and an hour in the company boozer.

[Harry Smith reflects on a few things about the three-day duration of Operation Smithfield: Dozens of recent graves were found, several being large enough to hold up to ten bodies. Although the graves were shallow, they were not dug up, as that task would have been not only distasteful but also unnecessary— it was obvious what they were. These graves were not added to the Long Tan body count statistics. Several hastily constructed but very useable delaying positions were found—many obviously recently occupied and only evacuated in front of the advancing troops. This indicates that, though badly damaged, the VC and NVA were still a coherent and dangerous fighting force. The fact that they chose not to come into contact with the pursuit forces would indicate that Long Tan had, at least for the time being, knocked the 'fight' out of them. In fact, there were no contacts with the enemy at all over the three days of Operation Smithfield.]

Back in base the mood was subdued as the diggers moved back into the tent lines where the kit of the casualties was glaringly missing. In Dave Sabben's tent, which he shared with Gordon Sharp, half of the tent was now just an empty bed. 'I sat and stared at it for a while, coming to grips with the implications. Would, some day, someone sit and look at my empty bed in the same way?'

Despite the events of the past few days the routine of the Task Force area had to be re-established. There were too few troops available for another unit to take over our FDL defences, so each platoon provided a MG sentry roster and we looked to our own FDL duties. The company was somewhere between half and two-thirds of effective strength, so a major reorganisation with transfers, promotions and reinforcements was needed. The officers and senior NCOs began reforming the company on paper. However, Delta would be used on base camp duties until reinforced.

In the diggers' lines, there were many letters being written home that night. Those not writing were drinking and talking quietly over dim lights in the tents. There was a notable absence of noise and frivolity, which was understandable. The healing process was not able to begin out on the battlefield, but would begin now they were back, confronted by the empty beds.

The following day the company warriors went to Vung Tau for leave. To get drunk and talk about their experiences among themselves, to remember missing mates. Some were feted as heroes by the Americans, though I don't think there was one of them who even considered that. Most were thankful to be alive and not wounded. The Yanks entertained a lot of them and being Aussies some played up to everything they could. There were a few non-Delta Company fellas about, all non-operational base wallahs. Some cheeky ones tried to get on the bandwagon for free drinks. They were soon caught out. Most of Delta Company diggers sat quietly by themselves or in small groups and pondered the whole thing, missing their mates.

Morrie Stanley chose not to go to Vung Tau but instead accepted an invitation to visit the Battalion HQ officers' mess for the first time.

I really enjoyed the company of the many officers whom I had known in earlier years and proceeded to relax. Later, I said to Harry Honnor that I would return to Delta Company area for the night and he asked me if I knew where it was. I had to admit that I didn't and even if I did I would not have been able to navigate my way in the dark. He offered me a 'bed' on the floor of his tent. That was home this night.

'I never visited Vung Tau and never asked to be part of the hospital visiting team,' recalls Bob Buick.

The line between commissioned and non-commissioned officers can be wide. I, as acting officer in command of 11 Platoon, stayed at Nui Dat to sort out the not so pleasant duties. Confirming certificates of death— 'Private so and so died from a small arms bullet entering his right shoulder and exiting near his left hip'—all that type of administrative detail.

Many stories come back to him.

The one about our wounded visiting the club at the air base brought smiles and humour to a saddened camp. The story goes that they had left the hospital in pyjamas and slippers to get on the grog, all bandaged, some on crutches, one in a wheelchair and others pushing a trolley with drip bottles attached. A truck driver, an American, crashed his truck as he looked in amazement at this band of crazy Aussies going on the piss. Some were refused entry to the club because they had no shirts or tops. It did not take long before their mates returned with jackets and they all had a good time. When the doctors and nurses got wind of it there was all hell to pay but no retribution. This was the first time the Yank hospital, the 36th Medical Evacuation Hospital, had had so many Aussie patients at one time. Our Delta Company blokes set the tone for future patients at the 36th Medevac Hospital.

CHAPTER SEVEN
WHERE ARE THEY NOW?

LIEUTENANT COLONEL HARRY SMITH, MC (RTD):
FORMERLY OC DELTA COMPANY AT LONG TAN

In August 1967, almost immediately after our Vietnam tour, most of our National Servicemen were discharged and returned to civilian life. I was posted back to Special Forces and given command of 1st Commando Company at Georges Heights, Sydney, until December 1969. With 1 Commando I was able to qualify at free-fall parachuting and improve my qualifications in other skills, such as rappelling from helicopters, small craft operations and the like.

I don't want to dwell on Vietnam experiences after Long Tan, other than to say my company saw more than its fair share of action in 1966–67. The total of killed and wounded was indeed depressing, not just for families and loved ones, but for all of us who served. Apart from Long Tan where Delta Company lost seventeen KIA and twenty-one WIA, the tragic New Zealand artillery accident in early 1967 took another four KIA and fourteen WIA. Add another two KIA and twelve WIA in other actions and the total of 70 casualties for a rifle company of around 120 strong was a massive and very sad 60 per cent. 11 Platoon was the worst hit, with thirteen KIA and eight WIA at Long Tan and out of a nominal active strength of about thirty, suffered fourteen KIA and twenty WIA over the year.

While much has been said about post-traumatic stress disorder in Vietnam veterans, I have to say that in 2003 I know of very few Delta Company survivors suffering from the problem. Yet they would have more cause than most, certainly more than those veterans who never saw a shot fired. Nevertheless, I know I, and most others, get very emotional when I think of those we lost and how the rest of us were lucky to survive. As with other Delta Company veterans, a tear or two comes to my eyes whenever I dwell on the tour, or hear the familiar and sad bugle call of the 'Last Post' at commemorative services. Many of us prefer to stay away from such ceremonies. I keep well away.

Back home in August 1967, the war behind me, I was fortunate to have several attachments from 1 Commando to SAS Regiment in Perth, one trip to an SAS Squadron in PNG, and an SAS parachuting exercise up at Port Hedland, one of the hardest drop zones I ever encountered. It is no wonder I am 50 mm shorter now than in 1966! In Perth I qualified as a rappelling instructor. An RAAF Iroquois pilot, Geoff Banfield, almost dropped me into the local sewage farm by way of his idea of a joke. I dangled on the end of a 50-metre rope with my feet just on the top layer of wet compost as part of a 'hot extraction' technique exercise. Geoff had been one of our most supportive 9 Squadron pilots in Vietnam, always willing to drop into our company LZ or deliver supplies into difficult jungle landing zones. Unfortunately, he passed away due to cancer at Noosa in 1996.

Army activities and exercises did not decrease and Kathleen was sick and tired of following me around from posting to posting, twelve months here, eighteen months there, living in all sorts of married quarters accommodation, such as sub-standard high-rise Housing Commission flats in Melbourne. Tired of trying to raise three young children, with no stable friends for her and the children, she wanted a home base, along with my resignation from the army to take up some civil vocation and be like a normal husband. This plea had been made before, but it was only after Vietnam that I had saved enough money to be able, with the aid of a War Service housing loan, to purchase a house in a suburb outside Sydney for Kathleen and the children. I had no civil vocation or trade and loved the army, so we agreed to separate and went our own ways. I am still on very good terms with my three children and five grandchildren.

While with 1 Commando in Sydney and through my diving association with the RAN Diving School, I was able to live on board HMAS Penguin at Balmoral. Here, at a RAN sailing activity, I met a WRAN officer, Anne, the lady who later became my second wife. The navy used very heavy Bosun dinghies and I became involved with the task of introducing lighter and faster Corsair yachts to the three armed services. I was involved in all sorts of peculiar activities, such as submarine operations and underwater demolitions, as well as free-fall parachuting. I recall being the first army guy to trial a new Drager oxygen underwater breathing apparatus for the army. I tested it in a water jump at Port Stephens, dropping out of the parachute harness as I hit the water. I swam underwater for some time, but then started to feel quite ill. I surfaced, signalling the Zodiac rescue boat, and then found that no 'Sodasorb' gas absorbent had been placed in the canister by the maintenance team and that I had almost expired from CO_2 poisoning! Nevertheless I really enjoyed my two-year posting to 1 Commando, despite long hours with night and weekend work conducting various commando courses mainly associated with amphibious and airborne raids.

I met and admired many devoted CMF commando soldiers, such as Mike Wells and Ian McQuire, who both served full-time duty tours in Vietnam. Ian was my Delta Company 2IC later in 1967. I considered the commando soldiers were a cut above the average part-time or 'weekend warriors' who seemed to be wasting a large percentage of the Defence budget and in many cases were employed in protected industries and could not go to war anyway.

I was selected for the 1970 Staff College course at Queenscliff, a year of quasi-university type work with military subjects. As a result of my active service experience, I qualified 'psc' (passed Staff College) near the top of the course. Anne was able to follow me to Victoria by being posted to a navy appointment in Melbourne. After Staff College, I was posted to my first-ever staff appointment as DAA&QMG (senior administrative staff officer), HQ Western Command, Perth. As there were no navy officer postings in WA, Anne left the navy and moved over to work and live with me, although I was not yet divorced. I managed to organise the Western Command Army Sailing Club with the newly acquired Corsairs. I took out the WA Corsair Champion Title in late 1971 and then skippered the 15-metre yacht *Siska* on loan to the Army Club. With the support of the commander, Brigadier George Larkin, I was able to delegate most of my daily duties to my army and public service staffs and concentrate on sailing, with ample reward to the army by way of excellent public relations both on the water and in the media. As well as weekend club races, we sailed three or four twilight races each week with up to 25 passengers, mainly army families, and at 50 cents per sail, we were able to raise funds to maintain the yacht.

It was in Perth that Alan Bond sailed the first *Apollo*, then the fastest racing yacht in Australia, and was to take on the Americans for the America's Cup in the larger 12-metre type yachts. Alan wanted the army to provide logistical support for the venture, with my army guys crewing a pace yacht, and to have equal chance of representing on the challenger. This was all approved in principle by the then Minister for the Army, Bob Katter Snr, but an election campaign frightened the politicians, fearing they might be seen to be wasting public funds. So ended the army involvement. It pleased me to see the services become involved in 'adventure training' in later years, including sailing, along with fully paid Whitsunday Islands charter sailing as adventure training. Why not?

At the promotion and selection committee interview in late 1970, my marital status and my 'non-union' attitude was frowned on by the 'establishment' and saw me placed on the 'Y—reconsider' list for promotion, despite my professional record. But in 1972, after serving my penance, I was selected to be the first commander, or chief instructor, of the Army Parachute Training School to be taken over from the RAAF at Williamtown RAAF Base, near Newcastle. I was then promoted to lieutenant colonel and posted to the UK, Canada, and USA for thirteen months of Joint Warfare (JW) training and considerable parachuting work. This was all done discreetly under the guise that initially I would be the army senior instructor at the Joint Warfare Centre at Williamtown, but my briefings were quite clear as to my future. Apart from various JW work, I spent most of my time parachuting in the UK, Canada and USA, including HALO (high altitude low opening) jumps from 25 000 feet over Salisbury Plain in the UK. As it was an 'accompanied' posting I was able to prevail on the Civil Court for a decree absolute and marry Anne so that we were able to see the world as well as undertake all the work required of me.

Unlike Australian public servants, I found our overseas military mission staffs were extremely helpful and able to arrange all sorts of visits to various military establishments in a way that we were able to utilise the available allowances and travel arrangements. I bought and sold a lovely 1964 Jaguar car in the UK for £500 and a V6 1964 Ford Mustang for $500 in the USA, selling both cars on to other army colleagues at nil loss. The 'system' was able to convert my airfares into cash mileage allowances, which enabled us to drive to most areas, making life very pleasant. While I had to pay for my wife's expenses, US army and air force base accommodation in furnished apartments was just $2 per night. In those days allowances were minimal and public service claim regulations made life difficult until less-stringent attitudes were adopted in later years when staff found they were dealing with human beings rather than cans of bully beef!

We arrived back at Williamtown RAAF Base in NSW in March 1973. While there was some resistance from the RAAF, army policy prevailed and I eventually formed the Army Parachute School with about 100 staff and we got on with training and introducing new equipment to meet the role of training army airborne forces. A company of 3RAR commanded by Major Tony Hammett was the first to be trained there—a project devised by Colonel Owen O'Brien (formerly OC Administrative Company, 6RAR, who flew in with the ammunition resupply at Long Tan) at Army HQ, and myself. My philosophy in 1973 was that the army needed mobile forces that could be delivered by parachute or amphibious means.

I was personally very fit and active. I enjoyed jumping, up to five times a day when we had courses. I formed the army 'Red Berets' free-fall parachute display team which gave displays at all RAAF air shows and various army displays around the country. For my spare time, I bought a 10-metre yacht hull which I set up in the back yard of our RAAF married quarters home and spent some eight hours at work and another five to six hours a day fitting the yacht out.

The yacht was visible from the officers' mess and most RAAF officers were somewhat bemused by this army officer who jumped out of serviceable aeroplanes, who was married to an ex-navy officer, and who lived in a house on a RAAF base with a yacht in his back yard! They were also convinced I had little idea of what I was doing with the building of the yacht and I was given all sorts of help by RAAF officers who donated their time and labour, plus some surplus RAAF stores to assist with various items. I recall the radio officer, Kev Maddox, insisting on doing all the electrical wiring for me.

In late 1975, I was test-jumping a new free fall parachute from 12,000 feet and it initially failed to open after I pulled the ripcord as my twin altimeters indicated rapidly passing 3,000 feet. When I rolled over to deploy my small reserve parachute, the main chute came away off my backpack, but opened up between my legs. It caused me to come to a rapid stop from a 200 kph free-fall. This created a massive whiplash, which caused damage to my lower spine, neck and other joints. I was eventually medically downgraded from FE (fit for everywhere) to HO (home only) and unfit for infantry field service. Although I might have been able to continue to serve in some clerical-type work, my aspirations of commanding an infantry battalion and later a task force completely disappeared. My planned military career had evaporated.

I chose to leave the army and resigned to preserve my superannuation benefits rather than take a basic medical pension. I sadly left the service in March 1976. I took up an office job with a Sydney firm known as Beaufort, marketing sea safety equipment for a couple of years until my old injury problems caused me to leave work in 1978. I had bought a house at Bilgola Plateau with the aid of a War Service home loan and long service money, but without an income we chose to live on the yacht and rent the house to supplement my small superannuation income. We slowly sailed up and down the coast to the Whitsundays each year, becoming involved in research for a guidebook to be used by charterers called *The 100 Magic Miles of the Whitsundays*. Our names are still recorded in the Acknowledgments section of the latest edition.

Peter Smeaton, former OC Alpha Company, 6RAR, and I renewed friendships on the water when we were sailing off the Queensland coast in 1985. He unfortunately passed away due to cancer in 1990 after returning from a Melbourne–Osaka race. Charles Mollison, OC Alpha Company at Long Tan, was on his yacht *Dalliance* in the same area at the same time, and he had already spent many years cruising around the world. After twenty-odd years, I was to hear their voices again with their very formal radio procedure on an otherwise colourful coastal radio net punctuated by fishermen's procedures— mainly four-letter words! I introduced my boat on radio and we all met up in Bundaberg's Mid-Town Marina in July 1985.

That year I went back to school in Brisbane and gained a Marine Master 4 Qualification and took up some light work driving charter boats, along with moving home to Airlie Beach in North Queensland, but could not get permanent work—I was too old and infirm! I began cruising the north and researching another guidebook for the waters between Whitsunday to Weipa, which was to be called the *1000 Magic Miles*. Apart from the research, which entailed plotting depths and describing uncharted areas using a satellite navigator and sounder linked to a notebook computer, we had a great time beach-combing, all the time keeping well clear of the many crocodiles and wild pigs. In company with another boat crewed by Jim and Mavis Purcell of Gladstone, we were able to locate about 400 Japanese glass fishing floats plus all sorts of flotsam and jetsam from dinghies to diving gear.

In 1994 my married life was again under pressure, this time not from the army lifestyle, but on account of my obsession with boating. I agreed to sell our boat and home in the Whitsundays to retire to Nambour, Queensland, so that Anne could be near her family. Fate moved in and I had to take a sailing yacht as a trade to sell the house. That led me back to racing. One of my crew, Felicia Smith, was an attractive and fit lady introduced by Anne's sister. Little did I realise we were to become close friends, and some six years later, loving partners. I went into a high-tech Jarkan 40 Grand Prix racing yacht called *On Silent Wings* with ten crew to do all the hard work. With several ex-servicemen in my crew we did very well. Re-named *Midnight Special* in late 1997 by new owners, she was lost off Eden in the 1998 Sydney–Hobart race. I bought a smaller MASRM 31 and kept on racing—my main hobby in 1950!—and now, another 54 years later!

Aided and abetted by Bob Buick, I launched this book project in October 1997. It flowed on from Bob's own biography and a video presentation by Bob, Dave Sabben, Morrie Stanley and Bob Grandin at the Australian War Memorial. I had declined to take part, as was my usual custom of keeping away from military-type events. But, when we viewed the video portraying the battle in chronological order, my wife said I should have been involved and suggested the main players could put the story down on paper in book form. I was aware there was a resurgence in interest in the Vietnam War and that there was room on bookshelves for the story of Long

Tan to be told by those who were actually there on the ground on the day. Apart from the details of the survival of my company against all odds, there were many peripheral issues that could be aired. Although I have no desire to criticise my senior officers, it is best that we voice the true story. This includes why we were sent out to face a VC regiment, to why senior officers were decorated for their role in a battle they never saw, especially as it was at the expense of junior commanders who were there.

In 1998, just after my 66th birthday, my six crew and I took out most of the trophies for the season at the Mooloolaba Yacht Club, in Queensland, on the MASRM that we called *Crow Bar*. At the same time, I sadly received the news of the loss of two of my former Vietnam soldiers, Bluey Moore and Lance Larcombe, with the Big C. Unfortunately, Anne and I parted after thirty years due to irreconcilable differences. Sadly, both Anne and Felicia's estranged husband would lose their battle with cancer inside the next two years. Felicia and I continued sailing together, but sold the racer in favour of a Cavalier 345 cruising yacht and cruised to the Whitsundays in 2000, then to Lizard Island in 2001 and 2002. On 20 September, 2003, Felicia and I were married in a garden ceremony in Hervey Bay.

I also continued to pursue the matter of Imperial Awards for Long Tan with the Vietnam End of War List Review Committee, which agreed there was a case to review awards downgraded in Vietnam, but of course did nothing concrete to achieve such a review. I also made a submission to the SEA Awards Review, with no success. In 2002 I wrote to the Chief of Army, General Cosgrove, suggesting he might initiate a review, but that fell on deaf ears, despite his approval of truckloads of awards in East Timor.

In mid-2002, I saw the demise of the third attempt at producing this book, caused mainly by arguments over different versions of the facts by Charles Mollison, which did not agree with those told by Adrian Roberts and myself, and those recorded in the After Action Reports. It was impossible to continue and I terminated the project. The authors' team later regrouped with Dave Sabben as Chairman, Bob Buick as

Secretary and Bob Grandin as the new Editor. I continued sailing. Given that Adrian Roberts was the commander of the APC Relief Force, we decided (unanimously) to use the contributions of various officers and soldiers of Alpha Company to outline the matters relating to their Company.

In 2004, I am glad to see the book published. I remain very proud of the courage and tenacity of all my Company, and all those who supported us, especially the Gunners, Helicopters and the APC Relief Force with Alpha Company on board. I am still saddened by the horrendous loss of life at Long Tan; not just our own losses, but the many hundreds of Vietcong and NVA we killed or who died of their wounds. I am still cynical at the way in which our senior officers manipulated the honours and awards at the expense of those who actually fought in the combat.

MAJOR GEOFF KENDALL (RTD): FORMERLY 10 PLATOON COMMANDER AT LONG TAN

After Long Tan, the rest of the tour in South Vietnam was something of an anticlimax, not only I believe to me, but to most of the company. When the awards for the battle were announced the company was stunned. The officer who commanded the most significant action of the Australian Forces in the Vietnam War got a decoration normally awarded to junior officers for successful small actions and it went on down the line. Senior officers received decorations without any apparent involvement, from our perspective. It was hard not to feel that we had been screwed.

Sadly for my military career, I became a bit of an *enfant terrible*, celebrating my award of a MID by getting involved in an argument with some military police in Vung Tau. You can't win those sorts of arguments and the OC chose to make an example of me. The end result was my transfer out of Delta Company to Bravo Company. About this stage I requested a parade to the CO and endeavoured to put my case. This interview was terminated in an interesting fashion when the CO jumped up and ran out to his sleeping quarters!

In 1967, on patrol in the sand hills area near the coast two of my scouts were killed by VC hidden in a camouflaged bunker firing through a slit. I attacked the bunker with the rest of the section but the VC had bolted out the back door. The next day I was sitting on the tray of an APC when in response to some shots fired the driver did a hard left stick and threw me onto the other side of the hatch splitting my lip and cutting my forehead. I was casevaced (casualty evacuated) to Task Force where an excellent medical officer whose name I have never known did a great job sewing my lip and forehead. When I got back to the battalion area, the OC Admin Company—a nice guy whose name escapes me—suggested I take a couple of days R&R in Vung Tau until the battalion got back from the operation. By the time I had a few drinks in the bachelor officers quarters (BOQ) I was an accident waiting to happen. I decided to go out to the back beach for a swim to sober up. Not having transport, I took the first Land Rover I saw parked outside the BOQ.

The practice of 'borrowing' Land Rovers was fairly prevalent in Vietnam; usually it was troops from Nui Dat units 'borrowing' vehicles belonging to Vung Tau support units. Sadly the practice was frowned upon by the powers that were and by the time I arrived back at Nui Dat half the province was looking for the officer with the stitched-up face. A further episode where I was a passenger in a 'borrowed' vehicle did not improve my chances of becoming a field marshall. Looking back I was a very silly young officer, but in some ways I got a lot of the Vietnam and Long Tan crap off my chest before I got home to Australia.

On return to Australia I was posted to JTC Canungra as an instructor on Battle Wing. There is probably another book in my experiences there, but let me tell you just two stories about JTC. These I feel illustrate my contempt for and frustration with a system that continues to teach soldiers tactics and doctrine that have been proven fallible on countless occasions. One night I had a platoon of trainees doing a night ambush at Lever's Plateau in the JTC training area. At about 2.00 a.m., the senior instructor of Battle Wing crept into the rear of my ambush trying to find someone asleep. The first trainee to see him waited, as he had been taught, until he couldn't miss and then fired his weapon (blanks, naturally). The senior instructor was both startled and embarrassed, but immediately proceeded to dress me down because he hadn't been challenged for the password. I tried to explain that once an ambush was set, anything that moves until it was unset, was enemy. This officer, who had served in South Vietnam, albeit not with Australian troops, imagined I would allow the rear protection element of one of my ambushes to say to someone coming up on it, 'Halt! Who goes there?'

The second example occurred about ten years later when I was doing a tactics course required for promotion to major. During discussion on an exercise company attack one of the Staff College graduate instructors suggested that it might be necessary to clear a minefield in front of the enemy position by passing a platoon over it. Thinking I had misheard, I asked if he were seriously proposing to use Australian soldiers as a sacrificial tool to clear a minefield. When assured that this was the case, I'm afraid I said some rather rude and uncomplimentary things. To the budding field marshals who are no doubt scoffing at my naive sentimentality while reading this, I have only this to say. The Australian Army has been incredibly successful throughout history *despite* the efforts of some of our alleged professional officer corps. This is due almost totally to the natural fighting ability of the Australian soldier. We don't have many of them so let's please not waste what we've got.

Back to my life after Long Tan. In 1969 I did a Chinese course at the RAAF School of Languages at Point Cook and after graduation I was selected for further training in Hong Kong. In Hong Kong I attended the British Ministry of Defence

Language School at Lai Mun, famous in the Second World War for the massacre of Hong Kong volunteers by the Japanese. The course was not as intense as the Australian one and I quite enjoyed the British Army attitude and in particular their sense of humour. An example: the Australian officer selected for the Mandarin training the year before me had not completed the course and as I knew he was a good linguist I wondered why. I finally asked the chief instructor, a very pukkah British Education Corps officer. 'Well, Geoffrey,' he said, 'it was like this. One morning the commandant and I were walking around the school doing a casual inspection. We noticed that one of the doors on a small studio classroom was closed, so we knocked and entered. We were surprised to see a student and a female teacher having it off on the desk. We apologised and left but the commandant was furious. "Get rid of that student," he told me. I said, "Oh sir, I can't. Firstly, he's Australian. Secondly, he's by far the best linguist on his course." "Well, get rid of the teacher." "Can't do it, sir, she is by far the best instructor we've ever had." "Well—get rid of the bloody desk!" '

Lai Mun was a composite base and with the student population drawn from various British regiments a formal dinner was something to be seen. After the passing the port stage, the band commenced playing the marching songs of the various regiments and corps (in strict seniority, of course). Suddenly they broke into 'Waltzing Matilda'. As the only Australian present that was real lump in the throat stuff.

The week after we moved into our apartment in Hong Kong, I needed a bit of paint for some touch-up work. I had noticed a sort of convenience store just down the road, so after several practices I walked in and in my very best Mandarin said, 'Do you have a tin of paint?' The Chinese guy behind the counter said in the broadest of Australian accents, 'Why the bloody hell would you come into a grocery store to buy paint?' He had been born and raised in Melbourne and had come back to Hong Kong to find a wife!

After graduation from Lai Mun I was attached to the Joint Service Intelligence Service at Victoria Barracks in Hong Kong. My boss was a British major, John Hunt-Smith—a great guy, also not short of the English sense of humour. About the second day I was there he raced into my office, threw a Chinese People's Army magazine on my desk and said, 'Give me a quick translation of that article.' At Point Cook we had been taught not to bother translating the titles of similar articles, which are often stylised and bear little relation to the text, but to get straight into the meat of the article. After about half an hour of wading through fairly graphic descriptions of what might be termed female plumbing, I checked back to the title. The vital piece of intelligence for which the whole Western world was apparently waiting, was an article by a female 'barefoot doctor' entitled, 'How I Cured My Urinary Incontinence Using Only Acupuncture and Chairman Mao's Thought'!

By this time I had transferred from infantry to intelligence where I spent the remainder of my 24 years' service. Intelligence work in Australia wasn't quite as exciting as in Hong Kong. However, I did manage to get posted as the OC of the 1st Division Intelligence Unit, a company-sized unit. This was by far the most enjoyable posting in the Australian Intelligence Corps and I thank the many excellent officers and soldiers who passed through the unit while it was my privilege to command it.

On leaving the army I bought a small hardware store, which for ten years struggled from crisis to triumph to tragedy and back in the fashion of most small businesses in Australia. My 24 years in the army were a superb preparation for running a hardware store. For the first couple of months I thought most of the customers were speaking a foreign language—sadly, neither English nor Mandarin. One day, very early in my hardware career, a Middle European gentleman with a thick accent came into the shop and said 'Vair iss clagshaw?' I remembered as a kid a glue called Clag, so took him to the Selleys bar. He got angrier and angrier as I tried to establish what kind of glue he needed. Luckily, at that moment one of my staff, a semi-retired gem of a guy called Fred Bennet came around the corner. 'Fred, can you help this gentleman with some clagshaw, please?' I said, and decamped to the till. About three minutes later the guy walks up to the counter and says, 'See—clagshaw!!' and shook a hacksaw under my nose. Strangely he continued to come into the store, although he seemed to prefer being served by someone else! I finally sold the hardware store after eleven years and retired to my home on Bribie Island, north of Brisbane.

On some occasions, for instance recently when the subject of the Long Tan awards was raised again, I get a little bitter about it all. At times like this I try to remember that I have had more than thirty years that eighteen of my mates didn't get. I live with a wonderful lady in a comfortable house in one of the nicest parts of the world. My mirror tells me I'm not exactly starving and I just lost a stroke off my golf handicap. Would I do it all again? No bloody way!

WARRANT OFFICER CLASS ONE
BOB BUICK, MM:

PLATOON SERGEANT OF
11 PLATOON
AT LONG TAN

I remained with the battalion and moved to Townsville from Brisbane in the November of 1967. I went to Bravo Company as a platoon sergeant anticipating a return to Vietnam in a year or two. I had no burning passion to go back there in the same job and expected to go to Mortar Platoon in Support Company. Robert, our son, joined our family during April 1968 as part of what seemed a massive baby boom. It seemed that just about every wife of those who went to Vietnam with the battalion was expecting an ankle-biter at the same time.

A year later I was posted to Ingleburn near Liverpool in Sydney, as an instructor in the Battle Wing at the Infantry

Centre. Ingleburn was the home of the Infantry Corps where all the corps qualification and training courses were conducted. During the two and half years at the centre, I completed a senior mortar course, the qualification course for warrant officer class two (company sergeant major) and a number of other skill training courses. During this time at Ingleburn I was asked, if required, would I return to Vietnam with the 8th Battalion as a mortar fire controller. I said that I would but indicated that the war was winding down and that I would only go if really needed. A month or two later I was asked if I would go with the Australian Army Training Team (AATTV). I said yes, but insisted that I select the 'team group' to which I would go. There were some on the Team I wouldn't have a beer with, let alone trust them to be there if the shit started to fly. George Chinn, DCM, now an officer, but who was my regimental sergeant major from 1965 to 1967 and ex AATTV, visited me. He was sent to find out my requirements for going to the Team. After some fifteen minutes he agreed with my assessments and said that I had done enough and I would not be returning to Vietnam. I never was asked again, so I reckon George spoke with the right people in the right places.

After the couple of years at the 'School of Insanity' I was promoted to WO2 and posted to Bunbury, Western Australia, as the Regular Army cadre staff to Delta Company, 16 Royal Western Australian Regiment (RWAR). The job I had with this unit was to be the link between the CMF and the army's requirement for correct administrative and training procedures. This was the system throughout the army within all corps, and possibly half of the warrant ranks were involved with the CMF nationwide. After three and half years we left Bunbury for a posting to the Royal Military College, Duntroon near Canberra, as a field training and infantry instructor.

RMC could be classified as the pinnacle of an infantry soldier's career. There were only eight WO2s posted as instructors. We were responsible for the teaching of all weapons training, field and infantry tactics, plus battle training. It was a rewarding job and I enjoyed the two years there. After RMC it was off to Brisbane and back to 6RAR, the old unit, as CSM to Bravo Company. Later I moved to Logistic or Administration Company.

The life and duties in the battalions had changed since I left eight years before. In the mid-1960s it was Vietnam and counter revolutionary warfare (CRW), now ten years later it was 'continental defence and open warfare'. 6RAR trained hard and long with the emphasis on night warfare. All battalion attacks and other phases of war concentrated on night operations. This training is not dissimilar to jungle warfare as many of the difficulties and problems are similar. Observation, control, navigation and movement are restricted in both. There was no urgency in the training during this time. The Government had been reducing military spending, to boost social security expenditure. Spare parts and service equipment was a problem and this could be seen through the skill reductions of the individuals and units, shooting skills and battle training being the first to suffer. It was the start of the rot as far as I was concerned and it was then I decided that when I attained the rank of Warrant Officer Class One (regimental sergeant major, RSM), and after completing twenty years I would retire.

I completed the RSM's course and was promoted in 1978 and posted to the 1st Training Group, an Army Reserve Headquarters that conducted officer and NCO training for all non-Regular Army members. The main manning was by Regular Army officers and non-commissioned officers, who planned and conducted most of the training. As the RSM I was not involved with this day-to-day tasking, but kept a judicious eye on all matters. The defence cuts were starting to affect all facets of training and I bided my time, planning for the phase of my life as a civilian.

In May 1980 I retired from the Australian Army and Defence Force, completing twenty years of service in the army and air force. It was time to start again and to promote some domestic stability for my family, especially for Tracey and Robert who had not forged strong peer relationships. I was offered employment by a private school, Brisbane Boys College, Toowong, as an assistant bursar. I was responsible for all maintenance and cleaning of the college and some fifteen staff that went with this job. It did not take too long before I became disillusioned with what they had offered and then expected from me. In the army, all is cut and dried, everyone had a job and we all cooperated. It was not so when working for this religious school. If you show any willingness to assist and do extra, within a few months you were responsible for that too. No extra money or remuneration for the extra time devoted, of course. It was time to change and as it is said, 'I went into real estate'!

Selling houses and achieving satisfaction knowing that I had helped someone to get their first home was gratifying. I really enjoyed the challenge, but in the early 1980s the nation was plagued with questionable politics and high interest rates. Labor under Hawke came to power in 1983 and soon there was high inflation and higher interest rates imposed on all. The challenge was not to find the home for the buyer but a buyer who could afford to buy a home. An opportunity came my way to establish, open and manage a liquor barn for a New Zealand bloke I met through real estate. That was a challenge and in the first year the barn turned over $1.2 million worth of beer, wines and spirits. This job did not last long, accounts were slow to be paid and as the 'front man' the gun was pointed at my head. I felt the owner and friend was treating me extremely badly. One day I gave immediate notice and left. Back to real estate, but I noticed that the business world was changing. Honesty and integrity were being replaced by deceit and lower business ethics by many in the industry.

I stuck with it for a couple of years until one day I decided that to be successful—that is to make money—I would have to join the others. Never being one to follow the herd, I became a security guard. During this time, until I retired in 1996, I went to work, did my time, had no problems with my conscience and planned for retirement.

In 1995 my son Robert gave me his old clunker computer. I used this as a word processor only and started to write my life story. A friend read about my Vietnam experiences and encouraged me to concentrate on a book about my time there. This I did and it has been published under the title *All Guts and No Glory*.

The army has been half of my life, but Long Tan was the turning point. I now have become distrustful of politicians and refuse to take life too seriously. I suppose I have determined that, if you have no control over something, endeavour to influence change but don't kill yourself doing it. This book was spawned through my manuscript and the need for the Long Tan story to be told by those who commanded the troops in the battle. This has now been done. At last those who were on the ground, in the rubber, wet, miserable and terrified of being killed or wounded, have completed the true story. I take immense satisfaction knowing that in a small way I played a part in the most significant battle in which Australians were to be involved in Vietnam. I have encouraged others like myself to tell their story in what is now possibly a unique book. A look at military history, a battle, written by the commanders in the battle.

The future from here is semi-planned by Bev and myself. Our children are now adults and we are extremely proud of them and their chosen partners. On 22 November 2002 Tracey and Scott brought into this world Liam, a brother to Daniel, born on 5 March 2001. Robert and Alana had moved to Sydney the same year and Georgia was born on 12 November 2001. We are all a family in the true sense of the word and should I depart this life sooner than expected I could not have asked for more. I have taken my opportunities and made the most of the roll of the dice in the game of life. I am proud to have known and served with many fine Australians during my time in uniform, especially those in Delta Company, 6RAR during the period covered by this story.

Late 1999 Bev and I sold up in Brisbane and purchased a home on the Sunshine Coast of Queensland, 100 kilometres north of Brisbane City. Here we intend to stay and enjoy the years left after an eventful, fruitful and happy life together. Having completed my personal contribution to the manuscript about my involvement with this unique battle story there is little I have not accomplished. It is time to find new horizons or travel again some of the old roads looking at the changes.

I completed the twelve-month tour and returned to Australia, a dozen of us remaining from the original 12 Platoon I'd taken to Vietnam. To ensure the military experience was not wasted, I joined the CMF and spent a further four years as a platoon commander with 17RNSWR. In the process, I qualified for captain, but business forced my relocation and I never got to wear the rank.

I returned to my reserved occupation in the advertising industry and found that my platoon leadership and management experience held me in good standing in civilian life: I quickly advanced to team and then department managing positions.

Changing from retail advertising to newspaper advertising, I again advanced through the ranks and was managing a small weekly newspaper in Wollongong in the early 1970s.

In a total lifestyle change, I then became a professional puppeteer, learning the ropes ('strings?') for two years and then setting up a marionette theatre with my schoolteacher wife, Sue. We toured NSW with two marionette productions and two small children until the children needed to go to school, after which we settled down again to 'normal' jobs, both in the computer industry.

Divorce after twelve years of marriage forced a change in location but not occupation and I moved to Queensland with the children and worked for a time in Brisbane. After a year, Sue remarried and with no immediate prospect of marriage for me, I returned the kids to a stable, two-parent environment and moved on, this time to Melbourne.

Advancing within the computer industry I found that computer projects utilise all the same leadership and management principles as commanding a platoon, without (usually) the live ammunition. I was soon a team leader and shortly after that a project manager.

Eight years after the divorce, I remarried. Di and I live in Mt Eliza, Victoria. Di runs a travel agency and I am wafting gently into semi-retirement, but still managing mainframe computer projects, mainly on Tandems and mainly in the finance industry.

The two children from my first marriage are both settled in NSW. Four grandchildren will, I hope, ensure a full and active life after retirement.

When I reflect on whether I would do it all again, I think I certainly would. I believe now as I did then that the citizens of a nation are responsible to and for their nation. Those not prepared to defend the nation (its freedoms as well as its territory) are doomed to lose what they can't or won't defend. National Service was flawed in many ways, but it was a step in the direction of making the citizens understand that there are responsibilities to and for the nation beyond taxation.

I attribute any business successes in my life to the officer training I received at 1 OTU, Scheyville. It taught me the value of self-discipline, the essence of leadership and man-management. Such diverse concepts as situation analysis, giving and taking orders, being responsible for things, accepting authority oneself and respecting it in others stood me in good stead. It was also at 1OTU that I first challenged my own concepts of how long, how far, how difficult. I subsequently understood the applicability of military 'do or die' decisions into the civilian arena. I attribute any shortcomings to myself only.

If I consider my priorities today they are my home and my family life. The titles I enjoy and respect most are brother, husband, father and grandfather. To me, these and health beat the hell out of any other status, influence, titles or assets.

While I was in Vietnam, my wife and three sons aged eleven, seven and four were moved by the army from Hamilton to an army house in Papakura Camp, to where I returned. For my first few months back in New Zealand I was posted as second-in-command of 16 Field Regiment, after which my substantive appointment was on the HQ of 1st Infantry Brigade Group as DAA&QMG (senior administrative staff officer).

In my opinion, my experience in Vietnam made me a better officer. I was more self-confident and had a better understanding of the military and the needs of soldiers in combat. As a result, I really enjoyed my brigade appointment, especially during exercises where we deployed three battalions and all the supporting arms and services. During that period I was fortunate to participate in an exercise in Singapore and northern Malaya for a few months to practise cooperation between British, Australian, Singaporean, Malay and New Zealand units. My role was generally to ensure that the administrative services were operating effectively.

At the end of 1970 I was asked whether I would like a fairly 'tough' job as defence liaison officer in Melbourne for four years. I was to be accompanied by my wife and family and we did not need to consider that offer for very long. The New Zealand High Commission, including the head of the New Zealand Defence Staff, was in Canberra and until I was posted, New Zealand Air Force officers had filled the Melbourne position. As I was the first army officer to be appointed it was necessary for me to attend briefings at

Defence HQ, Wellington, before I took up the appointment.

I was to be responsible directly to Wellington for the location, ordering and delivery of material and services required by the NZ Navy, Army and Air Force from Australia. Purchases covered a wide range of commercial and military items and included orders for the overhaul and repair of major items such as aircraft engines. My duties also involved the exchange of information with Australian services and the administration of uniformed and civilian members of the NZ Defence Department in Victoria plus, occasionally, in other States. My appointment as a diplomat in Australia, where I had carried out my officer training and had met my wife, was very satisfying. It meant that I spent eight years living and working in Australia while I was in the NZ Army.

During the Melbourne posting I had to make a decision about my future service. The choice was between a posting to Wellington or to Auckland and then retirement. We chose the latter and I was appointed to HQ Field Force for the last year of my service until my 45th birthday in 1976. I decided to retire because I expected there would be better prospects for another career while still relatively young. Even so, many people in this situation experience a period of concern about what they are going to do and what sort of a job they would like or could obtain. The first job I applied for in Auckland was in the education area. I duly attended for an interview by a board and having been asked what I considered to be a stupid question, advised the receptionist later that I was withdrawing my application. A poor start indeed.

My wife noticed an advertisement in the daily paper of a vacancy in a major hospital. What the hell could I do in a hospital? Well, after inquiring, I found that hospital systems were similar to those in the military, and consequently I applied for the job as an administrative officer. The manager and two other senior people comprised the interview panel and after some introductory chat, I was asked whether I smoked. I thought this was a trick question, but even so I said, 'Yes I do, thank you.' Well, imagine my relief when a member of the panel offered me one and we lit up. I felt quite comfortable with those people and the feeling must have been mutual because I got the job. That appointment was very enjoyable and set me on the path of hospital administration.

After nearly three years in the hospital, I was appointed to the Personnel Department in the head office of the Hospital Board, which at that time employed about 13,000 staff. Later, I was promoted to other positions, including personnel manager, and I specialised in organising appointments to senior positions and to medical posts. I continued to work in the health service for nearly sixteen years until 1992, when I retired. I still have an association with the service through my appointment as a director of an association that offers medical insurance for health workers.

I meet many returned servicemen and when they or anybody else express interest in the Vietnam War, I do not withhold my views or avoid discussion, and I will never be ashamed or embarrassed at having served. My parent unit and the one to which I was attached served with distinction. 161 Battery RNZA was awarded the United States Meritorious Unit Commendation and the Vietnam Cross of Gallantry with Palm Unit Citation. Delta Company, 6RAR and my FO Team were awarded the most prestigious United States Presidential Unit Citation for extraordinary heroism.

In 1986 I attended the Special Commemorative Parade at Enoggera that marked the twentieth anniversary of the battle. Before I travelled to Brisbane, I had thought deeply about my Delta Company flag and where it would be best placed for the years to come. There was no doubt in my mind that it should return to Australia and I was pleased to present it to the OC 6RAR for preservation and permanent display in the unit museum.

Of all my military experiences, therefore, the one that will always be uppermost in my mind is when I was the artillery forward observer with Delta Company, 6RAR at the Battle of Long Tan, 18 August 1966.

After my year in Vietnam I was posted to Armoured Centre as a tactics instructor, which was a marvellous experience, but regrettably cut short by a posting as adjutant to 1st Armoured Regiment; a very demanding position since a tank squadron was warned for service in Vietnam shortly after I arrived.

In 1969 I was lucky to be posted as an adjutant to 10 Light Horse in Western Australia which, while not a great career move after 1st Armoured Regiment, allowed me my only home posting in 26 years. I was very happy to bring training ideas into the regiment in which I'd been a trooper.

In 1970 and early 1971 I went on an extensive series of courses to fit me for service in AATTV. 1971 saw me in Vietnam serving with 1 ARVN Armoured Brigade on operations in I Corps, literally from Danang to the Demilitarised Zone. I had eight months in this area until, with the so-called Vietnamisation, Australian advisers were withdrawn from I Corps. In December 1971, I joined US Special Forces on the FANK project to train an instant army for Cambodia in South Vietnam. This brought me back to Phuoc Tuy after the 1ATF had departed and I saw at first hand the inevitable way the NVA and VC were taking back the country, a reality I had already begun to see in I Corps. The waste of human life, effort and resources appalled me. If ever I had a field marshal's baton in my pack, it fell out then.

On my return to Australia I had three wonderful years as an instructor and senior instructor at OCS Portsea. The curriculum for cadets had become impossibly packed with subjects. Their study was far beyond the time available to cadets, yet the curriculum really represented the minimum knowledge needed by a young officer to survive in modern warfare.

I also became aware of the limitations of training staff who are constrained by prescribed solutions to tactical or leadership problems, which were usually contained in staff notes (pinks). Such solutions represent conventional wisdom and too often deter lateral thinking. They are easy options and make for lazy training methods and staff; more importantly, they are 'walls' against new thought.

I encountered this problem in every training school I attended in the army including UK Staff College. The only exception was the German Army's encouragement of thinking in its tactical training, which I encountered during a visit to the German Armoured School in 1983.

At OCS I became aware of the conservative tendency to stick to what we had experienced despite its irrelevance, so that Vietnam situations were being played out on the open range area of Puckapunyal despite the differences in observation and engagement ranges plus the fact that the war was over. Some years later, while a tank squadron commander at Puckapunyal, I saw RMC cadets being debussed from APCs 1000 metres short of their attack objective and then moving on foot to attack the position. I asked their staff why. The answer was that the APCs were out of enemy RPG range. No one seemed to care that these now dismounted officer aspirants had been placed in the area of the best range for enemy MG fire to kill them. The point of APCs and the reality of terrain had been completely overlooked, largely because the Vietnam experience was being applied without thought. One can only hope that those RMC cadets reflected on their experience.

Much as my family and I enjoyed the posting I should have gone to 2 Cavalry Regiment at the end of my second year but I felt I was contributing to the army at OCS.

I was lucky enough to be selected to attend the UK Staff

College. At Royal Military College, Shriveham, I almost learned to spell 'science' and at Camberley, I maintained a delicate balance between tourism and study. The highlight of my year was probably set designs and graphics for the pantomime, plus the battlefield tour of the Normandy landings. I felt Brits were on a different journey and my Australian identity became important to me.

In 1977 I had my first taste of life in Army Office serving in the Office of the Chief of General Staff, then returned to the 1st Armoured Regiment as a squadron commander for a year, then a year as regimental second-in-command. My advice to young officers is never become a second-in-command. I thoroughly enjoyed my time as squadron commander and I tried very hard to teach my men to think on their feet.

Vietnam had taught me the danger of calcified, carefully choreographed tactics that seek to endorse the status quo. Hence, the real need to exercise in such a way that the technology at hand is fully exploited. Also, commanders are exposed to the unexpected and must be able to seize the tactical initiative. Finally, the need to tolerate high levels of ambiguity. These were lessons I tried to incorporate into my tank squadron's training.

I returned to Army Office for a year in Operations Branch in 1979, writing operational requirement documents. Sadly much of the effort was wasted for the Waler dream to build our own armoured vehicles foundered. Promoted to lieutenant colonel in 1980 I had two interesting years in Materiel Branch looking after armoured vehicle matters.

In 1982 I became CO/CI of Armoured Centre, which was a significant posting. The politics of life in the army now became more demanding and my tendency to care more about those under my command than those in command of me proved a weakness. Still, it was a period when the new Armoured Centre building began and a marvellous school was created. Separation from my family to facilitate my children's education, as in 1978–79, proved an erosive and stressful experience that came to an end when I returned to Army

Office. Sadly for me, I found myself back in the office of the CGS initially as an SO1 then on promotion to colonel in 1984 as Director of Army Information and briefly Director of Coordination, before returning to Materiel Branch as Director of Equipment Management Planning. At this point I had decided life in the Army Office 'curia' was not for me as we desperately tried to make a dwindling budget buy the army's wish list. I found little comfort in the conservative closed world that so valued conformity; in any event, I was aware my health was beginning to decline.

Accordingly, I resigned in January 1988 and in a burst of idealism returned to teaching only to find that my memories of teaching in 1962 were unreal. Nevertheless, until ill health forced my retirement in 1996, teaching young men gave me a real sense of achievement. There is something nice about meeting young men whom you have taught either in the army or more recently at school and hearing of their achievements in life. Looking back that would be the most rewarding part of my working life, whether army or civilian. Somehow the values that we aspired to as cadets at OCS seem to have disappeared over the years, victims of ambition and the struggle for achievement, which in the ultimate end is pointless; death doesn't care whether you were a colonel or a private. When I was a young officer, a senior officer told me that I was 'too altruistic'—gradually altruism gave way to cynicism. Now as I sink beneath the waves of anonymity I take comfort that teaching gave me back some level of the altruism I had lost.

I am not a pacifist. I realise that war will always have a place in human activities. But, when I reflect on the ultimate futility that was Vietnam, I can only hope that the leadership of the day thinks with rigour and has morality in mind before committing its youth to such folly in the future.

I now live in quiet retirement.

After returning from Vietnam I returned to 9 Squadron in Canberra and did routine army training missions for a few weeks before being sent to Sale to do a flying instructor's course. Towards the end of the course there was concern that I would not conform to the rigid training schedules outlined in the manuals, as I often used different procedures to teach the various skills. As I would not promise that I would 'toe the line' I was suspended. My comment at that stage was, 'I was a teacher not a robot.'

My subsequent posting was to the Transport Support Flight in Butterworth, Malaysia. The Director of Postings, my old rugby coach from the academy, was doing a refresher course at Sale before heading off to Butterworth (where he disappeared one night flying a Mirage) and organised my 'second prize'. In Malaya we did supply dropping to mountain villages and delivered cargo and personnel to the various locations that the Australian fighter squadrons operated from in Thailand, Singapore and Malaysia. We also transported the various VIPs who visited South-East Asia on their tours and provided the transport support for all the region's Australian ambassadors as they carried out their duties. This was a great opportunity to see South-East Asia in depth. Strangely, we flew back into Vietnam on diplomatic missions, flying the ambassador to visit places where Australia had spent aid money, seemingly with a special permit that said we were not in the war and should not be shot down.

I returned to Australia to take up a post as a flight commander at the RAAF Academy, Point Cook in January 1970. My main role was administrative; however, I completed my Bachelor of Science during the next three years in this position. I found working with the cadets pastorally, educationally and in sport very enjoyable and fulfilling. In contrast, I found the bureaucratic ways of the service frustrating and the lack of control over my own life's direction unacceptable. As a consequence I decided to resign and seek other employment. This took effect sixteen years after I had joined on 22 January 1973. (Just before Gough Whitlam made it attractive to serve twenty years.)

I considered commercial airlines, but felt it was bus driving, and you were away too much. I spoke to ex-air force friends in helicopters, but again felt the time away from home was not what I wanted or flying to oilrigs uninteresting. I was offered a job with IBM as a computer consultant to government departments, but another ex-RAAF friend in the company identified this job as selling your soul to IBM, which was not attractive. So I took the lowest-paying job of teaching mathematics at a private school in Melbourne, Carey Baptist Grammar School. Here I started my life working with young people—often as exciting and dangerous as Vietnam.

However, I continued to move around. After building a new home in the Melbourne suburb of Bullen, I sold up after a year and moved into the Dandenong Ranges as we did not like the pressure and insecurity of the suburbs. We lived in a caravan on four hectares while we built ourselves a log cabin home. We created the 'self-sufficient' farm, a misnomer of course, and enjoyed the lifestyle immensely, despite driving eighty kilometres to work each day. I left Carey after five years and went to work at the Armidale School, NSW, so we could have a bigger 'hobby farm'. This 50-hectare property still did not prove to be enough and we bought 1000 hectares after two years. I had become the OC of the University of New England Company, Army Reserve during this time, allowing me to see things from the other side! I also commenced a Master of Educational Administration, which I completed many years later.

I resigned from teaching and became chief pilot of Armidale Air Charter in conjunction with developing our new property into a significant Angora goat stud. We were back to living in a caravan, but this was one of the most enjoyable places in which we had chosen to live. After a few months, the onset of a drought caused a severe reduction in flying and I took a position as deputy principal of Longreach Pastoral College, rather than go broke. We attempted to operate our property, with some help, from 1,600 kilometres away. After two years we recognised that this wasn't working so I took a job teaching mathematics at Brisbane Girls Grammar School. We sold the property in New England and bought a house in the suburbs and a shop in Brisbane called 'Just Lace' for Jan to operate.

During this year I accepted the role of principal of St Barnabas' School, Ravenshoe, in Far North Queensland, which uprooted the family once again. At this stage Brett, my eldest son, had been shipped off to the army to become a driver in artillery, upholding his grandfather's tradition. This boarding school was a farm and catered for unsettled children, including a 50 per cent indigenous population. I remained there for six years. Unfortunately, the diocese chose to close this school in a financial restructure. I had one year in Cairns at Trinity Anglican School before accepting the principal's job at Slade School, Warwick in South-Eastern Queensland. The girls, Cathy and Jodie, had by now gone to university and Cathy had a job teaching with the Education Department. I established this struggling school as an 'alternative' to traditional schooling and managed its transition from a boarding school predominantly for indigenous students, to a school strongly supported by local students. I remained for the next seven years and during this time completed a Doctor of Education on children's experience of learning.

Following its closure in December 1997, once again for economic rationalist reasons, I went to the USA and worked with Professor Christine Johnston on a 'Let Me Learn' program. I had met her in Greece while I was on a sabbatical trip visiting educational institutions around the world. I was sponsored by the Association of Independent Schools of

Queensland and worked with teachers in their schools for the rest of 1998.

I worked in support of Professor Johnston in the USA from Australia for the next two years, travelling to participate in teacher training institutes on three occasions. I also did short-term teaching contracts during this time. In 2000, she was successful in obtaining support to establish a centre for the Advancement of Learning at Rowan University in New Jersey. I was appointed to the position of researcher in the schooling side of the work carried out by this centre. I worked in schools and pre-schools, assisting teachers to gain the skills to focus on the diversity of learners in the classroom. I also taught post-graduate classes in curriculum development. I was in the USA on September 11, 2001 and experienced a nation moving to a war footing as it prepared for further terrorist attacks. This was not a pleasant experience and highlighted the separation that we felt from Australia. When we visited home for Christmas 2001, we decided that Jan would stay at home and I would terminate my contract at the end of June 2002.

I have started to write more; in particular, I am writing about the conflict between the demands of set schooling curriculums and the diversity of learning needs of the children in classrooms. This, I believe, is the root cause of much of the inequity in outcomes that is apparent in children as they leave school. I am hoping that, once again, I can make a difference to the aspirations of those with whom I am working.

CHAPTER EIGHT
THE OTHER BATTLES OF
LONG TAN

The Battle of Long Tan is a significant part of Australian military history. Like so many events of this time, it has a series of other stories associated with it. Accountability has become a modern catchcry and investigative reporting has dug deep into the decisions associated with many issues of our time. Reflection allows us to question why many things happened, while freedom of information provides access to secret decisions of the time. But some of this investigation by third parties has allowed myths and fallacies to distort what really happened at Long Tan.

This section of the book seeks to set the record straight. It attempts to refute misconceived assertions that the Battle of Long Tan was the result of an enemy ambush; it examines the nature and extent of intelligence available to the Task Force prior to the battle; it reveals how shabbily Long Tan participants were treated with respect to awards and decorations; it analyses the relationship between air force and army; it reflects upon the limited use of armour and the role that could have been played by US artillery; and asks why 18 August has not been maintained as the day of remembrance for the Battle of Long Tan and its veterans.

When the initial hype about Long Tan faded a little, I started to hear stories about all the evidence that was available before the battle to show there was a large VC force out there. I have no doubt other authors might dwell on the finer detail, but suffice to say I became aware of a range of intelligence information that should have cautioned the use of a company only on Operation Vendetta. These included the signals intelligence that had tracked a VC 5 Division radio to the Long Tan area and radio interference that had been passed off lightly. There were reports of large groups of VC passed off as unreliable or misconstrued as being caused by our own movements. The mortaring and the Main Force 75 mm artillery fire on the Task Force were obviously not just undertaken by D445 alone. In later years, especially when a video presentation was made at the Australian War Memorial in 1996 by Bob Buick, Morrie Stanley, Bob Grandin and Dave Sabben, I heard of all the intelligence that was held by HQ 1ATF before Long Tan. But, for reasons of secrecy or incompetence, this information was never assessed correctly and passed down the line, resulting in Delta Company going out to face an NVA-reinforced VC Main Force regiment.

A summary of this intelligence was provided in *Duty First*, *January 1970*, by Lieutenant Colonel R.R. Hannigan. Prior to the operation there had been low-grade reports and other indications of enemy activity in the area of Xa Long Tan YS4865 and Nui Dat YS4868. The main events were:

1   8 August: A police agent reported that 300 VC dressed in greens, with crew-served weapons, were in the vicinity of YS487687 on 1 August. (On 1 August Delta Company, 6RAR had patrolled within 200 metres of this grid reference and it was thought that the report could have been referring to our troops.)
2   11 August: An aircraft reported sighting approximately 150 civilians moving south from Xa Long Tan.
3   11 August: An agent reported a VC battalion at YS485670

and a VC company at each YS490650 and YS488625. (Reports of VC battalions at various locations were quite common at this time.)

4 11 August: A 6RAR patrol made contact with a VC section at YS4767.

5 12 August: A VC company was reported moving south from YS4767.

6 13 August: A Sioux (H13) aircraft flying over Xa Long Tan received radio interference. The glide path indicator in the aircraft indicated that the transmissions were emanating from the southern base of the Nui Dat feature.

7 17 August: From 0243hrs to 0305hrs the enemy shelled and mortared 1ATF base area. Suppression and interdiction missions were fired between 0250hrs and 0410hrs.

With the exception of the enemy mortar and artillery attack on 17 August there was little in these events that differed significantly from previous indications of enemy activity in this or other parts of the Task Force area of operations. 6RAR patrol activity in the area north, south, and east of Nui Dat feature YS4868 disclosed no unusual activity. There were, however, other indications of increasing enemy interest further to the east, which resulted in attention being directed towards this area. The area east of Long Tan was believed to be one of the base areas of the VC Provincial Mobile Battalion D445. It was in this area, bounded by the 65 and 59 northings and the 49 and 54 eastings, that 6RAR had fought an estimated two companies of D445 during Operation Hobart, between 24 and 29 July 1966.

Highly classified intelligence from the 547 Signal Troop at Nui Dat has only recently become available. The following is drawn from the Royal Australian Corps of Signals publication, Chapter 5, 'Specialist Signals'. During their time in Vietnam, the intelligence received from 547 was only passed to the commander and operations officer. Two weeks before the Battle of Long Tan, 547 identified the radio call sign of 275 Main Force Regiment, a fresh unit in Phuoc Tuy Province and under the control of HQ 5 Division. On the day of the battle they fixed the location of 275's transmitter near Nui Dat 2, just north of the Long Tan rubber plantation. From the initial location a couple of kilometres north of Xuyen Moc the transmitter was tracked moving in steady deliberate stages, as though moving tactically, taking sixteen days to cover the seventeen kilometres to the area of Nui Dat 2. The analysis of this information by the Troop OC, Captain Trevor Richards, was that something significant was in the offing. However, this information appeared to become lost in the reams of intelligence information received at Task Force Headquarters, and was not passed on to battalions due to its classified nature.

The following quote is most significant. 'At 1700 hours as the besieged D Company were requesting a desperate resupply of ammunition by helicopter, another significant event occurred. The Commander, at last, called the OC of 547 Signal Troop to his side and asked for his analysis of the enemy attacking D Company.'

One wonders if this briefing was the cause of the commander's reluctance to release the Alpha Company relief force. However, it paints the picture of a serious oversight of the value of this Troop's intelligence-gathering capacity, something that changed from that day forward.

Rumours and accusations that SAS patrols knew, or should have known of the VC 5th Division move into Long Phuoc were common in 1966–67, but in 1999 there was no indication in my research in Canberra that the SAS knew anything of note. To my knowledge, the only patrol out east at the time was that led by Sergeant A.G. Urquhart. His patrol report (Ops 34/66) was located at the AWM in May 1999 by former SAS Trooper Greg Pullin. It showed the four-man patrol was located some 11,000 metres to the north-east of Long Tan from 17 to 19 August and saw no movement of large groups of VC towards the south-west. I also spoke to former SAS officer Peter Schumann, who had commanded a patrol that returned on 16 August. He confirmed that the former squadron commander, the late Colonel John Murphy MC, had discussed the subject widely in earlier years and concluded the SAS did not have any knowledge of the VC build-up near Long Tan.

Too often at this time (1966) intelligence was regarded with a low level of respect, as contacts had been minimal despite many stories of the presence of the enemy. While the engagement at Long Tan changed the leadership's attitude to planning and support of future patrols, there is still this burning question: how could so many staff officers overlook the evidence and risk so many lives?

WAS THE BATTLE OF LONG TAN A PLANNED VC AMBUSH OR DID THE VC INTEND TO ATTACK THE AUSTRALIAN BASE AT NUI DAT?
—DAVE SABBEN

It is never possible to revise 'history' to everyone's satisfaction. On one extreme, the 'facts' cherished by the majority are examined, found to be in error, and an attempt is made to rectify those errors. On the other extreme, the 'facts' cherished by the majority are, in fact, accurate, and an attempt is made to falsify the records. Most attempts at revising history probably fall somewhere between these two extremes, with facts missing or unclear, experts in dispute, motives and decision processes misunderstood and so on.

Whichever way it happens, somewhere along the path, someone's long-held beliefs are going to be overturned. Nobody wants to be shown they've been wrong. Those guided by intellect and logic may reconsider the proposed revision, examine the new evidence, re-examine the old evidence and decide whether to accept or reject the revision on the basis of their evaluation. Most, unfortunately, guided by ego, vested interests, or for whatever other reason, would reject the attack on their current beliefs regardless of the merit of the attack and would cling to their previous beliefs regardless of their accuracy. Mostly, the victor writes 'history'. Those who know better—those of the 'silent majority'—either know the truth, so don't believe it really matters, or don't care enough to be the voice of dissent. They do not want to challenge the status quo and draw attention to themselves by disputing the perceived authority on the matter at hand.

Such a case is the Battle Of Long Tan, fought by 105 Australian and three New Zealand soldiers, well supported by ANZAC and US artillery and a couple of RAAF helicopters, one monsoon-drenched afternoon in August 1966, in South Vietnam.

Those who were there on the day, those in support, those who had a hand in the events or their aftermath, their families and friends, even the extended armed forces at large, all 'knew' what happened. We all 'knew' that everyone else 'knew', so there wasn't any need or desire to write it all down in detail. After all, how could anyone *not* 'know'? It was all just common and accepted knowledge. The facts were simply so obvious. How could it ever be that a lie could be substituted and accepted by others who weren't there?

How could anyone take seriously the VC claims that we so lightly laughed off? Their claim that they'd ambushed us and enjoyed a major victory. How they'd had very few casualties and killed a whole Australian battalion. We laughed it off because it was so ridiculous. We looked around the battlefield as we buried some 250 VC bodies and laughed at their claims of 30 casualties. We laughed, along with the rest of the 'wiped out' battalion in the Task Force base, for the rest of the tour of duty. We laughed at their claims of success as we built up and further developed the Task Force base right in the middle of their 'home' territory and which they never thereafter challenged or attempted to attack. We laughed at their claims of success when ANZAC forces searched the province for several years and heard of them only when they tried to target the civilian population or attack some remote and obscure ARVN outpost.

From 1966 to 1972, we all 'knew' what had happened. Then the Australians left Vietnam. The 'war' was over. The VC (well, the NVA, actually!) were the 'victors'. In time, they wrote their 'history'. It was written in the late 1970s and the early 1980s.

It was shortly after this (in the mid-1980s) that two Australian academics (supposedly independently) took the VC

DANGER CLOSE

view and were determined to produce their own versions of the battle. Research on a video production prompted the writing of a book on the same subject and sure enough, a video documentary and a book were produced in 1986. Both took the VC view of the battle! Both stressed the alleged 'ambush' nature of the event. Both presented substantially the same sources and references, and both omitted many of the sources and references that could have been used to disprove their 'ambush' assessments. Unfortunately for them, both included enough of the accurate information that their own products (the video and the book) could be used to disprove their own cases! And this is precisely what has been achieved in a three-hour presentation made to the Australian War Memorial on 1 November 1996.

It was common knowledge after August 1966 that the VC had been foiled in their plans to mount a regimental-sized assault on the Australian Task Force base at Nui Dat. Their plans were foiled by the accidental meeting with D Company, 6 Battalion. The VC were in the area of the Task Force base before a planned assault. That this meeting was accidental has been questioned, but not from an 'ambush' perspective. Many believe that the Task Force commander was (or at least should have been) aware of the general VC plans and therefore be expecting a large VC troop movement towards the base sometime in the near future.

Whatever the circumstances, the fact is that the company patrolling away from the base met at least a part of the VC force. The meeting was unexpected by either side. The VC thought they had clear access to their assault start line and the Australian company was patrolling with orders to search out a VC mortar team of less than platoon strength and was following tracks by then 36 hours old.

All the evidence presented to the War Memorial came from sources already published—no new evidence was presented. Much of the strongest argument came from the video and book previously mentioned. But other books on the subject were referred to, including the War Memorial's own Official History, *To Long Tan*. The findings were, basically, that the VC had a need to attack the base and they had the strength to do so. Their actions and dispositions before and during the battle indicate they were prepared for a different kind of engagement. The aftermath supports the view that they'd been critically defeated on the day. The only thing missing from the whole argument is the actual assault plan, and the VC would never release this.

Why? Because the VC propaganda machine was forced to twist the facts to suit the events:

- The battle occurred at Long Tan, so couldn't be acknowledged to be an assault on the Nui Dat base (five kilometres away) that failed.
- The battle occurred under the ANZAC artillery umbrella, so had to be justified as being planned, rather than a VC mistake.
- The battle caused hundreds of VC casualties, so again had to be seen to be the result of a VC plan, rather than by having been caught and out-fought by the Australians.

So, without the real VC/NVA plan, we will make do with what I believe to be a reasonable approximation of it. What follows is an 'insider's attempt' at producing the sort of plan that the VC commanders could have been working to in late July and early August 1966 in effecting their assault on the Australian base.

Background
Since the arrival of the Australian and New Zealand forces and the establishment of their base at Nui Dat in May, their presence had disrupted the VC lines of supply and the VC influence in the hamlet of Hoa Long. The VC had suffered a number of casualties from the US attacks on the villages of Long Tan and Long Phuoc during the preparations for the Australian arrival. Since their arrival, the Australian patrols and ambushes had inflicted more casualties on the VC infrastructure and had limited the movement of VC forces around the province. Several VC supply stores and installations had been discovered and removed. The VC were losing influence with the provincial population.

It was essential to the VC that they did not lose the initiative. This would happen if the Australians were permitted to remain. They had to stop this decline of control. They had to win the important political war. They had to attack the Australians in their base.

Australian/NZ/US forces at the base

The 1st Australian Task Force (1ATF) comprised two battalions of infantry, supported by eighteen 105 mm artillery pieces, six 155 mm artillery pieces, about 30 APCs, a company of engineers and the usual administrative supporting services. In all, there were about 2,500 troops in the base—not all of these were combat troops. Their helicopter support was based in Vung Tau, so was not available to the base outside of daylight hours.

Artillery

The artillery was concentrated at the south of the base, with thin wire defences and no minefields. Their forward defensive lines were not adequately dug in and the artillery units themselves had to look to the manning of their own forward lines, even when a fire mission was in progress. This meant that when the gunners were manning the guns, their own forward defensive lines were very lightly manned.

The six US 155 mm mobile guns were tank-like artillery pieces that also looked to their own defences. They were not dug in, but rather, were parked within light screening bays and, again, had a very light wire fence around the position, and no minefields.

APCs

The APCs were on the western perimeter. Again, their defences were limited and they were not dug in. These units were not normally required to do perimeter defence, but rather formed internal reserve positions. An infantry platoon manned the APC forward lines each night, stretched thinly to cover an area that really required a company to defend.

Infantry

The infantry units were very thin on the ground. One battalion was often out of the base on an operation, but even when this was not the case, the hectic patrolling and ambushing schedule ensured that some

50 per cent of the infantry forces were outside the base at any given time. Each company of both battalions occupied a perimeter position—there were no depth positions. Each company front was actually never defended by more than a single platoon. With some 3,000 metres of front protected by just eight platoons of usually less than 30 men each, this represented less than one man per ten metres of front.

As with the other units, there were few defensive works. The wire fence was anything from one to three metres deep, there were no mine-fields, the weapon pits were for the most part open and without linking trenches and behind the thin front line of weapon pits there were no defensive works at all.

Other units and reinforcements in the base

There was an engineer squadron on the perimeter, to the south of the base, between the artillery and infantry forward lines. There was a small detachment of SAS troops in depth, without perimeter respon-sibilities, and a small reinforcement unit likewise. The rest of those on the base were non-combat and headquarter units.

Relief forces available from outside the base

The forces most likely to come to the aid of the base if under threat or attack were the 173rd Airborne Brigade and the US 11th Cavalry Regiment.

The 173rd Airborne was based at Bien Hoa, about half an hour helicopter flying time away. If the base were attacked at, say midnight, it was not expected that this unit would be able to react until dawn—six to seven hours later.

The 11th Cavalry could move from their base twenty kilometres to the north, but there was only one route south to the Australian base and that was along Route 2. This was ideal for VC ambush activities and several French and RVN convoys had already been ambushed along this route in previous years. Their reaction time would be less than the 173rd, but they would be at much greater risk.

Other factors concerning the base

The Australians were newly arrived in the province. Their enemy had been operating over the province for up to twenty years. Most of the local,

DANGER CLOSE

district and regional (provincial) VC forces were locals who had grown up in the area. Most of the NVA had grown up in similar environments.

Most of the Australian soldiers were young, inexperienced and had never seen action before. Most of the VC and NVA regulars had had several years of war experience behind them.

Defensive stores were severely under-supplied. There were no spare machine-guns or radio sets. There was no concrete or otherwise hardened bunkers or strong points in the whole Australian base. The base was weak, undermanned and unprepared.

VC and NVA forces

The main NVA unit operating in the province was the 5th VC Division. This comprised 274 Regiment, about 2,000 strong based in the north-west of the province, 275 Regiment of 1850 based in the north-east and three regional (provincial) battalions: 860 Battalion of about 550, D445 of 600 and D440 of 800. There were several district companies and local platoons, as well as a large force of political cadre, supply and administrative units and District HQ units. In all, there were some 6,000 combat troops under the direct command of the NVA commander in the province. In addition, an NVA battalion was attached for use as a reserve element.

The divisional and regimental units were not always up to full strength in their heavy weapons holdings. But there were units of 60 mm and 82/120 mm mortars, 75/82 RCLs, 57/76 anti-tank guns, 7.62 mm HMGs and some 12.7/14.5 mm anti-aircraft machine-guns, which were suitable for use against troops and vehicles as well as aircraft.

Ammunition, hand grenade and mine supplies were never as plentiful as the VC would have liked, but also were never less than adequate. The Main Force units were well equipped, well trained and well motivated. Their base areas were well developed and their morale was consistently high.

Weather and environment

The months of June, July, August and September—the most vulnerable time for the newly established base—were monsoon months. Heavy rain usually started mid-afternoon and lasted until an hour or two before or after midnight. For VC operations, the monsoon meant cover from air observation and a reduced risk of detection during night moves due to noise and visibility limitations. Being more lightly equipped than the Australians, they were able to move faster in the wet conditions.

During these same three months, the new moon occurred in about the third week of each month, so the darkest nights would be between the 14th and the 21st.

Main objectives of an assault

1   Inflict as many casualties on the Australians and as much damage to the Australian materiel and installations as possible.

2   Capture the Australian commander and as many staff officers of the rank major and above as possible. For political impact, capture would be better than having them killed.

The general plan

275 Regiment (of three battalions) with D445 Battalion, D440 Battalion and 860 Battalion (making six battalions plus supporting units) would make a night assault on the Australian base. One of the 274 Regiment battalions would provide a diversion attack and the remainder of 274 Regiment would place an ambush on Route 2 at the north of the province in anticipation of an 11th Cavalry rescue mission.

The date was to be the night 18/19 August to take advantage of the monsoon and the new moon. H-Hour would be midnight, 18/19 August.

Two days before the assault night, VC mortar and RR units would bombard the 1ATF HQ area from the east. This action was calculated to be so provocative and intolerable as to force the 1ATF commander to send out a reaction force. The VC would leave clear indications that the bombardment group was about platoon strength to ensure the Australians would send out a whole company. The VC would leave clear trails from the bombardment sites out to the north and north-east so the Australian follow-up would be well out of the way when the assault forces closed in on the base from the Long Tan area, due east of the base. Not only would this reduce the base defenders by about 20 per cent for the VC assault; but they would be in the path of the VC as they withdrew on the morning after the attack and without support from their guns, they'd be easy prey for the with-drawing VC forces.

The main assault force would approach the base and be in position some five kilometres east of the base by noon of 18 August, in the vicinity of the village of Long Tan. There, out of directed artillery range, they would await the onset of the monsoon rain, due at about four o'clock in the afternoon. Under cover of the monsoon, they would begin their move in.

Their route would take them through the Long Tan rubber plan-tation, across the Suoi Da Bang and into the old village of Long Phuoc. There local VC guides would lead them to their assembly points between the base and Hoa Long village.

At H-Hour minus 30 minutes the diversion attack by a battalion from 274 Regiment, supported by an Anti-aircraft Machine Gun (AAMG) Battery, would be mounted. This false attack would take place on the north-west perimeter of the base, with the AAMG fire being directed onto Nui Dat itself and into the APC position. This would have the effect of the base artillery being manned and swung to face the threat in anticipation of an all-gun fire mission.

The main attack would be a multi-phased assault from the south. At H-Hour the main attack supporting fire would start and the VC would attack through the artillery perimeter. The guns would be manned by then, so the gun perimeters would be at their weakest.

The VC supporting fire would be from their heavy weapons units, which would approach the base from the west. The anti-tank guns and the RCLs would target the 155s and the APCs. The mortars would target the artillery with anti-personnel rounds to kill the defenders without damaging the artillery pieces. The HMGs would fire both direct and indirect patterns into both perimeter and depth positions.

The multi-phased assaults

There would be five assault groups. The first and second assault groups would be from D445 Battalion. Being the local provincial unit they would be best able to move through Long Phuoc village and into the attack area as well as being best able to communicate with the Hoa Long cadre. They must be the ones seen by the villagers to have attacked the Australian base and to be victorious. The rest of the

*attack would be screened from the villagers, so they would believe that
this has been a local force victory.*

The first assault group of three companies of D445 Battalion

The objective was to attack the 105 mm gun area on a one-company-wide front. The ratio of assault troops to defenders would be greater than 9:1. As well, it would be expected that these guns would be committed to firing north against the diversion attack. There was only a three-strand cattle fence for their defensive wire, no minefields and few strong points manned—all the gun crews would be with the guns.

Once the guns were taken, the first assault group would secure the flank areas of the gun position and expand outwards. The second assault group would pass through to attack the 1ATF Headquarters.

The second assault group of three companies of D445 Battalion

Its objective was to pass through the first assault group and attack the Australian Base Headquarters. There would be resistance but largely only from non-combat troops and again, the ratio would be at least 9:1. The group responsible for the capture and removal of officers would be with the lead elements of this wave to identify possible prisoners. This group would be the remaining two companies from D445 and a company attached from 5th VC Division HQ.

With the second assault group, there would be three other special task groups:

1   *A team of experienced artillerymen from 5th Division's artillery and heavy weapons units would take over the guns once the gun area was secured. They would turn the Australian guns on their own infantry in support of their own further assaults.*

2   *VC engineers would form a group that would destroy the artillery once the VC had finished with them, remove as much communications equipment as possible and secure as many vehicles as possible to carry the wounded and captured equipment.*

3   *The VC intelligence and political cadres would be pooled to form a group to identify and capture officers above the rank of major*

and to secure and remove those officers from the base area as quickly as possible. On-the-spot interrogation would reveal the location of ammo dumps, fuel stores and radio facilities etc. for destruction by the sappers.

The third assault group of two companies of D440 Battalion

Its objective was to assault the engineer unit on the east side of the guns. Resistance would be expected as these troops were trained in combat roles. The VC sapper demolition teams would destroy any plant equipment that could not be removed for VC use. The ratio for this and all other rear attacks was at least 3:1.

The fourth assault group of one battalion of 275 Regiment plus two companies of D440 Battalion

Its objective was to pass through D445 when they had secured a path through the Headquarters area. These forces would have two aims: the D440 companies would attack the occupants on Nui Dat Hill; the rest of the group would assault the infantry on the north perimeter of the base (5RAR). Both of these assaults would be from the rear on to positions known not to have wire, mines or strong point defences in depth.

The fifth assault group of two battalions of 275 Regiment

Its objective was to pass through the engineer area when that had been secured, to attack the rear elements of the infantry battalion facing east and south (6RAR). Again, these assaults would be from the rear onto positions known not to have wire, mines or strong point defences in depth.

Security and POWs

The remaining company of D440 Battalion would be allocated to POW security, vehicle and equipment collection and casualty aid post protection duties. They would follow the fifth assault group and secure the casualty aid post on Route 2 opposite the Base HQ area.

Reserves

The attached NVA battalion would be the mobile reserve, to follow the *fifth assault group and be available for reinforcements if the VC met unexpected strong points.*

Medical and casualty evacuation

All casualties would be evacuated first to Route 2, where they would receive first aid. All captured vehicles would also be taken to Route 2, for collection of wounded for evacuation up Route 2 and thence to the Nui May Tao mountains. The D440 company would coordinate.

Withdrawal

Vehicles with casualties would move north as soon as Route 2 was cleared. The local VC units, D445 and D440 Battalions, would move to Hoa Long village as soon as the 'disengage' signal was made, or at 4.30 a.m. at the latest. The villagers would know what had been happening and would be prepared to receive the victorious VC units. The villagers would see the captured Australians in VC hands and would be in the destroyed base before daylight, looting and deliberately getting in the way of relief efforts. The VC units would then scatter over the next few hours and be well clear of the area by daylight.

The heavy support weapon units with their protection and porter parties would disperse to the north-west, joining the diversion battalion as it moved to the VC sanctuary areas at the province boundaries.

The VC/NVA elements which assaulted the infantry units would exit the base heading north and east.

Summary

The attack described never took place, so it's not possible to know how close this scenario might be to the one that was planned. However, it is clear that all the elements of this theoretical attack were consistent with the circumstances known at the time:

- The above plan abides by all the VC/NVA attack doctrines of the day (assault ratios, etc.);
- The VC/NVA commander did have these troops at his disposal;
- The VC did have detailed knowledge of the base, strengths, dispositions, etc.;

- It is known that the VC had prepared to attack the base earlier, in mid-June, but at the last minute had decided to ambush an aircraft they had shot down instead;
- The descriptions of the base and its defences are accurate for mid-August 1966, including the assessments of weakness, lack of defensive stores, and so on;
- The weather and moon phase for the time are accurate;
- The base area was bombarded in the early hours of the 17th and a search company was sent out to locate the base plate position and follow up the bombardment team;
- Clear tracks were left by the normally careful VC of the bombardment team as they withdrew;
- The artillery forward lines were denuded for fire missions, rendering their defences weak;
- Elements of 275 Regiment, D445 and D440 were identified in the battle area on the 18th/19th;
- The VC at Long Tan did not have heavy weapon units in the area to fire in support;
- The VC and NVA were heavily laden with ammo and grenades, but had no claymore mines;
- There were no ambush diggings or preparations found on the battlefield;
- 274 Regiment was in an ambush position north of the base on 18/19 August;
- A VC company was protecting a crossing point on the Suoi Da Bang on 18 August;
- An AAMG did fire on helicopters from a position just 500 metres west of Route 2 opposite Nui Dat hill—exactly where the diversion battalion would have been;
- Despite attempts to call the VC casualty rates into question, they are accurate.

If the VC plan was to initiate an ambush, then we have to ask:

- Why did the VC not trigger the ambush and catch the Bravo Company patrol on the 17th or 18th?
- Why were the opening shots of the supposed VC ambush fired by the Australians?

- Why, in their supposed ambush position, were they forced to manoeuvre while the 'ambushed' Australians defended?
- Why, if it was an ambush, were only two Australians killed in the whole first fifteen minutes?
- Why were there no VC weapon pits in the 'ambush' position?
- Why were there no VC command detonated mines used or found on the whole battlefield?
- Why did the VC not ambush the APC relief column at the only point where it could cross the Suoi Da Bang?
- Why did the supposed ambush last more than three hours and only end at nightfall with the arrival of a second company on APCs, leaving the Australians undefeated?
- Why did the VC site the supposed ambush within the Australian artillery umbrella, yet not provide either fire support for their own forces or counter bombardment fire into the artillery positions during the supposed ambush?

If the 'ambush' scenario is therefore proven invalid and if the VC plan to assault the base was anything like this one, then the likelihood of success would have been more than any Australian would have wished. It is acknowledged by all sources—including both of the above-mentioned academics—that:

- the base was ill prepared and too under-manned to resist a determined assault;
- the VC had the numbers, equipment and ammunition to badly damage the base;
- the circumstances (moonless night, monsoon season, raw Australian troops, newly established base, lack of wire and mine defences, etc.) favoured a base assault rather than an ambush out in the open, within ideal artillery support range;
- there was an obvious lack of preparatory diggings, command detonated mines, etc. on the battlefield, indicating against a planned VC ambush;
- the conduct of the VC battle indicates against a planned VC ambush.

The subsequent events indicate that the VC suffered a defeat far greater than they owned up to. It must be asked:

- Why these self-styled 'authorities' persist in supporting such a discredited scenario as the possibility that the Battle of Long Tan was a planned VC ambush?
- Why, for instance, do they believe the VC and NVA would risk over 2,000 troops to ambush just 100 Australians?
- Why would the VC use two whole battalions to ambush Route 2 in anticipation of a major US Cavalry relief force when they expected to hit the Australian company, engage them for no more than an hour, annihilate them and melt back into the bush? Did they really think the Americans would react to such an insignificant event in such a massive way?
- Why would the VC ambush the Australians, who had artillery support, yet make no arrangements for artillery, RCL or heavy mortar support for themselves?
- Why, when the VC tactic under artillery fire was to close with their enemy, were the VC unable to close with their enemy, which they were supposed to have trapped in an ambush?
- Why did the VC not at least set an ambush for the local relief force that had to cross a river to get to the battlefield, and could only cross at one point on that river?
- Why would the VC set an ambush where the ambushed troops would be forced to defend against the VC probes and attacks? Wouldn't it be more likely that the ambush would have required the ambushed troops to attack the ambushing force? Yet there were no diggings prepared on the battlefield. No set mines. No prepared fire lanes!

Any reader who may be interested in the full presentation is asked to contact the Australian War Memorial.

HONOURS AND AWARDS—HARRY SMITH

There are three aspects of this issue that cause me great concern.

Firstly, I feel that the imperial honours and awards for the battle were inappropriate given the nature and scope of the action. Secondly, I am at a loss to understand why awards offered by the US and South Vietnamese Armies were not accepted.

Thirdly, given the lavish number of awards presented to Australian forces in Vietnam, I do not believe the participants in the battle were adequately recognised.

Back home the loss of so many National Servicemen in one battle became a political problem. The Australian Government decided to urgently generate awards and decorations to placate the public outcry by recognising those who had fought in the battle, especially as the US Army wanted to bestow their own awards on participants.

My surviving platoon commanders and I were caught up in the difficult process of trying to decide who should be recommended for honours. Rather than be given time to consider all eligible nominations, it had to be done with all urgency, I was told. I believe it was the night of 21 August when my field telephone rang, near midnight. The call was from Colonel Townsend, explaining to me the pressure from Canberra and requesting my citations the next day. Accordingly, as the company commander at the battle, I deliberated with my platoon commanders and CSM and submitted appropriately typed and signed citation forms to Battalion HQ. I recall a discussion with Colonel Townsend that I had too many and that there was a ration of one decoration per 150 troops per six months, and as we were just into our first six months, there might not be any left for others. One per 150 meant that my company of 109 would qualify for less than one decoration—what rubbish!

I recall arguing with Colonel Townsend that the Brits wrote the book about awards and in a decent stoush were the first to throw the book out the window. I had had a little to do with the conditions of honours and awards when I was adjutant of the Infantry Centre in 1962. I suggested that the total strength of the force in the theatre of war was the number to be used and that as the large majority of soldiers in base areas were never likely to see action, then it followed that most awards should go to the combat units. I also suggested the nature of the Long Tan battle required immediate awards and special consideration, perhaps to the point of requesting a special allocation of awards. I also remember saying that it was

Some of the members of D Company who received gifts in lieu of Vietnamese awards and decorations (Back L.-R) 2Lt Geoff Kendall, Sgt Bob Buick, Pte Geoff Peters, Cpl 'Bluey' Moore, Cpl Barry Magnussen and Pte Ian Campbell (Front L.-R) Pte Noel Grimes, Pte Allen May, Pte 'Yank' Akell, Pte Neil Bextram and Pte Bill Roche. (AWM CUN.66.0750.vn.)

difficult to try and recognise a few individuals when all my company had played a part in their survival.

After pruning some posthumous awards and a couple of decorations, suffice to say that I submitted the citation forms for what I considered the absolute minimum, expecting that all would be promptly approved. I was not told that any changes had been made to my recommendations. In fact, I heard nothing more for several months.

About a week later, a similar process of recommendations for awards offered by the South Vietnamese Government of the day became a priority. Again, citations had to be submitted in the shortest possible time. With this episode I was able to have more names mentioned than on the previous list. But the offer of Vietnamese awards became a farce and embarrassed the Vietnamese Government. We were told about an hour before the presentation parade that the Australian

Government had refused their offer of medals. At the big parade on 2 September 1966 we were presented with cigar boxes for officers, and 60-piastre (50-cent) Vietnamese dolls for the selected soldiers!

Back home, several newspapers gave a list of the original awards offered, showing Brigadier Jackson and myself with National Orders of Vietnam 5th Class, Crosses of Gallantry with Palm Leaves for Colonel Townsend, Captain Mollison and Sergeant Buick, and similar but lesser awards for various others on the list. The list included a few APC and artillery representatives, but not Lieutenant Adrian Roberts, who commanded the APCs carrying Alpha Company. The matter of the command of the relief force is also raised in citations for imperial awards where Adrian Roberts was awarded the MID (Mention-in-Despatch) but Charles Mollison was omitted. It is interesting to note Colonel Townsend's citation for the Cross of Gallantry on the Australian War Memorial list headed 'Awards to Australians for heroism at Long Tan': 'Commander of the Sixth Battalion who took personal command of the reinforcements which relieved the surrounded Company.' Yet it was Adrian Roberts who commanded the relief force, with Colonel Townsend only arriving in the rear in the last minutes of the final assault into Delta.

The Australian Government held firm to its policy that we were not able to receive foreign awards, yet only a few months later the policy was reversed; however, it was not made retrospective for my company and other recipients. In 1998, long after the 30-year secrecy period, I was still trying to get documentation to support those medals for my soldiers. I could never understand why the Government did not allow the medals to be presented for Long Tan, or at least be accepted but not worn. Not long after 1966, approval was given for US Army and South Vietnamese medals and citations to be worn by the Australian Army Training Team, but not made retrospective for the Task Force.

I have since been in contact with Charles Tran Van Lam, who was the former President of the Senate, Ambassador to Australia and Minister for Foreign Affairs of the Republic of Vietnam. In a letter dated 8 October 1999 he wrote the following:

I refer to your query regarding the Vietnam National Order awards. I would like to confirm that my former Government did intend to present Awards to some 21 Officers and Soldiers of the 1st Australian Task Force for their service and gallantry at the Battle of Long Tan at a parade held at Nui Dat on the 2nd September 1966. However, the offer was rejected by the Australian Ambassador in Saigon at the last minute on the grounds that the Queen had not given approval. Consequently, although embarrassed, our President went to Nui Dat but had to present gifts rather than the awards mooted for the officers and soldiers.

I understood the Australian Government of the day was to seek approval and make retrospective approval so that the soldiers could receive their awards as was the case in future years, and the desire of my Government.

My Government had also intended to present all the Soldiers and Officers of the Company with a unit Citation in addition to the awards for selected commanders, officers and soldiers.

While the content of this letter has been provided to the appropriate government departments and inquiries, it has not, however, been accepted as sufficient proof to change the rulings on foreign awards for the Battle of Long Tan.

It is interesting to note that individual foreign awards, as well as group citation awards were accepted in the Second World War and Korea—a precedent. And in 1998, it was also interesting to note the acceptance of individual French and Polish awards—albeit many, many years down the track. Medals were the minimum recognition for service, but maybe it was the old story—those who weren't there were jealous and blocked the awards.

During the late 1990s there were several committees

established to look into aspects of awards associated with the Vietnam War. We felt that we would be able to get a hearing at one of these. The first was the Review of Service Entitlement Anomalies in respect of South-East Asian Service 1955–1975, chaired by Major General the Hon. R.F. Mohr RFD ED RL, February 2000 (referred to as the Mohr Report). Dave Sabben, Bob Buick and I presented cases for different aspects of the Long Tan awards. Our cases were rejected as being outside his interpretation of the terms of reference. This we found difficult to understand, as Section 14 stated:

14) In extraordinary or unusual circumstances permission for the formal acceptance and wearing of foreign awards by Australians may be recommended to the Governor-General by the responsible Minister without a formal approach through diplomatic or other official channels to the foreign government concerned.

Major General Mohr told us to present our case to the three-man End of War List Committee, comprising Noel Tanzer, Major-General Peter Phillips and Clive Mitchell-Taylor. As we had made a presentation previously to this committee on behalf of the 6 soldiers that had rejected their Australian Award equivalent to the Military Medal we recognised that this would not be successful. Nevertheless, Dave Sabben, Bob Buick and I made individual representations, which were also rejected as being outside the terms of reference. In April 1999 I received a telephone call from Graham Edwards MP, a Vietnam veteran who has lost both legs in a mine explosion incident. Graham explained he had raised various anomalies relating to Awards announced in the End Of War List in 1998 and that a new Review of the List was to take place, under the chairmanship of Major General Peter Phillips (Rtd), also National President of the RSL. He suggested that I raise the matter of Imperial and South Vietnamese Awards with the Minister for Veterans' Affairs, Bruce Scott MP and ask the Committee to consider all awards for Long Tan. He was aware that my 1996 submissions to the Minister for Defence had fallen on deaf ears.

In that submission I was still fighting to get some of my original Long Tan recommendations for imperial awards recognised. Given my knowledge of the awards made during the Korean War and Malayan Emergency, I had recommended them for the only applicable decoration for their rank—for distinguished service under fire—the Military Cross (MC). I did this because my two surviving platoon commanders had led and commanded their platoons at Long Tan out away from the company area, against all odds and again in the big final defensive battle. There was no doubt in my mind then, as now, that the platoons each fought against overwhelming odds and firepower by themselves, until they joined in the company defensive position where they continued to fight off the assaulting VC waves. 12 Platoon went out into the enemy-held area to try and help 11 Platoon with only twenty soldiers and were successful in aiding 11 Platoon to withdraw. 10 Platoon also fought off a VC company before being ordered to withdraw. If it had not been for their training, their dedication, their tenacity, their team spirit and their leaders, all three platoons might not have survived and the company might have been annihilated. The APC relief force might then have been ambushed. The inexperienced young platoon commanders were recommended for awards, not just for themselves, but also for the gallant performance of their platoons. I compared their performance to those I saw in Malaya, where the MC was awarded for small patrol actions resulting in one enemy dead! There was no comparison. And what could have been a major military and political victory by the VC was turned around the other way by the platoons. I do not underestimate the effect of the artillery fire. But that was directed, in the main, by the platoon commanders in close support, advising the artillery FOO of corrections for maximum effect. While not my prerogative, I recall suggesting that both Adrian Roberts and Morrie Stanley be cited by their own commanders for the MC for their outstanding performance under fire. Further, had it not been for the encounter battle, the poorly defended Task Force base might well have been attacked with disastrous results.

The 11 Platoon commander was killed in action. Sergeant Buick took over command and his platoon was recognised by the Military Medal (MM). What the other two officer platoon commanders received in late December 1966 was the MID, which is *normally* for 'good service over a long period', or 'an act of bravery', but can be a posthumous award for heroism. And MIDs are not *normally* submitted as immediate awards. To diminish the effective value of the awards to my platoon commanders, they were on a list of recipients announced in December 1966 that included the same award for administrative services. It included MID awards to administrative officers both at the Task Force base and at ALSG, when administrative services were not well regarded. Unfortunately, at the time the catchcry around Task Force was 'punch a postie for Christmas' because of apparently slow service.

I had arguments with Colonel Townsend over this and he claimed that some 'superior' authority had downgraded my recommendations, along with rejecting some other recommendations. Two that come to mind are an MM for Corporal Moore, 11 Platoon and a posthumous award for the 11 Platoon commander, Gordon Sharp. 'Bluey' Moore died of cancer in Launceston in 1998.

The imperial award policy traditionally recommended commanders for awards on behalf of their commands and because people move on, the actual award is seen to become a personal award. Whereas in the original British system officers and senior NCOs remained with their regiments and the awards therefore remained in the regiment. Probably the USA, through the Presidential Unit Citation, made the best, and fairest, award to Delta Company later. This went to everyone in the company, plus the New Zealand artillery forward observer's party who served that day, recognising all, not just commanders at various levels. The citation is normally awarded at unit or regimental level, having been awarded twice before to Australian Army units, 3RAR, at Kapyong, Korea and the Papua and New Guinea Volunteer Rifles in the Second World War. It is rated as the highest unit award in the US system, equivalent to the US Distinguished

Service Cross. We of Delta Company all wear this citation, known colloquially as the 'Blue Swimming Pool', with honour and all those who currently serve in the company wear the award while they are so posted.

To my knowledge, this was the only time a Presidential Unit Citation was ever awarded to a sub-unit or company group. It had been awarded to a RAAF squadron at the end of the Second World War, albeit not presented to 2 Squadron RAAF until 1967 at a ceremony at Phan Rang, South Vietnam where the squadron was flying Canberra bombers.

In late 1996, after the 30-year official secrecy period, I was able to obtain what purports to be the original citation form for one of my officer platoon commanders, Dave Sabben, via the *Freedom of Information Act*. I found that my actual *original* citation form had either not been submitted by 6RAR or it was required that another be raised. In fact another form had been raised for a lesser award of MID and signed by Colonel Townsend, who was not present at the battle and there-fore did not see or really could not comment on what my platoon commanders did. Certainly it would have been appro-priate for the matter to be discussed with me rather than have me believe my recommendations had been processed, whereas Battalion and/or Task Force Headquarters, or both, had down-graded them. As can be seen from his letter below, the former personal assistant to Brigadier Jackson claims to have seen the citations for the MC for Dave Sabben, 12 Platoon, Geoff Kendall, 10 Platoon, along with one for myself, raised by Colonel Townsend. In addition, there was another raised by the commander of the APC Squadron for Adrian Roberts, who commanded the carriers at Long Tan.

In that case, Colonel Townsend did submit my original citations to Brigadier Jackson, but then something went haywire! It would be interesting to know just what discussions took place between Commander 1ATF, Commander AFV, and CO 6RAR at that time. While evidence suggests CO 6RAR initially forwarded my citations, he was obviously persuaded to change them. Then he saw fit not to pass that information on to me, the initiator. This was unusual behaviour for Colin Townsend because he was a very popular CO and while he and I had many differences of opinion as to how I trained and operated my company, I had the highest regard for him. It was only in 1996 when I discovered he had a part in the downgrading of the awards that I questioned his motives. Was he persuaded or directed by Jackson to denigrate the performance of his officers and soldiers?

The following 1999 letter is pertinent. The then HQ ATF liaison officer and personal assistant to Jackson, Lieutenant (later Major) David Harris, wrote:

Very soon after the extent of the Delta Company victory became evident the TF HQ received a request from HQ IIFFV asking us to prepare citations for U.S. Awards. This request was probably received on 20th or 21st August and was the reason for the urgency in preparing Imperial awards. No one had given much thought to awards at that stage and the IIFFV request was answered in the usual way by saying that we could not accept allied awards on an individual basis. We had received a similar request from HQ III Corps, which was answered in a similar way.

I remember the 6RAR citations arriving at TF HQ. After Jackson had read them they went to Ian Hutchinson who was doing the staff duties job at that stage. I contacted Major Bob Hagerty (OC 1 APC Sqn) and suggested that if Adrian Roberts was going to be cited then now was the time to act so he did not get left out. The four citations (yours, the platoon commanders and Adrian Roberts) were all for MCs.

I was unaware the citations did not leave HQATF until late September. I thought they went to COMAFV within days of arriving at TFHQ. I believe they definitely had a spell at HQAFV in the meantime. If the citations were held up or returned to TFHQ by COMAFV then it was under the table stuff. I was in a unique position at TFHQ in spite of my junior rank and I know that if the citations were 'in the system' then I would have known. My gut feeling in retrospect is that there was a cosy little deal done between

COMAFV, Comd 1ATF and CO 6RAR. There can be no other explanation for what happened and I remember how some of us were shocked at the outcome.

Signed David Harris (Letter to Harry Smith,
9th February 1999)

David Harris also wrote:

In the period between the citations leaving the TFHQ and the actual awards being made, I distinctly remember discussing them with other officers on the HQ and most agreed that yours should have been a DSO and the others MCs. When the actual awards were made months later we were dumbfounded when the platoon commanders and Adrian were downgraded to MIDs.

I am aware that individual awards are often difficult to recommend with fairness to all, especially when the award is the result of a team action, such as was the case with most of the awards at Long Tan. However, I also recognise from my observations over the years that awards can also be influenced by personal and command considerations. I am not sure what motives resulted in the downgrading of the awards for my platoon commanders. And many people have questioned the MC for the company commander when the appropriate award for the rank and the ferocity of the action was obviously the DSO. In fact a citation for DSO was raised by Colonel Townsend, countersigned by Brigadier Jackson, and later downgraded in Saigon by the late General Mackay (who was in Australia at the time of Long Tan attending the CGS exercise). This occurred on the same day, 5th October, he signed the recommendation for the DSO for Brigadier Jackson. But it added insult to injury when gallantry awards of the DSO for both Brigadier Jackson and Colonel Townsend were announced later on and that they both had Long Tan quoted in their citations.

In mid-1997 when we were hearing daily about rorting of government travel allowances, I could not help thinking how the medals system was rorted by those in 1ATF and AFV responsible for writing the citations for the senior officers under their command. Or did they all agree to write their own citations, as has been rumoured about decorations for the odd member of the Australian Army Training Team who served in isolated posts with US Army soldiers? While the award of DSO to Colonel Townsend may well have been warranted for his year's tour with 6RAR, his part in the Long Tan Battle should not have been misconstrued. Moreover, the conditions for the award of DSO shows it is 'normally reserved for Lieutenant Colonels and Majors' for 'conspicuous gallantry and leadership under fire'. In the case of senior officers it 'requires leadership over a period entailing gallantry'. Questions could be asked as to the qualifying service, especially for Brigadier Jackson, and how their awards were assessed and approved by general officers at Army Headquarters. There is an unmistakeable odour of RMC Club members being decorated at the expense of Delta Company's young OCS and Scheyville officers.

Dave Sabben, Bob Buick and I continued to write to the Minister, in fact Ministers as they were being regularly changed or the issue was shuffled between portfolios. The rejection of the South Vietnamese Government awards seemed to be based upon the fact that there was now no government of this name to authenticate the awards. We felt that Section 14 of the gazetted guidelines to wearing foreign medals covered this situation. The Imperial awards were not considered as they did not wish to review awards given 'in country' as distinct to those awarded from Australia. We maintained contact with Graham Edwards, who raised questions in the House of Parliament, which the government managed to brush aside, in line with their policy of avoiding the issue.

It was at this point that we received reliable information indicating that the files which would support our case, had been 'secreted' away within government departments. Additional time restrictions were applied before they could be released. In fact, we believe that the files are now held in the Department of Foreign Affairs, rather than Defence, Veterans' Affairs or the War Memorial archives, to make them less accessible. We have even been advised by National Archives that some apparently relevant files have been destroyed. All our attempts to gain access or to get an explanation for the difficulty of access have been thwarted.

In early 2004, after I had written to the Governor-General, we were told by the Hon Mal Brough MP, Minister Assisting the Minister for Defence, that he was processing a submission to both the Prime Minister and the Governor-General for the approval of the individual Vietnamese Awards announced in 1966. This approval was granted in June 2004, but the Cross of Gallantry Unit Citation on record was not approved. This was on the ground that as a unit award it was not covered in the Legislation. I will be pursuing this matter.

In August 2004 the ALP announced it would launch an Inquiry into Long Tan Imperial Awards and I have made representations to the new Minister, Ms Kelly MP, with a view to a review of all Awards in all units that were downgraded or not submitted in Vietnam. I hope that justice will be done for all.

Unfortunately, while it gives me no great pleasure to criticise senior officers' awards, some facts in their DSO citations are quite incorrect. The late Brigadier Jackson did not 'personally direct the Battle'. While my original DSO citation gave me credit for the command and control of the battle from start to finish, with Colonel Townsend not on the August list, his 1967 DSO citation indicated 'he moved out quickly, took command and fought with his battalion against a VC regiment for four days'. Colonel Townsend took over at Long Tan after the battle and not a single shot was fired in the ensuing four days. My Company Operation 'Vendetta' then became lost in the Task Force Operation 'Smithfield', which was written up as starting *before* the battle. It is a pity that General Officers in Canberra condoned all this.

RELATIONSHIP BETWEEN THE ARMY AND AIR FORCE—BOB GRANDIN

It is an unfortunate fact that inter-service rivalry manifested itself very significantly in the command and control of air power. While the

United States Army had its own aircraft, it was not policy or practical for each service to have its own 'other arms' within the Australian Defence Forces. Throughout history each service had acquitted itself honourably and worked in support of each other, but frustration remained over the issue of practical on-field control. This issue manifested itself at the Battle of Long Tan and has unfortunately continued to colour the relationships between the two services even after the transfer of some air power to the army.

From the position of one of the participants in the resupply of ammunition to Delta Company during the Battle of Long Tan, I feel it is very disappointing that this rivalry continues to cloud the issue of a critical part of the day's events. Recognition of the importance of the resupply is downplayed by all except those members of Delta Company by whom it is regarded as a life-saving event. A search of newspapers on 18 August 1996 illustrated this point. As the media portrayed the character of the events in the Battle of Long Tan, it was very difficult to find a mention of the fact that there was a resupply of ammunition by helicopter at a critical point in the time line of the battle.

These aircrews flew into the battle area knowing that it was a death-defying mission, with the odds stacked very heavily against them. They accurately delivered ammunition at a time when soldiers had expended all their rounds, or were very close to empty. These rounds enabled Delta Company to repel the concerted assaults of the enemy until the armoured personnel carriers arrived an hour later.

Why then was there a problem? What were the issues? Why has this animosity remained?

The commander of 9 Squadron, then Wing Commander Ray Scott, who was the most experienced helicopter pilot in the Royal Australian Air Force, provides some of the answers. He indicated that the helicopter is an extension of the normal fixed wing transport support and therefore the main air power principles governing the use of aircraft in transport and close air support are applicable. Unfortunately, many army officers failed to understand this simple fact and tended to regard the helicopter as a truck or artillery substitute. The basic tasks that the army nominated for the squadron were troop lifting, logistic support (lifting stores and equipment), and aero-medical evacuation. These operations were always planned as being into and out of a secure landing zone. Tasks were either within the capability of the aircraft or not and the decision on this issue always remained with the aircraft captain. It was this issue that created the first stumbling block. Higher ranking army officers believed that they could order the aircraft captain to carry out tasks that the captain believed were unsafe or a gross misuse of the aircraft. This included brigadiers. While more junior officers appeared to learn this principle quite quickly, others did not.

The fact that the squadron was based at Vung Tau, rather than at Nui Dat, also appeared to be a contentious issue. While the simple issue of the vulnerability of the aircraft was not well appreciated by those who had to expose themselves by living at Nui Dat, the operational requirements of servicing the aircraft appeared to be overlooked. There was a Task Force requirement of no lights or noise after last light, which would not allow repairs and servicing to be carried out at night so the aircraft were available again the next day. It was also impractical to locate all the logistical support required for this work on the aircraft in the Task Force area. Also, the co-location of the US Aviation facilities at Vung Tau allowed for access to some resources that would otherwise not be available. This was especially pertinent as the squadron carried out the major servicing of its aircraft, which could not be done in primitive conditions. There was also the enormous problem of storing and securing large quantities of fuel for use by a squadron of helicopters in this area. Response time from Vung Tau was only a matter of minutes, as well as the fact that aircraft were positioned at the Task Force at first light if required. But once again, the fact that they had to be requested to come appeared to displease some senior officers, who wanted them at their 'beck and call'.

The relative comfort of Villa Anna in Vung Tau, where the RAAF pilots lived, was one of practical expediency, rather than an effort to provide special conditions for the members of the squadron. Concern about this issue seemed to stem from jealousy, rather than fact.

The day of the Battle of Long Tan as recounted by Wing Commander Scott provides a view from the 'other side of the fence'.

Contrary to longstanding land/air warfare doctrine the Task Force HQ steadfastly refused RAAF participation in the planning of operations, nor did it provide the 9 Squadron Operations Room with up-to-date intelligence and situation data. Consequently, on the afternoon of the Battle of Long Tan I was unaware that 6RAR was conducting company-sized sweeps to the north-east of Nui Dat. When the usual afternoon monsoonal storms appeared, resulting in extremely poor flying conditions, I was not surprised when the Task Force HQ released the squadron from an alert status, other than the two aircraft transporting the Col Joye concert party.

About 5.00 p.m. I received a phone call from the Task Force air support officer, Group Captain Peter Raw. As the phone line was insecure Peter gave me a rather garbled message, which I interpreted as meaning that a situation had developed that required a maximum effort from the squadron as soon as possible. The maintenance staff worked wonders in rapidly readying five of the six aircraft remaining at Vung Tau. One minor problem was that, due to sickness of some crew, two of the aircraft could not be fully manned.

On approaching the Task Force LZ we were advised by radio to land and remain at the pad on stand-by until further advised. On landing we were then given our first inkling of the situation by the two crews that had carried out the ammunition resupply to Delta Company. After spending the next six hours at the pad, completely isolated from further information, Peter Raw arrived at the pad at midnight and advised that we were to pick up Delta Company casualties from a landing pad, which had been secured by

APCs. He also advised that as the enemy situation and intentions were unknown, Army would not sanction the use of landing lights on the approach to the pad, but an APC would have its lights on. I was satisfied with this as APC lights would be far superior to the primitive ground lighting normally experienced during field operations, which usually consisted of a torch, or flame from a Zippo cigarette lighter.

After a quick briefing of the aircraft crews, I got airborne shortly after a US Army dustoff helicopter, which was carrying out the initial pick-up of casualties. Visibility was very poor due to low cloud and the aftermath of the artillery barrage in the form of thick drifting acrid smoke. On locating the landing pad I noted that it was showing a bright light. However, almost immediately this was extinguished. I then realised that the US Army dustoff pilot had used his landing light, contrary to the instructions we had received.

I had great difficulty relocating the pad, as the only semblance of a light was a small red-purple glow that wavered and frequently disappeared. Slant visibility was so poor that at no stage during the approach did I sight more than one faint glow, which gave no depth perception whatsoever. Nor did I sight torchlight until I touched down on the landing pad. Following aircraft had similar problems. Whether the US dustoff pilot received the prohibition on the use of a landing light but chose to ignore it I do not know. 9 Squadron pilots were determined to avoid compromising the security of the troops on the ground. Hence, although it slowed the evacuation of the casualties, they carried out their landings and take-offs without the use of lights in extremely adverse conditions. That they were able to do so speaks volumes for their training and capabilities.

Early the next morning, the squadron evacuated the remaining dead. This was the saddest moment in my tour of Vietnam.

Folklore continues about the events of the day, perhaps as an enhancement of the fact that I was prepared to admit that my first reaction to the task was one of resistance. I do not recall others debating the issue. If Frank Riley had been alive to provide input to the many books on the issue I am sure he would have said, 'There was never any doubt in his mind and Bob was just like that, he questioned everything.' While Harry Smith is happy to say that if he had known he was going out into a conflict against overwhelming odds, he would not have gone with only one company, no one questions the integrity of his actions. Those of us who were faced with being tasked to go out on the resupply were doing so knowing about the overwhelming odds. We had to decide to go into this encounter without any of the usual support for air power, like gunship helicopters, and no possible support from ground forces. And then there were the quite horrific flying conditions. It is also possible to say that if we had been under command and directed to go that we would not have got there any sooner with the ammunition. The time line was very quick for the helicopter participation if it is compared to the time it took the relief force in APCs to be released from the Task Force Area.

However, the following account by David Harris, PA to Brigadier Jackson, may be taken as the other view.

I was in the HQ 1ATF Command Post Meeting area on the afternoon of the 18th August, then a second lieutenant as ADC to Brigadier Jackson. Those present were Jackson; Lt Col Cubis (Arty); Gp Capt Raw (RAAF); Lt Col Dick Hannigan, GSO2, and I think, Captain Trevor Richards of the Signals Intelligence Unit. The US Air Liaison Officer (ALO) was not there initially but I was sent to get him from the Air CP.

Delta Company, 6RAR had requested an urgent helicopter ammo resupply through their HQ. When we received it by phone Jackson called Raw into the CP and put the request to him. Raw refused saying that the risk to crews and aircraft from ground fire was too great. Jackson then moved from the CP into the meeting area with the others mentioned and a very heated discussion took place. I was sent to get the ALO and on return Jackson asked him how quickly he could get US Army helicopter support from Vung Tau and whether they would do the job. The ALO said it would take about twenty minutes and they would do it.

Jackson had been having trouble with the RAAF for weeks before this and would have been quite happy to forget them and rely solely on US Army Air. Air Vice Marshal Murdoch, Chief of the RAAF Air Staff, had visited us not long before 18 August with the purpose of sorting out the problems the RAAF were having with a real war. Now it was about to boil over again!

Raw recognised the serious situation he was now in. I distinctly remember him saying, 'We will do the mission if you [Jackson] will take full responsibility in writing for the consequences.' Jackson replied: 'Of course I will take full responsibility and you have plenty of witnesses to that fact'—and there was no written acceptance of responsibility from Jackson.

The following day I was talking to RSM George Chinn, who went in one of the helicopters, and he said he was aware of the incident in the ATF CP. He said to me that if the RAAF pilots had baulked he would have made them do it at gun-point!

It is unfortunate that sometimes comments made on reflection are taken as representing what actually happened at the time. We would never have been on 6RAR pad if we weren't going; at the pilot level there was no evidence of reluctance to go; and shooting the pilot doesn't help get the job done! Several stories of people threatening people with guns arose out of the day and perhaps each story fed on the other.

Similarly, it is disappointing that some thirty years later, when the facts are known, that stories disparaging the valour of the pilots are still perpetuated. Dave Harris recounted:

> It is an interesting anecdote that it became common
> knowledge that the RAAF initially refused the
> mission. The pilots were subsequently decorated for
> bravery, one with a DFC, essentially the RAAF equiv-
> alent to the MC for Harry Smith, and much higher
> than the MIDs for his platoon commanders, for a few
> minutes over the battlefield.

Harris was in full knowledge of the facts that it was an army
decision that the level of recognition to Harry Smith and his
soldiers was downgraded, as is discussed in the section on awards.
To dismiss the act of heroism on the grounds that there were
discussions at a higher level on the wisdom of the involvement is
to belittle the act of heroism. To try and put a time onto what
constitutes bravery above and beyond the call of duty is again a
disappointing way to recognise a critical act in the day's events.
The person who undertook to lead the resupply, on his own if
necessary, in defiance of the wisdom of the senior officer, was the
one who received the Distinguished Flying Cross (DFC) for his
performance during his tour of Vietnam. The pilot of the other
aircraft received the MID for this and other acts of flying during
his tour. Both were required to call on all their flying skills and to
work with their crews to successfully carry out the resupply under
the conditions of the day.

As we discussed the writing of this book, members of Delta
Company recognise that there were a series of critical events
during the day, without any one of which there would almost
certainly have been a different story about the Battle of Long Tan.
Most significantly, they would probably not be here today to tell
the story. One of these is the ammunition resupply. Like a house
of cards, take out one critical card and the whole thing falls in a
heap. So the participation of the RAAF on the day should be seen
as yet another act in which the army and the air force worked
together to achieve an excellent outcome in the highly demanding
circumstances of the day.

The singular lesson that APCs were an aggressive assault weapon was made clear to all who cared to think about such matters at the Battle of Long Tan. Unfortunately, the system of reflection and review of battle outcomes at the time did not objectively record the achievement or potential of 3 Troop.

I have often wondered why a company in APCs was sent to relieve a situation in which another company had been effectively pinned down by a force that had to be far greater in size than a battalion. Then, when in a position to envelop the enemy force, they were ordered to withdraw and secure the beleaguered company. What was required was a far bolder sweep to the east, approaching, say, north from the horseshoe feature toward and beyond the ruins of the village of Long Tan. Such a bold sweep could have been made using the balance of the APC squadron, forces which the OC of that unit had pressed upon HQ 1ATF but whose use was refused. The APC force, together with infantry from the sister battalion at 1ATF, would have required field manoeuvre by HQ 1ATF. Delay, presumably over the need to defend the base area, eventually ruled out such a manoeuvre as darkness and weather delayed reaction on a grander scale until 9.00 a.m. next day, by which time the enemy had left the field at his initiative.

The fact that the APC was introduced into the Australian Army battle order at a time when the whole army was undergoing rapid expansion created a significant problem in the timely training of infantry in the tactical use of this weapon. Battalions were fully committed in the training of their National Service recruits, as was 1APC Squadron in training its crews, but very limited opportunities arose for joint exercises. This is probably the reason for some communication breakdown on the command and control of the infantry company as it was being transported to Long Tan. I was never in doubt that I was in command of the APC troop and those inside the carriers until the troops dismounted into battle as set out in the squadron standard operating procedures (SOP). Unfortunately, the 1ATF SOP did not cover the situation and the extreme circumstances had not arisen in which the command situation would be tested. It was disappointing that both the imminent fall of darkness and the need to link with the beleaguered D Company prevented the full exploitation of the APCs' eastward assault into a continuing enveloping sweep across D Company's front to destroy the remaining enemy forces who might have been in that area.

In fact, I believe that Delta Company would not have faced the problem that it did on 18 August if it had been allowed to operate with APCs on that patrol. The mobility and firepower that APCs could contribute would have made the enemy situation less overwhelming in terrain that was for the most part suitable for APC operations. This sort of combined effort did take place after Long Tan wherever the terrain was open or able to be patrolled.

Another aspect of the aftermath of the Battle of Long Tan was that there was never any real attempt to debrief the participants after the battle. In isolation, each element created a record of the events as they perceived them.

There was a need for an objective, analytical, sceptical examination of events. It required an independent historian trained in operational analysis. This would involve canvassing the raw experience of participants and commanders at all levels, the records of radio logs and reports from every level, distilling a narrative for the historical record plus lessons that may modify extant military practices. At the time the War Diary was the principal method of recording events. At best the War Diary records the narrative of an action from the CO/OC perception of events. It may not be the record of an uninvolved, trained observer, expressed in unambiguous language. At worst such diaries may be the 'cobbled' records kept by overtaxed sub-unit staff.

The need for an objective record of events, free from 'political' consideration and human ambitions, is apparent in the story of the Battle of Long Tan. The existence of a history staff at formation level would provide the means to debrief participants and analyse an action for the record. The record of events also has a human face in that soldiers need to be recognised as having participated in such an event. While individual acts may be recognised by awards or 'mentions' there is no individual recognition for most participants. Without this record of events, many of the elements, whose participation was critical to the outcome, can be overlooked. Recognition of the individual by an appropriate Australian corporate award system that has true meaning and that is not debased by general issues is important in an avowedly egalitarian armed force which seeks to reflect Australian society.

USE OF THE US ARTILLERY

'If the 155 mm Battery had been commanded to fire Battery 5 (30 rounds per mission) at each target, the VC body count would have been much greater.'

Major Glenn Eure, US Army, took command of A Battery, 2nd Battalion, 35th Artillery early in 1966 at Fort Carson, Colorado. A Battery was his fourth company-level command, where most captains were lucky to command one in a career. With 2IC Lieutenant Barry Dreyer, RNZA and S.F.C. Duke, the chief of the Firing Battery, they delivered decisive firepower during the Battle of Long Tan. In his book about his experiences, Eure raised some issues about the under-utilisation of their potential support.

> The American and Australian procedures for employing artillery are different in one major respect. The Aussie artillery commander is with the infantry as opposed to the American method where the commander is at the guns and he sends forward observer teams, usually consisting of a junior lieutenant, a reconnaissance sergeant, and radio operator to the supported infantry. This makes all requirements for artillery for the Aussie infantry coming from the Aussie artillery battery commander (usually a major in rank) in the form of a 'command for fire'. The

American artillery battery commander (usually captain in rank) dispatches to the infantry forward observer teams who 'request fire'.

My job as the American battery commander was to become integrated into the Aussie system of doing things, which would make us as much help and support as possible. This philosophy worked well with one exception.

During the Battle of Long Tan, the fire missions for my battery were coming from the New Zealand battery commander, Major Harry Honnor, at 6RAR Headquarters. My battery forward observer, Lieutenant Gordon Steinbrook, and his team were with Major Honnor. They were well trained but inexperienced. Lieutenant Steinbrook's positive personality and competence made him a good choice for this job. However, his very junior rank and inexperience coupled with the Aussie system of command from the front and the spirit of urgency of getting rapid, accurate artillery support made it virtually impossible for me to influence the artillery except to make sure what was commanded arrived quickly and accurately.

Second Lieutenant Doug Mistler was assigned as forward observer to 5RAR until just days before the Battle of Long Tan when he was assigned to the 1st Field Regiment Artillery Fire Direction Centre. As soon as the battle started, he was also sidelined by the major in charge. I called Second Lieutenant Mistler and asked him to attempt to raise the number of rounds we were firing from 6 to 30 per mission, that is from Battery 1 to Battery 5 rounds. This is what Americans in the same situation would have done. I also called American Lieutenant Chuck Hendrichs at the Task Force Headquarters with the recommendation we increase the fire, but he was not in a position to act at that time. My recommendations never made it to the commanders conducting the battle.

I did not push the issue because we were not tested in the eyes of the Aussies. Our guns were much bigger than those they were used to and, of course, I believe Major Honnor was attempting to rain artillery on as many targets as possible as rapidly as possible. Had I been able to communicate through the American lieutenants on the spot—Lieutenant Steinbrook with Major Honnor, Lieutenant Heindrichs at the Task Force command post, or Lieutenant Doug Mistler at the Aussie Regimental Fire Direction Centre—and my battery had been commanded to fire Battery 5 rounds at each target, I believe the VC body count would have been much greater. I also believe the reason we didn't fire my guns as I would have was because I was at the guns and not up with Major Honnor in a position to lend my experience in this situation. I in no way intend this to be any form of criticism of the absolutely marvellous conduct by all concerned in the fighting of this engagement. My salute goes to all the Aussies at all levels for this battle.

If we were truly integrated and using the Australian system with the battery commander forward, my age and service experience could have made an impact in trust and understanding of our capabilities. As it was, I understand that had I made contact with Major Honnor who was up to his eyeballs in executing his artillery fire plan, I probably would have accomplished nothing more than becoming an irritant. He probably would have seen me as a meddlesome battery captain whose job it was to respond to his commands for fire, not advise him on how to fight this battle.

I've never discussed this with now Brigadier General Harry Honnor, now retired from the Royal New Zealand Army. I'm sure one of his major concerns was to hit as many targets as possible as rapidly as possible. If I could have influenced him as to the speed with which we could shoot, in retrospect it might have been an endeavour of overkill. As it was, the Aussies gave the Viet Cong a thorough thrashing. In my mind, the Aussies were heroes, every man, and the Yanks, to the man, performed in a manner of which they can be proud. Our intensive training and motto of 'check, double-check, take nothing for granted' paid off when put to the test.

THE DATE OF THE BATTLE OF LONG TAN BECOMES VIETNAM WAR'S DAY OF REMEMBRANCE

Another action that has always upset Harry Smith and other members of Delta Company is the 'hijacking' of Long Tan Day by the Vietnam Veterans' Association Of Australia.

In 1988, the Vietnam Veterans' Association of Australia (VVAA), without any approval or consent from the long-established Long Tan Veterans' Association (LTVA), jumped on the bandwagon and chose Long Tan Day as the day for all veterans of the war. In 1997, on 18 August, we saw yet another 'Welcome Home' march, this time in Townsville, with the true significance of Long Tan being lost in the rejoicing of all those who now hang their hats on the battle.

While some say that we should be proud that 18 August has become the date on which the Vietnam War is remembered, the original survivors and their families would rather have the day just to commemorate and remember those we lost and left behind. Individual approaches to the Minister for Veterans' Affairs and the VVAA have all fallen on deaf ears. It is inexplicable to me that the LTVA and 6RAR Association have failed to address the matter.

The clout exerted by the VVAA was illustrated in 1996 when a contingent was flown back to Vietnam to commemorate the thirtieth anniversary of the battle and to witness the erection of the 'Long Tan Cross'.

I had personally written in via the Long Tan Veterans' Association in 1995 to 6RAR to request that all the survivors of Long Tan be taken back to Vietnam in one of the RAAF VIP 707 jets to commemorate the battle while they were still young enough to do so. Also to be included were elements representing those units that supported Delta Company, along with minimum press, media and other dignitaries.

After a long delay and no advice, just before 18 August it was suddenly announced that a contingent was to be sent to Long Tan. However, it did not include Delta Company, but rather comprised a gaggle of Vietnam Veterans' Association people and public servants. Delta was to be represented by only one soldier, former Private Jim Richmond, who was found alive on the battlefield the next morning, and one of the next of kin, Susan Jewry.

While I might not have been too popular with the system, even Colonel Townsend failed to receive an invitation. We put it down to the VVAA lobbying the Minister for Veterans' Affairs, who also went along on the 'junket' trip.

It is also disappointing that the VVAA, like the 6RAR Association, has not given any support to the submissions for recognition of the SVN medals for Long Tan. This is despite many of their members, especially those who served with the AATTV, wearing a variety of foreign awards.

So we still have people jumping on the Long Tan bandwagon! And a side effect is that the survivors of Long Tan and their own Association shun the glory that should be showered on them. They want nothing to do with the politics, just to be left alone to recollect the day when they lost their mates in a rubber plantation, defending Australia's vital interests.

GLOSSARY OF TERMS AND ABBREVIATIONS

1 ALSG	1st Australian Logistics Group, Vung Tau
1 ATF	1st Australian Task Force, Nui Dat
1OTU	Officer Training Unit, Scheyville, NSW, which trained National Service officers
2IC	Second-in-command
2Lt	Second Lieutenant
AAFVHQ	Australian Armed Forces Vietnam Headquarters
AAR	After Action Report
AATTV	Australian Army Training Team Vietnam
AK-47	Automatic Kalashnikov 7.62 mm (short) assault rifle
Albatross	Radio call-sign for 9 Sqn RAAF aircraft
APC	Armoured Personnel Carrier, vehicle designed to carry troops into battle
ARVN	Army of the Republic of Viet Nam
ATF	Australian Task Force
Bdr	Bombardier (artillery corporal)
BHQ	Battalion Headquarters
Boozer	Wet canteen, soldiers' recreational hut serving alcohol
CAP	Company Aid Post
Capt	Captain
CH-47	Chinook, medium lift helicopter

Charlie	Viet Cong, from VC, 'Victor Charlie'
Chinook	Medium lift helicopter
Chopper	Helicopter
CHQ	Company Headquarters
Claymore	M18–A1 directional anti-personnel mine
Cpl	Corporal, commander of a ten-man rifle section, smallest fighting group
CO	Commanding Officer (Battalion)
CP	Command Post
CQMS	Company Quartermaster Sergeant, stores controller
CSM	Company Sergeant Major
CT	Communist Terrorist, guerrilla forces Malaya
DCM	Distinguished Conduct Medal, other ranks decoration second highest award for personal bravery in battle
Digger	Nickname for the Australian soldier, a legacy of First World War trench warfare
DS	Directing Staff
DSO	Distinguished Service Order, officer decoration for leader ship and gallantry
Dustoff	Aeromedical evacuation by helicopter from the field of battle
FOO	Forward Observation Officer, artillery officer who controls and fires the artillery
GPMG	General Purpose Machine-Gun (M-60, 7.62 mm)
Gunship	Helicopter armed with rockets and machine guns
HE	High Explosive ordnance
Helipad	Helicopter landing area
HMAS	Her Majesty's Australian Ship
Hootchie	Nickname for personal shelter or lodgings
HQ	Headquarters
Huey	Utility helicopter (derived from the military title UH-1H)
JTC	Jungle Training Centre, Canungra, Qld
KIA	Killed In Action
Kiwi	Nickname for New Zealander
LCpl	Lance Corporal
Lt	Lieutenant
LZ	Landing Zone for helicopter
M-16	5.56 mm assault rifle (also AR 15)

M-60	Section MG, 7.62 mm (GPMG) general purpose, belt-fed machine-gun
Maj	Major
MC	Military Cross, gallantry decoration for officers, unable to be awarded posthumously
MID	Mention-in-Despatches, an award for outstanding service, an oak leaf attached to the campaign medal ribbon
MFC	Mortar Fire Controller
mm	Millimetre (calibre)
MM	Military Medal, an other ranks decoration for personal bravery in battle
MP	Military Police
Nasho	National Serviceman, a soldier conscripted into the army for two years' service
NCO	Non-Commissioned Officer
NLF	National Liberation Front
NVA	North Vietnamese Army
OC	Officer Commanding (company)
OCS	Officer Cadet School, Portsea, Vic
OMC	Owen Machine Carbine, 9 mm, Australian-designed weapon during Second World War
OTU	Officer Training Unit, Scheyville, NSW, which trained National Service officers
PAVN	People's Army of Viet Nam
Pit	Entrenched fighting position for ground troops
Pl	Platoon
PLA	People's Liberation Army
PT	Physical Training
Pte	Private
PTI	Physical Training Instructor
QANTAS	Queensland And Northern Territory Aerial Services
R&C	Rest and Convalescence leave earned after injury or illness or arduous duty and taken locally
R&R	Rest and Recreation leave earned after six months on operations in South Vietnam and usually taken outside the country
RAA	Royal Australian Artillery

RAAF	Royal Australian Air Force
RAN	Royal Australian Navy
RAR	Royal Australian Regiment
RCL	Recoilless rifle anti-tank gun
Recce/ recon	Reconnaissance
Regt	Regiment, a battalion size group in friendly forces
Regt	Regiment, a brigade size unit in the NVA and NLF (VC) forces
RNZA	Royal New Zealand Artillery
RMC	Royal Military College, Duntroon
RPG	Rocket-propelled grenade
RSM	Regimental Sergeant Major
RTB	Recruit Training Battalion
SAS	Special Air Service, highly trained specialist, paratroopers etc.
SEATO	South-East Asia Treaty Organisation
Sgt	Sergeant
SLR	Self-Loading Rifle, standard issue rifle, 7.62 mm
SOP	Standard Operating Procedures
SVN	South Vietnam, Republic of
TAOR	Tactical Area Of Responsibility
TF	Task Force
UH-1	Utility helicopter (Huey)
USA	United States of America
USAF	United States Air Force
VC	Viet Cong, the name for most enemy personnel
VHF	Very High Frequency
WIA	Wounded In Action
WO1	Warrant Officer Class One (RSM)
WO2	Warrant Officer Class Two (CSM)
Yakka	Extremely hard work

AWARDS AND DECORATIONS

(Given specifically for the Battle of Long Tan)

MEMBERS OF DELTA COMPANY

MILITARY CROSS	Major	H.A. SMITH
DISTINGUISHED CONDUCT MEDAL	WO2	J.W. KIRBY
MILITARY MEDAL	Sergeant	R.S. BUICK
	Private	R.M. EGLINTON
MENTION-IN-DESPATCHES	Second Lieutenant	G.M. KENDALL
	Second Lieutenant	D.R. SABBEN
	Corporal	P.N. DOBSON
	Corporal	W.R. MOORE
	Private	W.A. AKELL

MEMBERS OF 1 ARMOURED PERSONNEL SQUADRON

DISTINGUISHED CONDUCT MEDAL	Corporal	J.A. CARTER
MENTION-IN-DESPATCHES	Lieutenant	F.A. ROBERTS

MEMBER of the Order of the BRITISH EMPIRE	Captain	M.D. STANLEY
MENTION-IN-DESPATCHES	Bombardier	W.G. WALKER

ROYAL AUSTRALIAN AIR FORCE

DISTINGUISHED FLYING CROSS	Flight Lieutenant	F. RILEY
MENTION-IN-DESPATCHES	Flight Lieutenant	C. DOHLE

AWARDED TO ALL MEMBERS POSTED TO DELTA COMPANY ON 18 AUGUST 1966

THE PRESIDENTIAL UNIT CITATION (ARMY) FOR EXTRA-ORDINARY HEROISM TO D COMPANY, SIXTH BATTALION, THE ROYAL AUSTRALIAN REGIMENT.

Following is an extract from an information paper supplied by the Department of the Army, The Center of Military History, 1099, 14th Street NW, Washington DC 20005–3402.

The Presidential Unit Citation (Army) (PUC), formerly the Distinguished Unit Citation, was established for heroism by Executive Order on 26 February 1942 for action against an armed enemy occurring on or after 7 December 1941. It served as the Army's only unit award for valor until 1966. The criteria for the awards were as follows:

'The unit must display such gallantry, determination, and esprit de corps in accomplishing its mission under extremely difficult and hazardous conditions as to set it apart and above other units participating in the same campaign. The degree of heroism required is the same as that which would warrant award of Distinguished

Service Cross to an individual. Extended periods of combat duty or participation in a large number of operational missions, either ground or air, is not sufficient. Only on rare occasions will a unit larger that a battalion qualify for award of this decoration.'

Two Australian infantry units have been awarded this decoration, 3RAR for that unit's participation in the Battle of Kapyong during the Korean War and Delta Company, 6RAR for the Battle of Long Tan.

The Distinguished Service Cross (DSC) is the second highest award for valour, the highest being the Medal of Honor. In reality the award of the Presidential Unit Citation to 3RAR and Delta Company, 6RAR signifies that each member posted to that unit on the day has been awarded the Distinguished Service Cross.

INDEX